FORMULA1 2019
TECHNICAL INSIGHTS

PAOLO FILISETTI

GIORGIO NADA EDITORE

Giorgio Nada Editore

Editorial manager
Leonardo Acerbi

Editorial
Giorgio Nada Editore

Layout and cover
Aimone Bolliger

3D Graphics
Didier Naim Delfi

© 2020 Giorgio Nada Editore, Vimodrone (MI)

DESIGNED & MANUFACTURED IN ITALY

Giorgio Nada Editore s.r.l.
Via Claudio Treves, 15/17
I – 20090 VIMODRONE - MI
Tel. +39 02 27301126
Fax +39 02 27301454
E-mail: info@giorgionadaeditore.it
www.giorgionadaeditore.it

Allo stesso indirizzo può essere richiesto il catalogo di tutte le opere pubblicate dalla Casa Editrice.

The catalogue of Giorgio Nada Editore publications is available on request at the above address.

Distribuzione
Giunti Editore Spa
via Bolognese 165
I - 50139 FIRENZE
www.giunti.it

FORMULA 1 2019 Technical insights
ISBN: 978-88-7911-781-4

SUMMARY

2019 Regulations — 4
Car table — 8
Tyres 2019 — 10
Brakes 2019 — 12
Seb and Charles' steering wheels: so similar, but so different — 14
Mercedes AMG F1 W10 EQ+Power — 16
Scuderia Ferrari SF90 — 22
Red Bull Racing RB15 — 28
McLaren MCL 34 — 36
Renault RS19 — 40
Sport Pesa Racing Point RP 19 — 44
Alfa Romeo Racing C38 — 48
Toro Rosso STR14 — 52
Haas VF19 — 54
Rokit Williams FW42 — 56
The 2019 season — **57**
    Australia — 58
    Bahrain — 62
    China — 66
    Azerbaijan — 70
    Spain — 74
    Monaco — 78
    Canada — 82
    France — 86
    Austria — 90
    Great Britain — 94
    Germany — 98
    Hungary — 102
    Belgium — 106
    Italy — 110
    Singapore — 114
    Russia — 118
    Japan — 122
    Mexico — 126
    United States — 130
    Brazil — 134
    Abu Dhabi — 138
2020: year of transition in emergency — 142
3D virtual tech to analyse and explain reality — 154

2019 REGULATIONS

In 2019, the appearance of the F1 cars was modified slightly with respect to their 2018 counterparts, with changes to the aerodynamic configurations introduced in order to reduce as much as possible the sensitivity of the cars to the wake of those in front when overtaking. The intention here was to reduce the variations in downforce induced by the turbulence deriving from the car in front and, at the same time, to increase the efficiency of the DRS, producing a speed differential that facilitated overtaking. Along with the new aerodynamic regulations, the minimum weight was also increased from 733 kg to 743 kg, including the driver, the weight of whom was established as 80 kg. In practice, the minimum weight of the car is obtained by subtracting the 80 kg that are reached in the case of a lighter driver through the addition of ballast.

The aerodynamic regulations can be subdivided into four macro areas that concern respectively: the front wing, the brake air intakes, the rear wing and the bargeboards.

The width of the front wing was increased in 2019 from 180 cm to 200 cm. All the additional upper flaps above the principal profile were eliminated. In parallel, the number of elements visible in the plan and frontal views was restricted to five, thereby outlawing partial or intermediate slits between the elements that multiply their number. There were modifications to the endplates, which were also simplified in terms of the profiles connected to them that were banned; the endplates were also taller than the preceding ones by 2.5 cm. The maximum width of the external footplate was 5 cm.

There were interesting restrictions placed on the brake air intakes. In this case, in fact, the FIA decided to restrict their use as an aerodynamic element as had been the case in recent years. The air intakes were to have a mouth 18 cm tall and no wider than 5 cm. Furthermore, all the profiles and winglets connected to the intakes through to 2018 and acting as turning vanes were banned.

For the record it should be emphasised that as a consequence of the modifications to the front wing, the management of the air flows exiting it was also very different. In practice, while in 2018 the aerodynamic configuration aimed to create an in-wash of the air flows investing the wing, deviating them inside the front wheels and thus permitting the exploitation of the Y250 vortex generated in the neutral section of the wing to feed the underside of the car, in 2019 there was a progressive shift to an out-wash configuration with the flows directed outside the front wheels. In reality this direction was not taken up by all teams, but was in any case justified by the greater complexity in managing the flows passing between wheel and chassis. The passage through the suspension elements of the flows directed towards the sidepod mouths and the leading edge of the floor in fact proved to be critical, which also explains the location five centimetres back with respect to the previous position. The height of the vertical vanes in this area was reduced in 2019 to a maximum of 35 cm compared with the previous limit of 47.5 cm. The reasoning behind this modification was prevalently commercial in nature as the reduced height permitted greater visibility for the sides of the car available to sponsors. The change did of course have clear repercussions in the designs of the bargeboards themselves and the leading edge of the sidepod inlets.

Turning to the rear of the car, the width of the rear wing was increased from 95 to 105 cm, with an increase in height with respect to the reference plane of 7cm, from 80 to 87 cm. In order to improve the efficiency of the wing the DRS the rear overhang was increased, that is to say the distance between the rearmost point of the wing and the axle, from 71 to 81 cm. Specifically, in the case of the DRS the height of the vertical section obtained between the open flap and the main plane was increased from 6.5 to 8.5 cm. In this way the difference in terms of drag between the wing of the leading car with the flap closed with respect to that of the car following in its wake with the open flap was increased.

In terms of the downforce produced, the initial simulations had indicated significant losses of up to 15% and beyond, but according to a number of engineers questioned over the course of the season, with the methods of calculation and the profiles of the various elements being refined, it emerged that the values with which the 2019 cars finished the season were close, and in certain cases superior to, those of 2018.

Frontal comparison: new front wing dimensions, elimination of upper flaps (additional profiles), and limitation of brake air intake section. New rear wing and DRS gap dimensions

The width of the front wing was increased from 180 cm to 200 cm. All the additional upper flaps above the main profile were banned. The maximum dimensions of the air intake were 18 cm in height and 5 cm in width. The width of the rear wing was increased from 95 to 105 cm, with an increase in height with respect to the reference plane of 7cm, from 80 to 87 cm. The height of the vertical section obtained between the open flap and the main plane with the DRS activated was increased from 6.5 to 8.5 cm.

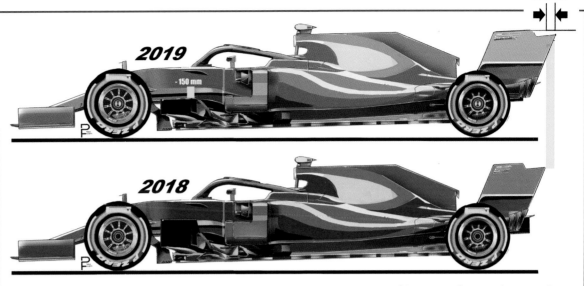

100mm

2019

2018

Lateral comparison: reduction in the height of the turning vanes and increased rear wing overhang

The height of the vertical vanes was reduced in 2019 to a maximum of 35 cm from the previous limit of 47.5 cm. The overhang of the rear wing was increased by 100 mm to improve its efficiency.

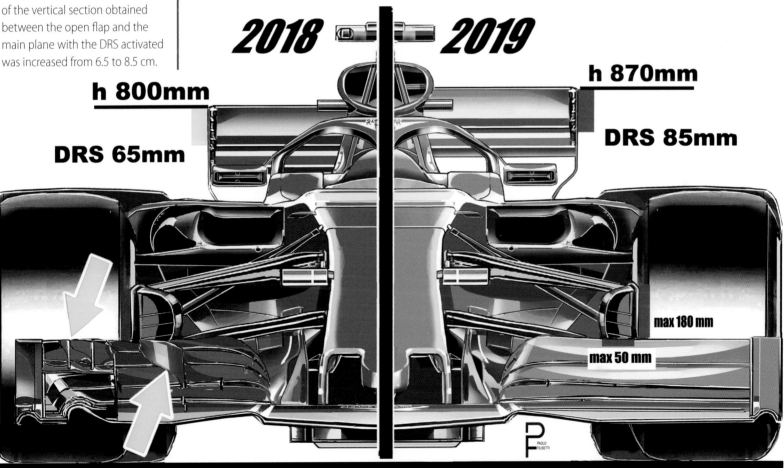

2018   2019

h 800mm

h 870mm

DRS 65mm

DRS 85mm

max 180 mm

max 50 mm

900mm   1000mm

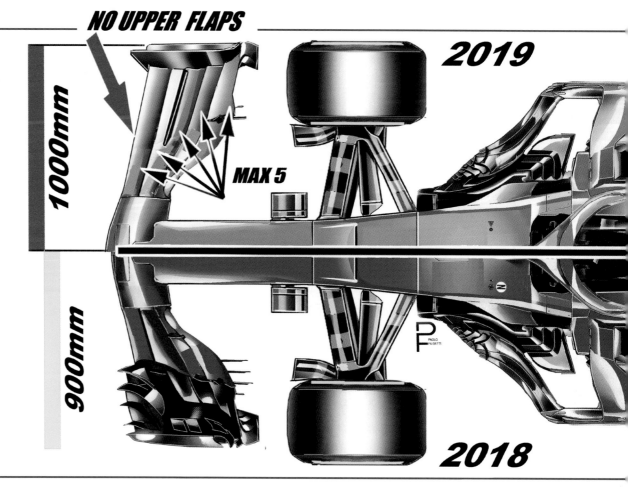

Overhead comparison

The increased width of the front wing, the elimination of the upper flaps and the maximum limit of five profiles are highlighted. The 100 mm increase in the width of the rear wing and its overhang.

NO UPPER FLAPS

1000mm

900mm

MAX 5

2019

2018

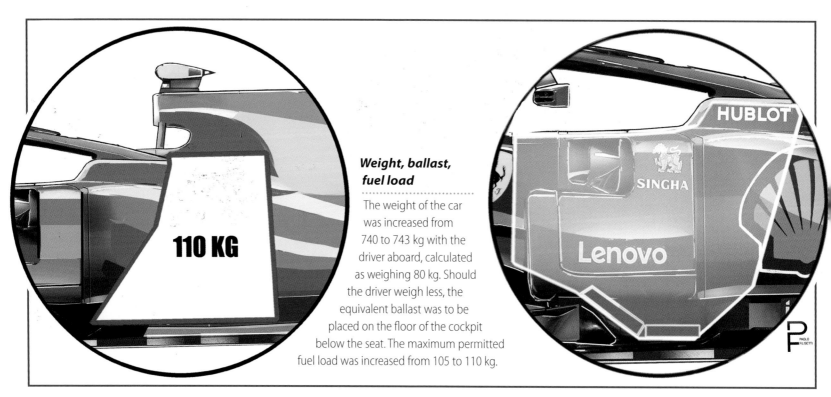

110 KG

Weight, ballast, fuel load

The weight of the car was increased from 740 to 743 kg with the driver aboard, calculated as weighing 80 kg. Should the driver weigh less, the equivalent ballast was to be placed on the floor of the cockpit below the seat. The maximum permitted fuel load was increased from 105 to 110 kg.

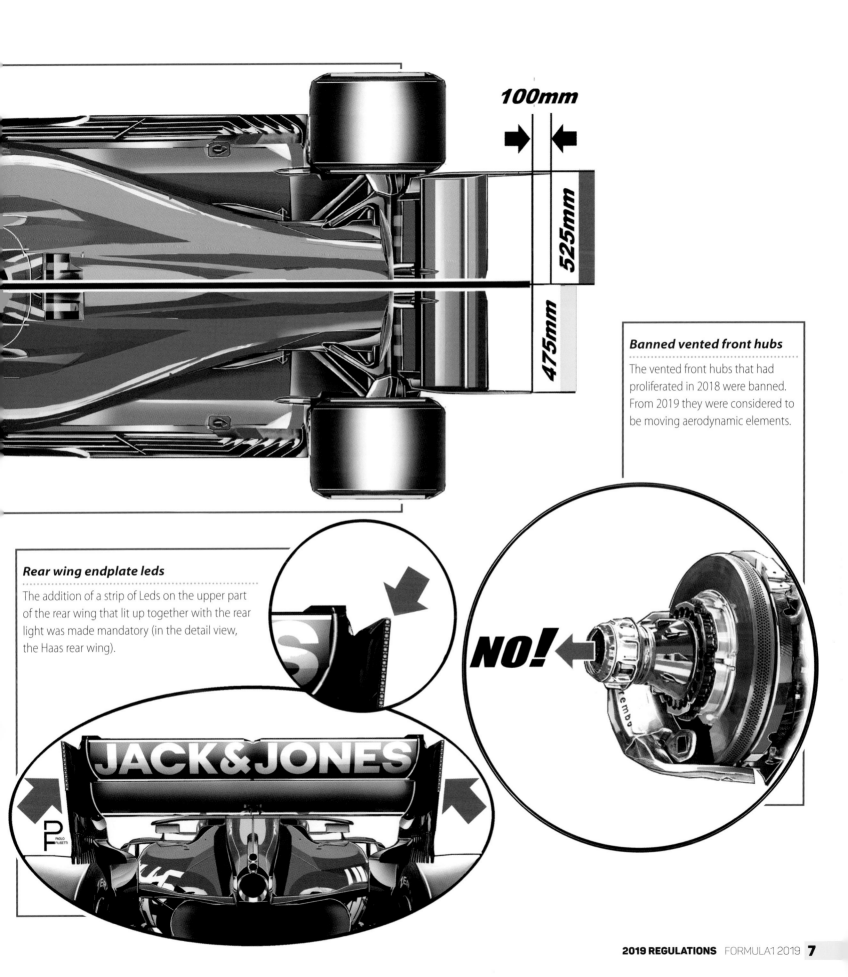

100mm

525mm

475mm

Banned vented front hubs

The vented front hubs that had proliferated in 2018 were banned. From 2019 they were considered to be moving aerodynamic elements.

Rear wing endplate leds

The addition of a strip of Leds on the upper part of the rear wing that lit up together with the rear light was made mandatory (in the detail view, the Haas rear wing).

NO!

JACK&JONES

PAOLO FILISETTI

CAR TABLE

	Mercedes-AMG Petronas W10	Scuderia Ferrari SF90	Red Bull Racing RB15	McLaren MCL34
Bodywork	Carbon fibre composite including engine cover, sidepods, floor nose. front wing and rear wing	Carbon fibre and honeycomb composite chassis. with halo fitted to the cockpit	Carbon-epoxy composite structure designed by regulation ard built in-house	Carbon-fibre composite. including engine cover. sidepods, floor. nose. front wing and rear wing with driver-operated drag reduction system
Front Suspension	Carbon fibre wishbone and pushrod-activated torsion springs and rockers	Independent suspension. Push-rod activated torsion springs	Aluminium alloy uprights, Aluminium alloy uprights, carbon fibre composite double sprirgs, anti-roll bar and dampers / Red Bull Racing	Carbon-fibre wishbone and pushrod suspension elements operating inboard torsion bar and damper system
Rear Suspension	Carbon fibre wishbone and pullrod-activated torsion springs and rockers	Independent suspension. Pullrod activated torsion springs	Aluminium alloy uprights, carbon fibre composite double wishbones With pullrods, anti-roll bar and dampers, springs / Red Bull Racing	Carbon-fibre wishbone and pullrod suspension elements operating inboard torsion bar and damper system
Dampers	Penske	ZF Sachs	Multimatic	Koni
Engine	Mercedes-AMG M10 EQ Performance	Ferrari 064	Honda RA619H	Renault E-TECH 19
Transmission	Eight speed forward. One reverse unit with carbon fibre maincase	Electronically controlled gearbox with quick shift. 8 gears + reverse	Eight-speed gearbox. Longitudinally mounted	8 forward and 1 reverse McLaren seamless shift. hand-operated
Gear Selection	Sequential. semi-automatic. Hydraulic activation	Servo controlled hydraulic limited-slip differential. Semi-automatic sequential	hydraulic system for power shift and clutch operation / Red Bull Racing	Electro-hydraulically operated seamless shift
Clutch	AP Racing, carbon plate	ZF Sachs	Red Bull Racing	Carbon multi plate. electro-hydraulically operated
Brake Discs	Carbone Industries carbon / carbon discs rear brake-by-wire	Brembo ventilated carbon-fibre discs rear brake-by-wire	Brembo carbon/carbon composites	Akebono carbon discs
Callipers	Brembo	Brembo	Brembo	Akebono
Pads	Carbone Industries carbon / pads with rear brake-by-wire	Brembo	Brembo carbon/carbon composites	Akebono carbon pads
Wheels	OZ forged magnesium	OZ forged magnesium	OZ forged magnesium	Enkei
Steering	Power-assisted rack and pinion	Ferrari Power-assisted rack and pinion	Red Bull Racing design	Power-assisted rack and pinion
Electronics	FIA standard ECU and FIA homologated electronic and electrical system	Ferrari/Marelli	MESL standard electronic control unit / Honda Racing	McLaren Applied Technologies. Including chassis control. Power unit control. Data acquisition. Sensors. Data analysis & telemetry
Cockpit Instrumentation	McLaren Electronic Systems MES	Ferrari/Marelli	MESL	McLaren Applied Technologies dashboard
Driver's Seat	Removable driver's seat made of anatomically formed carbon composite	Ferrari Removable driver's seat made of anatomically formed carbon composite	Red Bull Racing design	Removable driver's seat made of anatomically formed carbon composite
Seat Belt	OMP six-point driver safety harness	TRW/Sabelt	Sabelt	Six-point driver safety harness
Fuel	PETRONAS Primax	Shell	Esso Synergy	BP
Fuel Cell	ATL Kevlar-reinforced rubber bladder	ATL Kevlar-reinforced rubber bladder	Red Bull Racing Design / ATL	ATL
Lubricant	PETRONAS syntium	Shell	Mobil I	Castrol
Cooling System	N.D.	Secan/Marston	Engine oil & water radiators g/box oil radiator. hydraulic oil intercooler & Charge Air Coolers	Calsonic Kansei water and oil cooling

Renault F1 Team RS19	Scuderia Toro Rosso STR14	Racing Point RP19	Alfa Romeo Racing C38	Haas VF19	Williams FW42
Moulded carbon fibre and aluminium honeycomb composite monocoque	Carbon fibre composite including engine cover, sidepods, floor. Nose front wing and rear wing	Carbon fibre composite monocoque with Zylon side anti-intrusion panels	Carbon-fibre monocoque	Carbon-fibre monocoque	Monocoque construction laminated from carbon epoxy and honeycomb surpassing FIA impact and strength requirements
Carbon fibre top and bottom wishbones operate an inboard rocker via a pushrod system connected to torsion bar and damper units	Carbon composite wishbones with pushrod. Inboard torsion bars and dampers	Aluminium uprights with carbon fibre composite wishbones. Trackrod and pushrod. Inboard chassis mounted torsion springs. Dampers and anti-roll bar assembly	Double wishbone. Inboard spring and damper unit actuated by push-rods	Independent suspension. Push-rod activated torsion springs	Double wishbone, push-rod activated springs and anti-roll bar
Carbon fibre top and bottom wishbones, pullrod operated torsion bars and transverse mounted dampers inside the gearbox casing	Carbon composite wishbones with pullrod. Inboard torsion bars and dampers	Aluminium uprights with carbon fibre composite wishbones. Trackrod and pullrod. Inboard chassis mounted torsion springs. Dampers and anti-roll bar assembly	Double wishbone. Inboard spring and damper unit actuated by pullrods	Independent suspension. Pullrod activated torsion springs	Double wishbone and pullrod activated springs and anti-roll bar
Penske	Multimatic/Penske	Koni	Sachs Race Engineering	ZF Sachs	Williams Hydraulic
Renault E-TECH 19	Honda RA619H	Mercedes-AMG M10 EQ Performance	Ferrari 064	Ferrari 064	Mercedes-AMG M10 EQ Performance
Eight-speed semi-automatic carbon maincase gearbox with reverse gear	Carbon composite maincase longitudinally mounted. hydraulically actuated 8 speed	Mercedes GP 8-speed, semi-automatic	Ferrari 8-speed quick shift carbon gearbox longitudinally mounted	Ferrari 8-speed quick shift carbon gearbox longitudinally mounted	Williams eight speed seamless sequential semi-automatic shift plus reverse gear
"Quickshift" system in operation to maximise speed of gearshifts	hydraulic system for power shift and clutch operation	Sequential. semi-automatic. Hydraulic activation	Servo controlled hydraulic limited-slip differential. Semi-automatic sequential	Servo controlled hydraulic limited-slip differential. Semi-automatic sequential	Gear selection electro-hydraulically actuated
AP Racing, carbon plate	AP Racing carbon multiplate	AP Racing, carbon plate	AP Racing, carbon plate	AP Racing, carbon plate	Carbon multi-plate
Brembo carbon/carbon composites	Brembo	Carbone Industries	Carbone Industries	Brembo	Carbone Industries Carbon / Carbon discs. Rear brake-by-wire
Brembo	STR/Supplier bespoke calliper designs	AP Racing	Brembo six-piston callipers	Brembo six-piston callipers	AP Racing 6 piston. Front and 4 piston rear calliper
Brembo	Brembo	Carbone Industries	Brembo	Brembo	Carbone Industries
OZ magnesium	Apptech, Magnesium alloy	BBS forged wheels	OZ magnesium	OZ Racing	Apptech forged Magnesium
Power-assisted rack and pinion	STR Power-assisted rack and pinion	Racing Point Power-assisted rack and pinion	Alfa Romeo Racing Power-assisted rack and pinio	Ferrari Power-assisted rack and pinion	Williams power assisted rack and pinion
MES-Microsoft Standard Electronic Control Unit	Honda	FIA single ECU with in-house design electrical harness	MES-Microsoft Standard Electronic Control Unit	Ferrari/Marelli	FIA SECU standard electronic control unit
Renault	Scuderia Toro Rosso	Racing Point	Alfa Romeo Racing	Ferrari/Marelli	Williams
Removable driver's seat made of anatomically formed carbon composite	Removable driver's seat made of anatomically formed carbon composite	Removable driver's seat made of anatomically formed carbon composite	Removable driver's seat made of anatomically formed carbon composite	Removable driver's seat made of anatomically formed carbon composite	Removable anatomically formed carbon fibre seat covered in Alcantara
six-point driver safety harness	OMP/Sabelt	Schroth	six-point driver safety harness	Sabelt	six-point safety harness with 75mm shoulder straps
BP	N.D.	Pemex	Shell	Shell	Petronas
Kevlar-reinforced rubber fuel cell by ATL	ATL with Scuderia Toro Rosso internals	ATL	ATL	ATL	ATL Kevlar-reinforced rubber bladder
Castrol	N.D.	Ravenol	Shell	Shell	Petronas
Engine oil & water radiators	Engine oil & water radiators g/box oil radiator. hydraulic oil intercooler & Charge Air Coolers	N.D.	Engine oil & water radiators	Engine oil & water radiators	Aluminium oil. Water charge air. ERS and gearbox radiators

TYRES 2019

2019 was the ninth consecutive season with Pirelli as the sole supplier of tyres to Formula 1. In each of the previous years, Pirelli had always tried to introduce new compounds and carcass designs and in this sense 2019 was no exception. Some of the novelties were clearly visible and therefore easily understood by spectators at the circuits and the TV audience.

In the 2019 Grands Prix, the tyres were distinguished by just three colours: white for the hardest compound, yellow for the medium and red for the soft. In reality, there were actually five compounds available, identified from C1 (the hardest) to C5 (the softest). In defining the range of compounds, the principal aim of the Pirelli engineers was to guarantee a level of performance in line with that of 2018, while at the same time enhancing the reliability of the tyres. In order to reach these objectives various tweaks and modifications were introduced. Among them, one concerned the reduction of the maximum temperature of the rear tyre covers from 100° to 80°, while the maximum temperature of the front covers (100°) remained unchanged. This decision aimed to facilitate the warm up of the front tyres, reducing the risk of graining (the formation of debris on the tread), generally triggered with low asphalt temperatures. A consequence of

this configuration was the parallel reduction of the minimum rear tyre starting pressure. A second modification instead concerned the reduction in the thickness of the tread. On three occasions during the course of 2018, in Spain, France and Great Britain, tyres had been adopted with the tread thickness reduced by 0.4 mm. This decision was made necessary in that the circuits in question had been completely resurfaced. The new asphalt guaranteed such an elevated increase in grip that there would have been an excessive rise in tread temperatures. In order to prevent overheating that would have led to blistering it was decided to reduce the thickness of the tread, a measure that effectively solved problem, bringing the temperatures back within the safety range.

The experience gained in 2018 led the Pirelli engineers to extend the use of tyres with a reduced tread thickness (replicating the dimensions used in the three specific 2018 races) for every Grand Prix in 2019. This decision was also taken in view of a predicted increase in car performance that could be estimated at an average of over a second a year in the absence of substantial changes to the regulations.

The tyre carcass design was therefore identical for every race in 2019. Another by no means secondary change concerned the working range for each tyre

compound. It was in fact decided to increase the range in order to reduce the risks of overheating. In this way the operating windows were expanded, favouring increased versatility of their use by the teams. With regards to the green belt intermediate tyres, the 2019 version was designed to guarantee a crossover between the slicks and the full wets, extending their working range in both directions. The full wets for use in extreme conditions were also completely revised with a redesigned pattern that provided greater resistance to aquaplaning and increased driveability in the most critical conditions. At the start of the season, specifically on the occasion of the first test session at Barcelona, the surface sheen of the new tyres had aroused considerable curiosity. On that occasion, Mario Isola, Pirelli's racing manager, had explained that the effect was a consequence of the production process. In practice, in order to produce the 2019 tyres, moulds were used that had been subjected to a chromium treatment, used for the first time in 2018 to produce the tyres destined for Formula 2. The reason for the introduction of this technology was associated with the fact that in the production of the particularly sticky softest compounds slight imperfections were generated following the vulcanizing process. In practice, a dual result was obtained in both aesthetic and technological terms.

WORKING RANGE OF THE 2019 TYRES

C1 Gra	110-140°C
C2	110-135°C
C3	105-135°C
C4	90-120°C
C5	85-115°C

(C1 hardest, C5 softest)

TABLE OF COMPOUNDS USED IN EACH 2019 GRAND PRIX

	Race	Date	C1	C2	C3	C4	C5
01	Australia	17 Mar		x	x	x	
02	Bahrain	31 Mar	x	x	x		
03	China	14 Apr		x	x	x	
04	Azerbaijan	28 Apr		x	x	x	
05	Spain	12 May	x	x	x		
06	Monaco	26 May			x	x	x
07	Canada	09 Jun			x	x	x
08	France	23 Jun		x	x	x	
09	Austria	30 Jun		x	x	x	
10	Great Britain	14 Jul	x	x	x		
11	Germany	28 Jul		x	x	x	
12	Hungary	04 Aug		x	x	x	
13	Belgium	01 Sep	x	x	x		
14	Italy	08 Sep		x	x	x	
15	Singapore	22 Sep			x	x	x
16	Russia	29 Sep		x	x	x	
17	Japan	13 Oct	x	x	x		
18	Mexico	27 Oct		x	x	x	
19	USA	03 Nov		x	x	x	
20	Brazil	17 Nov	x	x	x		
21	Abu Dhabi	01 Dec			x	x	x

BRAKES 2019

The technical confines within which F1 braking systems operated in 2019 included for the first time the simplification of the front wing via the elimination of the upper flaps which guaranteed a tangible percentage of vertical downforce on the front axle. Consequently, there was a significant increase in straight line speed for all cars and a lengthening of braking distances, leading to a slight reduction in braking torque (to avoid undesirable wheel locking) and a contextual increase in the energy to be dissipated. In its 44th season in Formula 1, Brembo offered the teams it was supplying three different carbonfibre disc designs.

In the interests of greater safety and improved performance, the engineers from the Curno-based company retained the maximum torque values used on the static and dynamic test benches, substantially at the same levels as 2018, with aerodynamics generated by the car that were without doubt greater than those of 2019.

The increase in the energy to be dissipated, even though marginal, led to an increase in the temperatures of the braking systems. To reduce them, from 2018 Brembo had improved the cooling of the discs, adopting a maximum of almost 1,500 ventilation holes in the most extreme versions.

The majority of the cars used discs with thicknesses of 32 mm at the front and 28 mm at the rear. In relation to the ambient temperature of each Grand Prix and taking into account race strategies, each driver was able to choose from three Brembo disc options. Specifically, at the front the choice might range from the medium cooling option with 800 holes to the high cooling with 1,250 holes and the very high cooling version with 1,480 holes. The Brembo engineers also worked to provide a disc option with a reduced diameter on the rear axle, to be used on those circuits that were less hard on braking systems such as Le Castellet and Silverstone. This enabled optimum performance to be obtained from the carbonfibre.

In 2019, Brembo continued to work on the braking systems with the objective of miniaturising as much as possible the components in the Brake by Wire system and lighting the aluminium-lithium calipers. Brembo supplied seven teams with six-pot calipers, as required by the regulations.

The company also attempted to improve the response and reactiveness of its Brake by Wire systems used by four teams in the 2019 season. Of vital importance was the customization of the systems for each individual team. In practice, on the basis of the specific requirements of their cars each team defined, together with the Brembo engineers, the optimum weight and stiffness ratios for the brake calipers.

Using sophisticated design methods, Brembo was able to design for each team a brake caliper that achieved the desired ratio between stiffness and weight. The teams had different demands, with some privileging lighter but less stiff calipers, while others opted for less extreme specifications characterised by greater stiffness and consequently greater weight. It was therefore a challenge that implied an equilibrium that was obtained by Brembo's decision to develop a system independently and separately for each team.

The acquisition and subsequent analysis of data are fundamental in this process. The sensors mounted on the system provide the teams with disc and caliper temperatures in real time. In this way disc and pad wear could be calculated. Once the data has been analysed the driver can be instructed as to possible brake balance variations. This occurs in the event of anomalies with respect to the predicted situation. Over the course of a season, a team orders between 10 and 15 sets of calipers, a number sufficient to cope with an adequate safety margin with any accidents and periodic maintenance. Other teams instead opt for a reduced initial order, planning on development during the season and a second order with optimized quantities.

In terms of stress, on those circuits characterised by numerous repeated braking operations, the caliper temperature reaches 200°C. The working life of a Formula 1 caliper is no greater than 10,000 km, during which periodic maintenance is conducted directly by Brembo in its production departments. With regard instead to the friction materials, each team consumes between 150 and 300 discs and up to 600 pads over the course of a season.

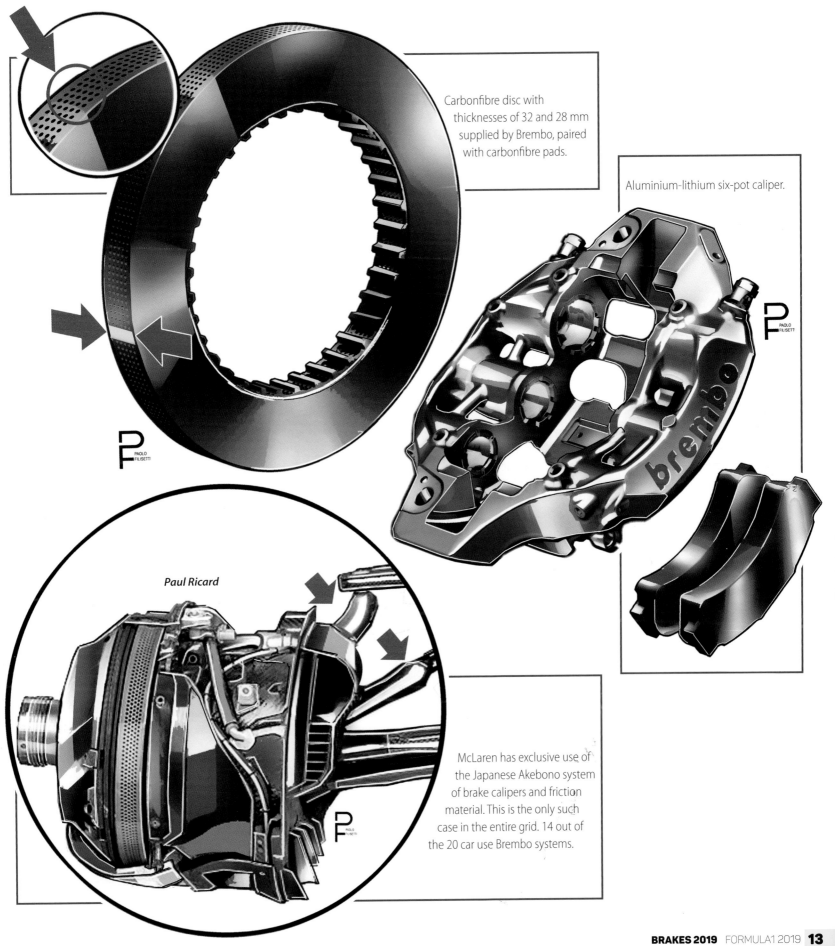

Carbonfibre disc with thicknesses of 32 and 28 mm supplied by Brembo, paired with carbonfibre pads.

Aluminium-lithium six-pot caliper.

Paul Ricard

McLaren has exclusive use of the Japanese Akebono system of brake calipers and friction material. This is the only such case in the entire grid. 14 out of the 20 car use Brembo systems.

SEB AND CHARLES' STEERING WHEELS: SO SIMILAR, BUT SO DIFFERENT

For some years now, the steering wheels fitted to Formula 1 cars have been transformed into control panels governing all the key areas of the car. Drivers can visualise and modify every parameter via the numerous switches, buttons and knobs positioned according to their preferences in terms of ergonomics, intuitiveness and frequency of use. Usually the component is characterised centrally by a large digital display on which alternate, according to the selections made, windows with specific information that can be consulted by the driver. The space that remains around and below the display is exploited to position the various controls and selectors. In theory, given the limited area available, there would appear to be little freedom of choice, instead what may at first sight appear to be marginal details, minor differences between two drivers of the same team, highlight different mental approaches and habits and permit each one to enjoy the greatest control possible and above all to maintain maximum concentration throughout the race, making specific adjustments or implementing instructions received from the team in the pits lap by lap. The wheels used by Sebastian Vettel and Charles Leclerc are at first sight very similar, especially in the part above the rim; nonetheless, the present interesting differences in the lower half, while others of no lesser importance can be glimpsed behind the spokes. Let's take a look in detail.

LECLERC

As mentioned, the upper part of the Monaco-born driver's steering wheel is practically identical to that of his teammate. From left to right, the **N** (NEUTRAL) button for neutral (1), alongside the explicit button that activates the **DRINK** pump (2), followed on the right by the one for communicating with the pits, **RADIO** (3). On the right-hand side (**10-**) (4) scrolls the display screen down while (**1+**) scrolls up (5.) "**P**" is the pit lane speed limiter and when actuated the

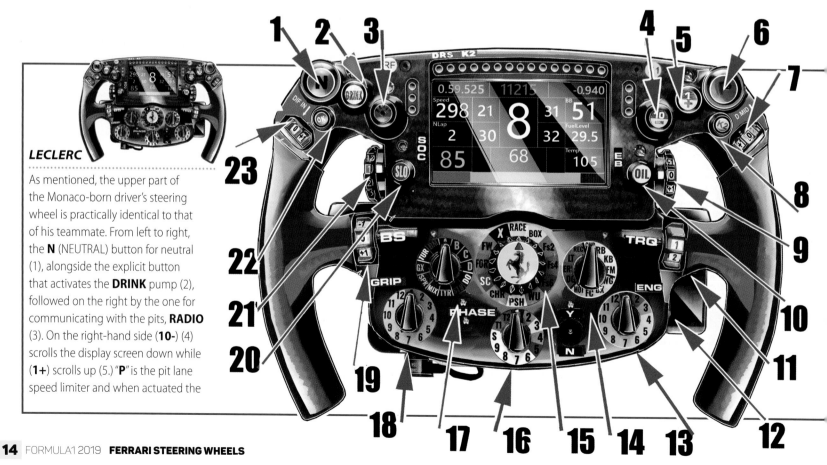

VETTEL

The **N** (NEUTRAL) button for neutral (1), alongside the C button that activates the drink pump (2), followed on the right by the one for communicating with the pits, **RADIO** (3). On the right-hand side (**10-**) (4) scrolls the display screen down while (**1+**) scrolls up (5.) "**P**" is the pit lane speed limiter and, when actuated the screen displays **PIT LIMITER** with the actual speed also shown (6). Below, the rotary selector controls the differential mid-corner (7). The **K2** button actuates the **DRS** (8). Hidden behind the right-hand spoke is a separate lever for the clutch (9) in alternative to the principal one. Engine braking (10) is highlighted by the **EB** (Engine Brake) sticker, while OIL actuates a supplementary oil pump to increase lubrication (11). The vertical **TRQ** thumbwheel controls engine torque (12). Button (13) controls a number of functions, including **ERS**, **REC** (Recovery) and **Mix** (air/fuel mix). **ENGINE** (14) allows the engine mappings to be selected, operating together with (15) which in its turn controls the various **ICE** modes. Among these are **WU** (Warm Up), **PSH** (pre-warm up +) and **PSHQ** (pre-warm up Qualif.). **INTERS/XW** handles certain torque modes relating to the use of intermediate or full wet tyres. Centre, the large rotating multi-function switch (16) controls the **SPK** that is the spark plug ignition advance, **Tur** (wastegate valve pressure) and recovery programmes, pre-set as A, B, etc. The selector (17) serves to choose the strategies for the hybrid part of the power unit. **GRIP** (18) together with **TRQ** controls throttle response. Positioned on the left, below the spoke, is the clutch lever (19). **BS** (20) controls the delivery of the battery charge. **K0** (21) is a switch that activates protection for the power unit's electrical component. The script **SOC** (State Of Charge) refers to the scale indicating the maximum desired/possible charging level, correlated with the specific conditions of the battery at that moment (22). The rotary selector (23) governs the differential when turning in. **OK** confirms the information received from the pits (24).

screen displays **PIT LIMITER** with the actual speed also shown (6). Below, the rotary selector controlling the differential mid-corner (7). The **K2** button actuates the **DRS** (8). The engine braking control (9) is highlighted by the **EB** sticker. **OIL** instead activates a supplementary oil pump increasing lubrication (10). The vertical **TRQ** thumbwheel controls engine torque (11). Positioned in this case on the right is the clutch lever (12) used only at the start. The selector identified as **ENG** allows the engine mappings to be selected (13). (14) instead controls various functions including **ERS**, **REC** (Recovery) and **Mix** (air/fuel mix); selectors that operate together with (15) the large central knob controlling the various **ICE** modes. These include **WU** (warm up), **PSH** (pre-warm up), **RACE** (literally race mode), **SC** (safety car) and so on. Centre, bottom, the selector for the **PU** hybrid strategies (16). Moved to the left and reduced in size compared to Vettel, the multi-purpose rotary switch (17) controls: **SPK**, the spark plug ignition advance, **TUR** (wastegate valve pressure) and recovery programmes pre-set as A, B, etc. The same position and colour for the **GRIP** (18) selector that together with **TRQ** controls throttle response. Both drivers have the same position and function for **BS** (19), which controls the delivery of the battery charge. **SLO** (20) instead selects the **VSC** mode. **SOC** indicated the maximum desired/possible charging level, correlated with the specific conditions of the battery at that moment (21). The rotary selector controls the differential when turning in (22). Finally, **OK** confirms the instructions received from the pits (23).

MERCEDES AMG F1 W10 EQ+POWER

Australia

W10 side view comparison: Australia and Japan

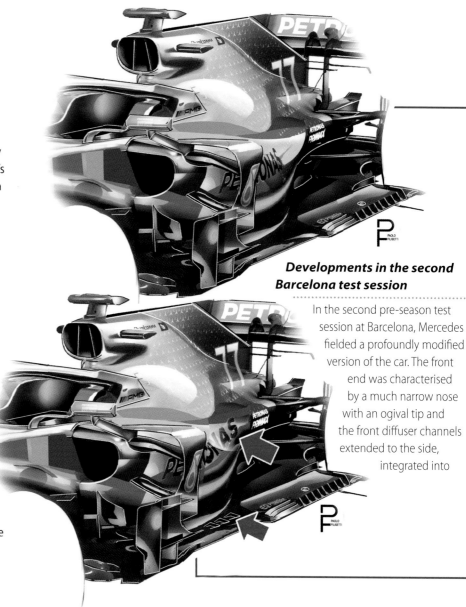

Developments in the second Barcelona test session

Y ou don't normally change a winning car, but this time was different. The aerodynamic philosophy was still based around the long wheelbase and the almost neutral set-up, but numerous elements had been modified. Following the Montmelò tests, the Mercedes hardly seemed to be the car to beat. Nonetheless, it had in the team's capacity to react a fearsome weapon, less so its now less than granitic reliability. The first factor was highlighted during the tests themselves. In the second session a "B" version of the W10 was fielded, demonstrating the enormous capacity for programming of the team led by Toto Wolff, along with the great technical and economic resources on which it can draw. In 2018, there had already been a clear demonstration with the redesigning of the rear suspension dynamics in the second half of the season, a factor that proved to be determinant from Singapore onwards. The introduction of the front diffuser (or cape) effectively brought forwards the long Venturi tunnel that previously terminated in correspondence with the splitter. This was part of the accentuated exploitation of the central area of the car traversed by the Y250 vortex that originates from the neutral section of the front wing. In order to maximize the quality and quantity of the flow, the front wing is principally configured for in-wash (the deviation of the flow between the wheels), with the flow downstream of it groomed by the series of profiles in the bargeboards and turning vanes flanking the sidepods. These elements were the object of extensive development throughout the season.

In the second pre-season test session at Barcelona, Mercedes fielded a profoundly modified version of the car. The front end was characterised by a much narrow nose with an ogival tip and the front diffuser channels extended to the side, integrated into

The two cars appear to be identical in overall terms, but in reality many elements were significantly different. From the front wing with endplates with a greater out-wash configuration in the final version, to the bargeboards and turning vanes area where the vertical elements were redefined both in terms of number and shape and were characterised by a series of horizontal slots. The rear wing was also visibly different in the conformation of the trailing edge of the endplates.

Japan

a single lower profile. The sidepods and the floor were also modified, with the former characterised by a deep diagonal taper to the upper part of the bodywork and the latter by the addition of a number of vortex generators to energise the flow of air across the lower part of the sidepods.

Suzuka

Front view Abu Dhabi version

Note the reduced section of the nose, preceded by the ogival tip joined to the lateral channels of the front diffuser. In this version, which debuted at Suzuka, note the horizontal profile above the intake mouths, separated by the vertical turning vanes, which effectively replaced the previous bridge configuration (see the circle).

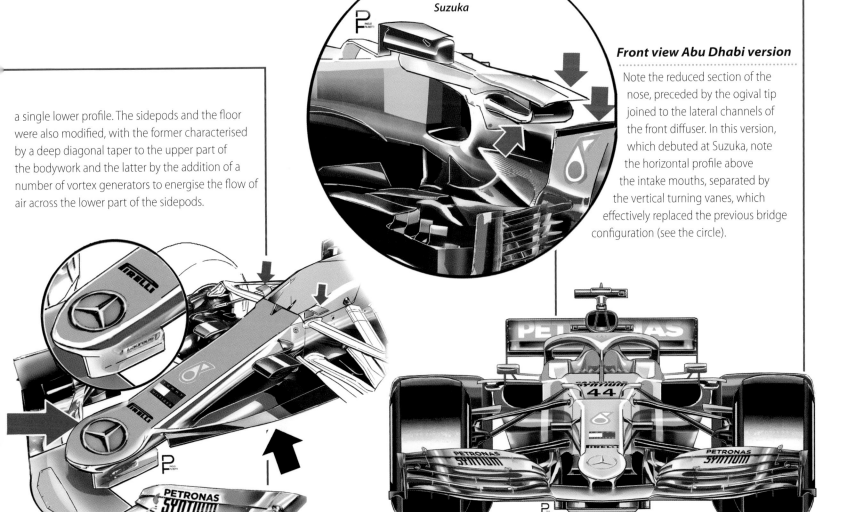

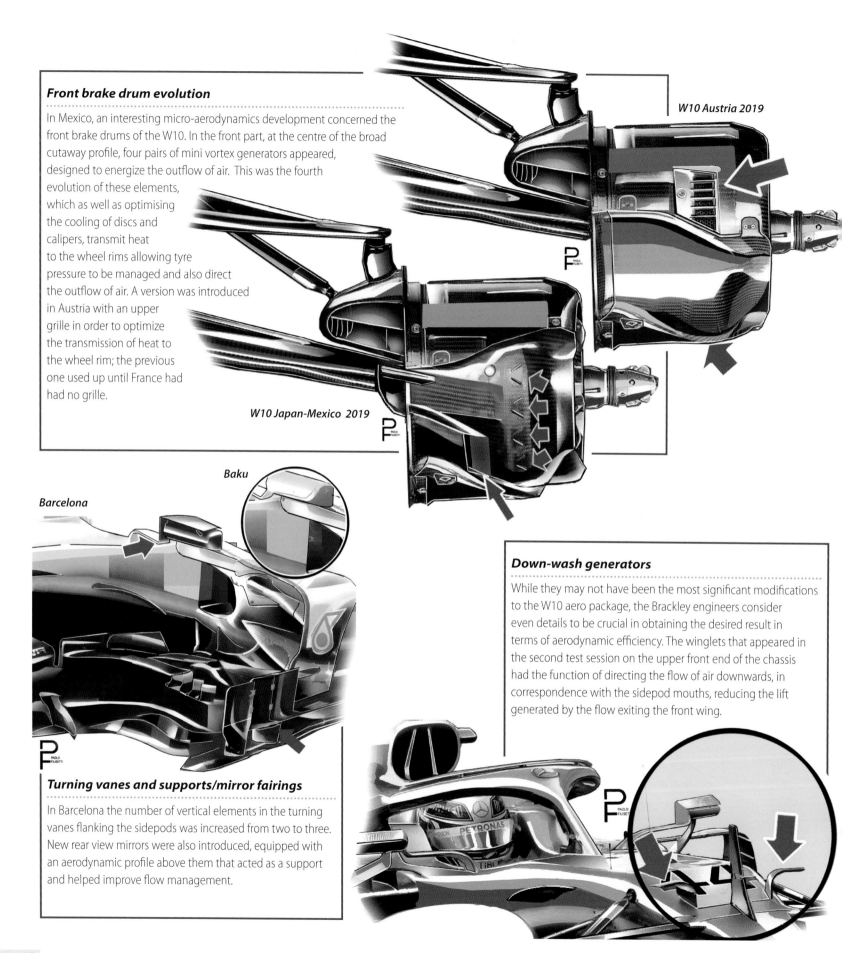

Front brake drum evolution

In Mexico, an interesting micro-aerodynamics development concerned the front brake drums of the W10. In the front part, at the centre of the broad cutaway profile, four pairs of mini vortex generators appeared, designed to energize the outflow of air. This was the fourth evolution of these elements, which as well as optimising the cooling of discs and calipers, transmit heat to the wheel rims allowing tyre pressure to be managed and also direct the outflow of air. A version was introduced in Austria with an upper grille in order to optimize the transmission of heat to the wheel rim; the previous one used up until France had had no grille.

W10 Austria 2019

W10 Japan-Mexico 2019

Baku

Barcelona

Turning vanes and supports/mirror fairings

In Barcelona the number of vertical elements in the turning vanes flanking the sidepods was increased from two to three. New rear view mirrors were also introduced, equipped with an aerodynamic profile above them that acted as a support and helped improve flow management.

Down-wash generators

While they may not have been the most significant modifications to the W10 aero package, the Brackley engineers consider even details to be crucial in obtaining the desired result in terms of aerodynamic efficiency. The winglets that appeared in the second test session on the upper front end of the chassis had the function of directing the flow of air downwards, in correspondence with the sidepod mouths, reducing the lift generated by the flow exiting the front wing.

Micro-wings below the halo

Micro-aerodynamic elements that were evidence of a painstaking attention to detail. The two small vertical vanes of a triangular shape below the halo permitted a separation of the flow, reducing drag and the buffering of the driver's helmet by turbulence.

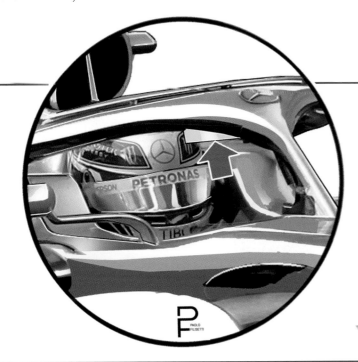

Third mechanical front damper

In Russia there was a further functional test of the mechanical heave damper on both cars, following the one conducted in Singapore. It was adopted for the full weekend in Sochi, replacing the hydraulic unit. The mechanical version, equipped with Belleville washers, made the front suspension of the W10 conceptually very similar to that of the W08 from 2017.

Front wing evolution

Various micro developments characterised the evolution of the front wing. At Shanghai, the endplates presented a sinuous cut-away of the rear corner which initially left the end section of the flap exposed. In relation to a recent FIA directive, no part of the flap could extend laterally beyond the endplate profile. For this reason, Mercedes had to apply an inverted L-shaped profile connecting the portion of the flap visible through the cut-away to the lower part of the endplate, creating a continuity with it (see the detail).

inwash

outwash

In Japan, instead, a small, inclined and curved profile was added to the endplates, close to the leading edge, in order to increase the out-wash effect (see the flow visualization detail).

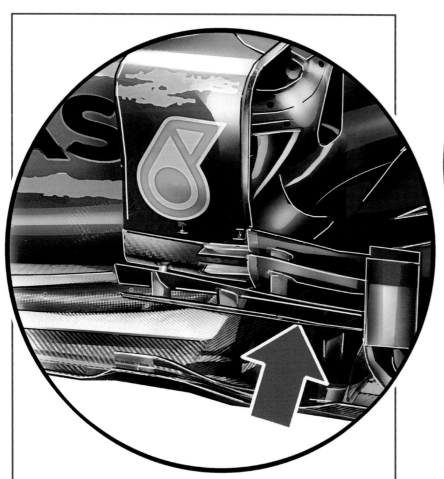

Bargeboard and turning vane development

Hockenheim saw the debut of an extensive aero package. The turning vanes flanking the sidepods and the bargeboards were modified. The first two vertical elements was replaced with a four-louvre horizontal grille (resembling a Venetian blind), inspired by those of Haas and Toro Rosso (see the detail in the circle). The rear-view mirror supports were also new and a triangular profile was added downstream of the upper wishbone.

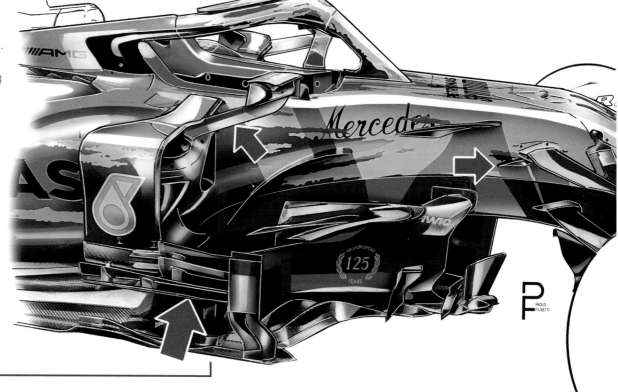

Increase in thermal exchange

In Mexico, Mercedes attempted to improve the reduced performance of the cooling system which was penalised by the rarefied air at the altitude of the country's capital city. In reality, there was a series of features including the addition of grilles either side of the cockpit for efficient heat dispersal, while the rear end remained fairly "closed" with the trailing edge of the bodywork lower than the upper wishbone.

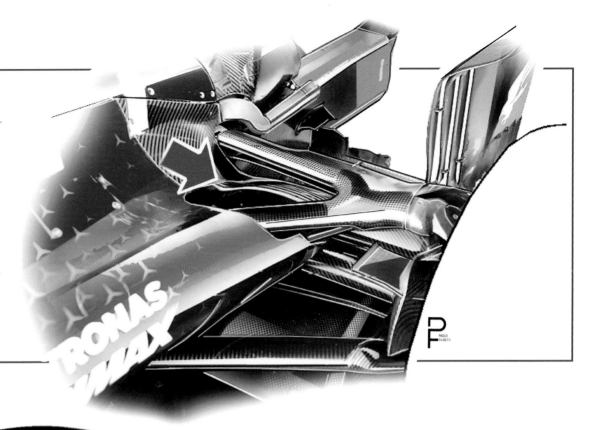

The Power Unit

The M10 EQ+Power, also produced at Brixworth, was perhaps not the car's strongest suit. Its limit was represented by the impossibility of running without reliability concerns due to the high internal operating temperatures. In certain cases (Austria), the drivers were obliged to make frequent lift and coast manoeuvres to keep them under control.

SCUDERIA FERRARI SF90

Side view comparison SF71H-SF90

The side views of the two car highlight how they were linked by a continuous conceptual thread, developed in accordance both with the regulatory changes that concerned the front wing and the progressive

The SF90 was an extensive revised evolution of the SF71H, the basic concepts of which were radicalized. They were also adapted to the new regulations that from 2019 governed the front wing. In detail, this last was characterised by flaps with a progressively neutral incidence in proximity to the endplates, becoming also neutral, thanks to a torsion of the profile. There was also a tangible reduction in the frontal section of the car. This involved a profound, almost radical refinement of the project that tended to dilute the family feeling with the SF71H. A strength of this car was the balance displayed with any set-up, independently of the fuel load carried and the tyres (and compounds) used. A further strong suit was the 064 power unit which boasted immediately and in evolutions 2 and 3 increased efficiency from the internal combustion engine and the ERS. Over the course of the season, the car's performance aroused suspicions and indiscretions among the rival teams regarding possible circumventions of the fuel consumption limits, encouraging the FIA to verify the SF90's *Power unit* compliance with the regulations at the end of the season. At the start of the 2019 championship, there was some concern over the car regarding reliability which in winter testing had been less than absolute. In the event, the problems suffered during the course of the season were actually rare.

"Rusticated" rear wheels

One particular feature that was only seen in testing and never used in a race was rear wheels with hollow spokes and a "rusticated" texture with droplet shaped protuberances inside the rim to favour the dispersal of heat produced under braking and to energize the air flow through their rotation. This feature was inspired by the one introduced by Mercedes at Spa in 2018.

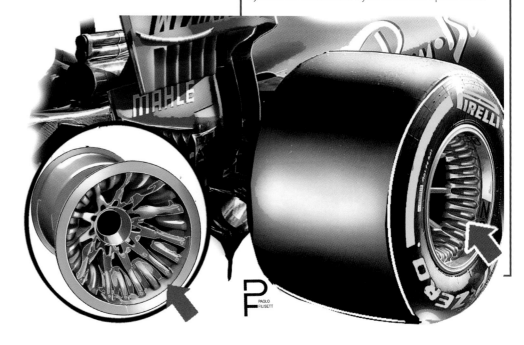

refinement of various features in favour of performance. With the front wheels removed we can appreciate the complexity of the brake drums open laterally with multiple ventilation ducts that clearly had a primary aerodynamic function.

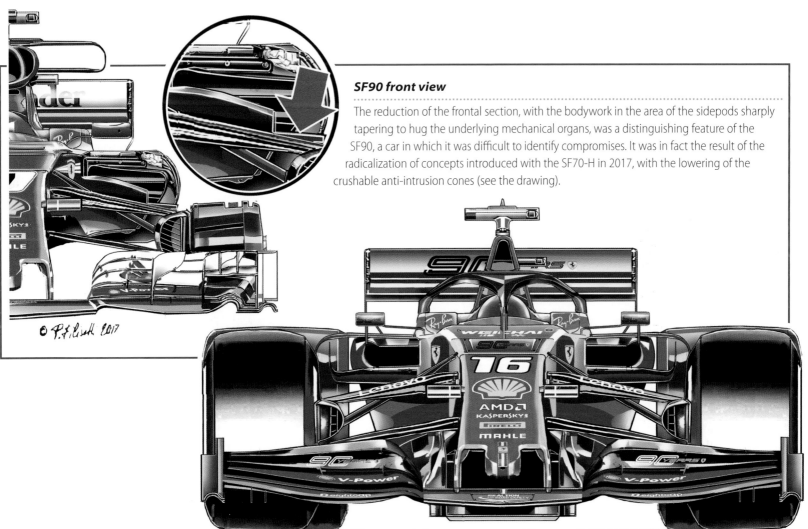

SF90 front view

The reduction of the frontal section, with the bodywork in the area of the sidepods sharply tapering to hug the underlying mechanical organs, was a distinguishing feature of the SF90, a car in which it was difficult to identify compromises. It was in fact the result of the radicalization of concepts introduced with the SF70-H in 2017, with the lowering of the crushable anti-intrusion cones (see the drawing).

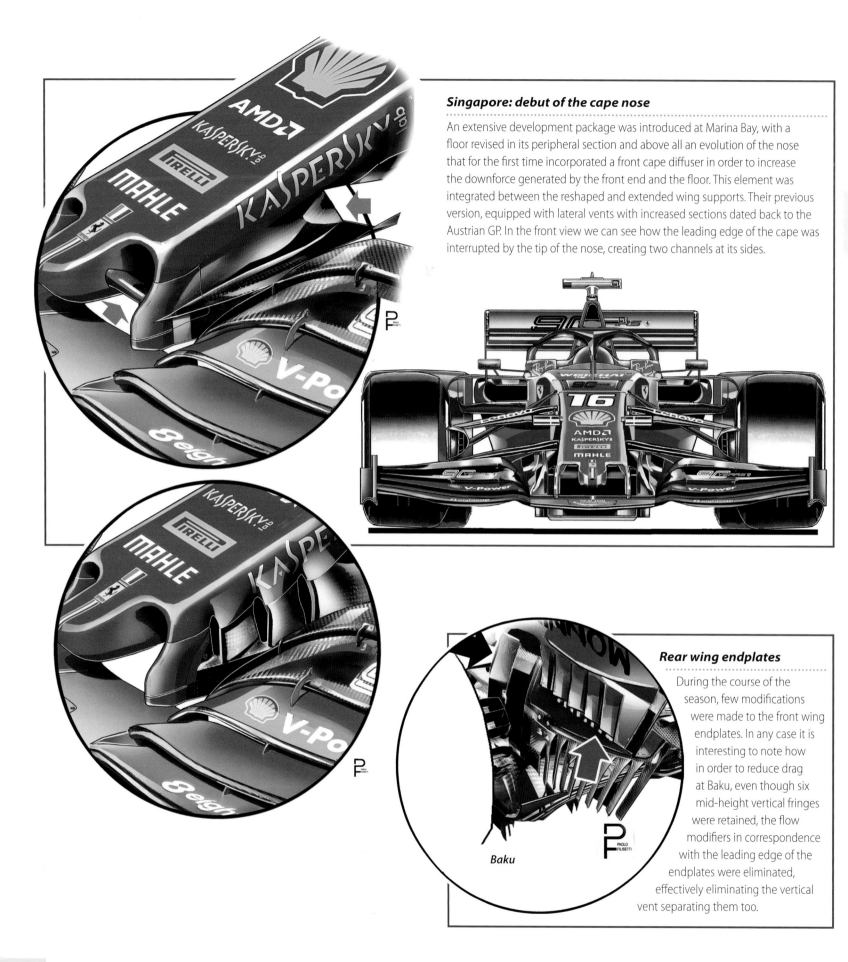

Singapore: debut of the cape nose

An extensive development package was introduced at Marina Bay, with a floor revised in its peripheral section and above all an evolution of the nose that for the first time incorporated a front cape diffuser in order to increase the downforce generated by the front end and the floor. This element was integrated between the reshaped and extended wing supports. Their previous version, equipped with lateral vents with increased sections dated back to the Austrian GP. In the front view we can see how the leading edge of the cape was interrupted by the tip of the nose, creating two channels at its sides.

Baku

Rear wing endplates

During the course of the season, few modifications were made to the front wing endplates. In any case it is interesting to note how in order to reduce drag at Baku, even though six mid-height vertical fringes were retained, the flow modifiers in correspondence with the leading edge of the endplates were eliminated, effectively eliminating the vertical vent separating them too.

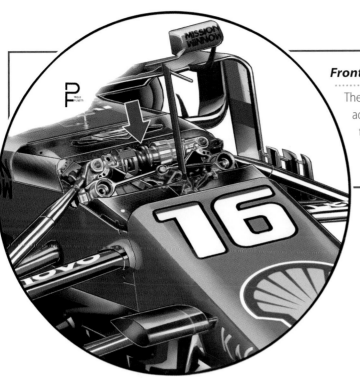

Front suspension

The front suspension retained the same configuration of the previous car. At Baku, where adjustment of the heave damper controlling ride height is particularly important, multiple tests were conducted during free practice, including the replacement of the anti-roll bar, facilitated by the layout of the system.

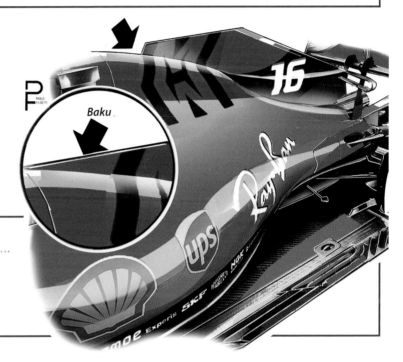

Baku

SF90 engine cover

A new engine cover was introduced in Spain, part of the first extensive aero package, with a cutaway in the leading section of the vertical fin designed to reduce the turbulence generated by the previous version which had been faired into the cover horizontally (see the circle).

Front wing evolution

The Paul Ricard saw the debut of a new version of the front wing characterised by a main plane with a more overt downwards curvature (1) close to to the endplates. The flaps (2) lost the torsion that reduced their incidence in the proximity of the endplates, now equipped with a rectangular cutaway (3) in correspondence with the upper rear corner. A triangular vortex generator was added to the footplate (4) in order to increase the out-wash effect (see the flow visualization drawing).

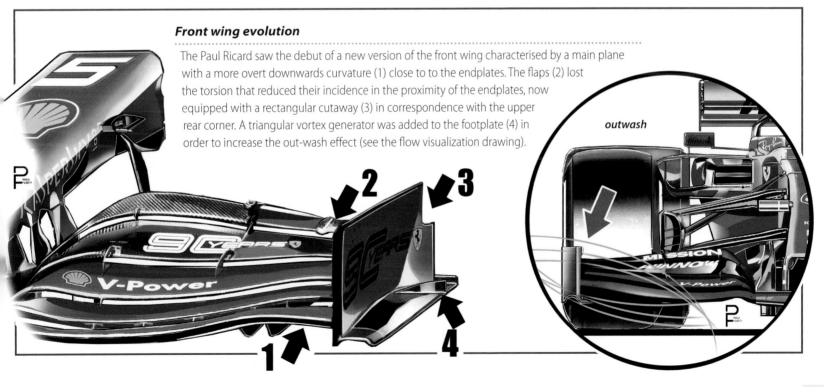

outwash

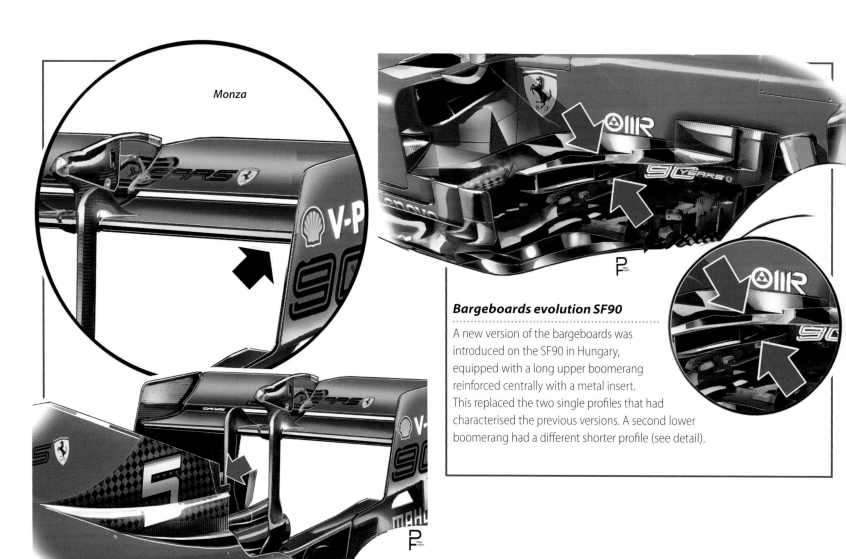

Monza

V-P

Bargeboards evolution SF90

A new version of the bargeboards was introduced on the SF90 in Hungary, equipped with a long upper boomerang reinforced centrally with a metal insert. This replaced the two single profiles that had characterised the previous versions. A second lower boomerang had a different shorter profile (see detail).

Low-downforce configurations

At Spa, the aero configuration provided for a rear wing featuring a main plane set very high in order to reduce the incidence of the flap and with the T-wing eliminated to reduce drag. At Monza this configuration was taken even further with the reduction of the incidence of the flap and the main plane set even higher (see the detail).

Rear bodywork and pressure sensors

In Mexico, the rear trailing edge of the SF90 bodywork was modified with a cutaway in order to increase the section of the vent for the air leaving the radiator packs and to guarantee adequate heat dispersal in the rarefied air of Mexico City. Also of note was the strip of pressure sensors fitted to the floor ahead of the diffuser "elbow"; a test was conducted to measure the magnitude and the pressure of the air flow with the version of the floor introduced in Singapore.

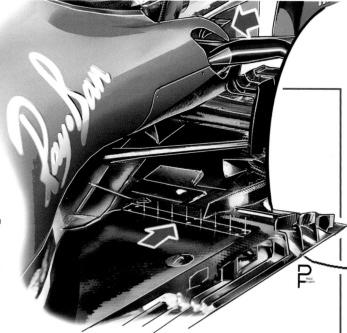

Ferrari ERS module position

The detail drawing shows the position of the sandwiched radiators and the ERS module on the Ferrari SF90. A location far from sources of heat and vibration such as the engine. The problem suffered by Charles Leclerc in Bahrain was actually caused by the characteristics of the last iteration of the module adopted.

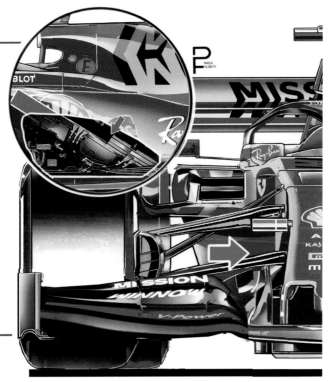

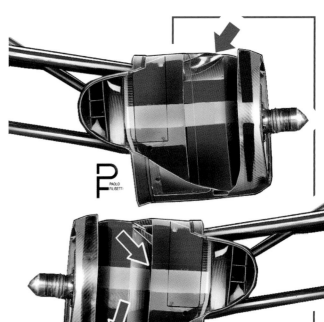

Asymmetric brake drums

The adoption of asymmetric front brake drums on a number of circuits was interesting and designed to optimize differentiated cooling and distribution of heat to the wheels rims. In Melbourne, for example, the SF90 presented a dual parallel vent along the circumference of the right-hand drum, with the exception of the lower part where the caliper was located. Note also, the two small channels in the lower part. On upper part of the left-hand drum, we can see a deep groove that reveals the path taken by the air towards the outside of the wheel.

Dual wastegate exhausts tested on the SF90

Abu Dhabi saw a test conducted with dual wastegate exhausts set above the principal exhaust exiting the turbocharger, with a slight upwards inclination at a

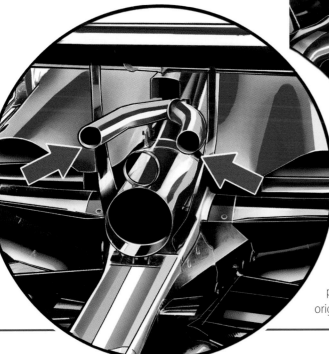

maximum of 5°, as per the regulations. The aim was to harvest data regarding the effects of the venting in the areas to the sides of the wing pylons. In the comparison with the standard version we can see the ring on the principal exhaust that contained the wastegate exhaust in the original position (see the detail).

RED BULL RACING RB15

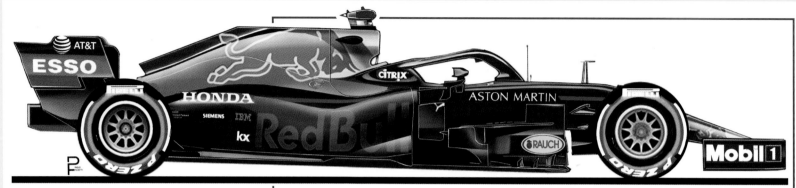

RB15 side view

The RB15 was characterised by reduced sidepod volumes, even smaller than those of the previous car. The bargeboards were already more complex at the car's debut, effectively being a development of the last 2018 version.

Despite changing power unit from Tag Heuer (Renault) to Honda, the team fielded a car that kept faith with the design canons of Adrian Newey. His hand was clear in every detail, even though certain elements were borrowed from other cars (Ferrari SF71H), albeit in highly modified form. The unknown quantity at the start of the season was the Honda power unit in terms of reliability and performance, despite the extensive mileage covered in testing. Overall, the RB15, thanks in part to the reduced dimensions of the Japanese unit, followed the prevailing aerodynamic dictates that demanded a significantly reduced frontal section. It appeared that in spite of uncompromising choices, the efficacy of the cooling system satisfied the Honda engineers and there was also an improvement in performance that placed the Japanese engine on a higher plane than the Renault six-cylinder.

Melbourne

Front view

The overall front view of the RB15 highlights how this car was initially characterised by a wing with a main plane extending the full width to the endplates with a configuration that was only slightly sinuous. This was a single profile notable for the absence of a clear demarcation between the neutral central and the lateral elements. In terms of flaps, the shaping indicates a principally in-wash configuration with the flows directed inside the wheels. From Melbourne, however, modifications to the endplates were designed to facilitate partial out-washing. The detail drawing shows, indicated by the arrow, the rectangular cutaway on the upper rear corner of the endplate. The tip of the upper flap can be seen, acting as an outboard "invitation" for that portion of the flow skimming the inner face of the endplates. The inner leading edge of the two upper flaps have a steep downturn with a very accentuated cusp.

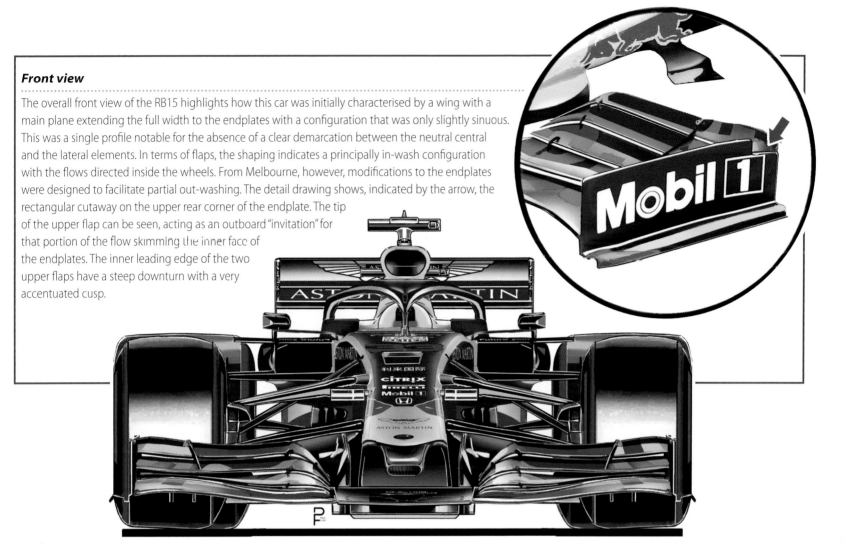

Sochi

Bargeboards evolution comparison

Micro-aerodynamic tweaks also affected the turning vanes ahead of the sidepods. In particular, there was an interesting introduction of vertical vents in the lower front turning vane support, integrated at the top with the lower lip of the intake mouths. These vents were designed to energize the flow over the lower part of the sidepods, ensuring that it remained attached. At Sochi, the bargeboards and the leading edge of the boomerang were modified. In detail, the profile of the bargeboard was no longer straight, but now had a sinuous cutaway that reduced the surface area in the lower part. In the comparison we can see the difference with respect to the previous version used through to Singapore.

Rear wing comparisons

It is interesting to note how there were macroscopic differences between a high-downforce wing, such as the one for Monaco, and a low-downforce one. Of particular note among the latter due to the extremely low incidence of the flap was the one for Monza compared to the one used at Spa.

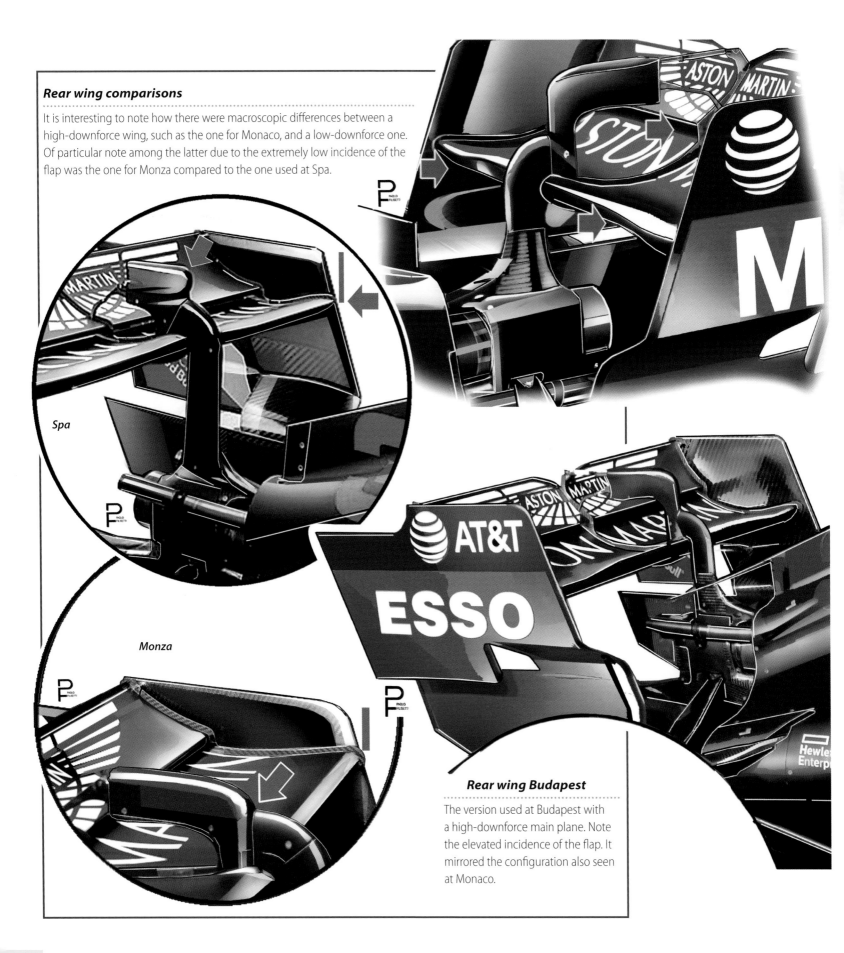

Spa

Monza

Rear wing Budapest

The version used at Budapest with a high-downforce main plane. Note the elevated incidence of the flap. It mirrored the configuration also seen at Monaco.

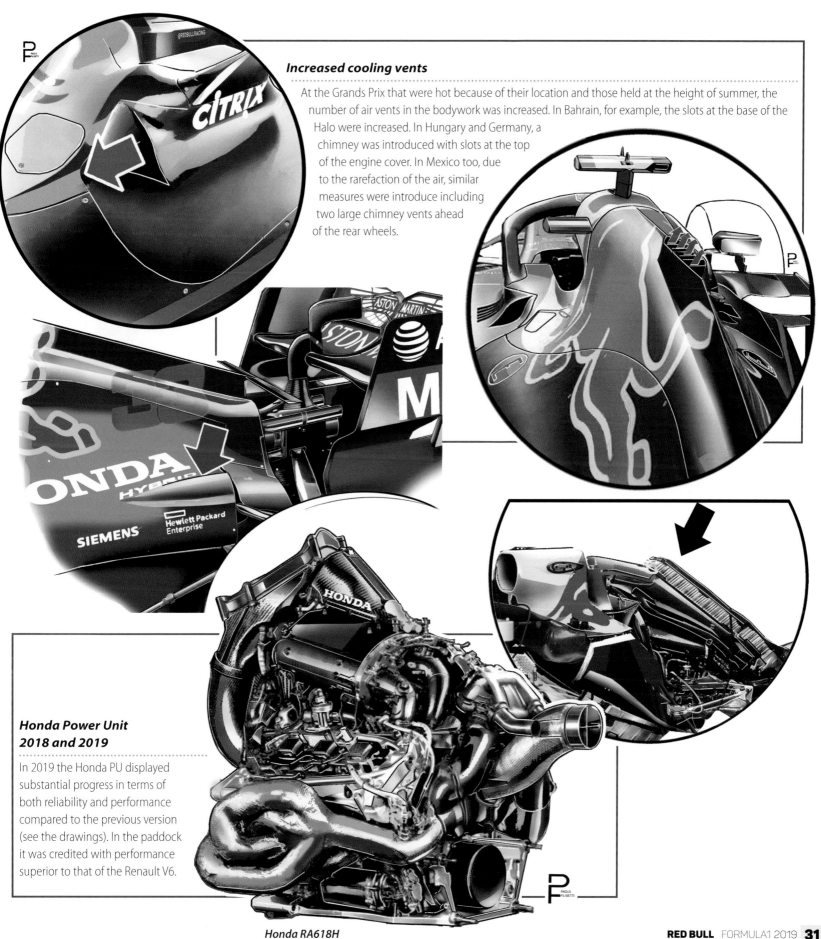

Increased cooling vents

At the Grands Prix that were hot because of their location and those held at the height of summer, the number of air vents in the bodywork was increased. In Bahrain, for example, the slots at the base of the Halo were increased. In Hungary and Germany, a chimney was introduced with slots at the top of the engine cover. In Mexico too, due to the rarefaction of the air, similar measures were introduce including two large chimney vents ahead of the rear wheels.

Honda Power Unit 2018 and 2019

In 2019 the Honda PU displayed substantial progress in terms of both reliability and performance compared to the previous version (see the drawings). In the paddock it was credited with performance superior to that of the Renault V6.

Honda RA618H

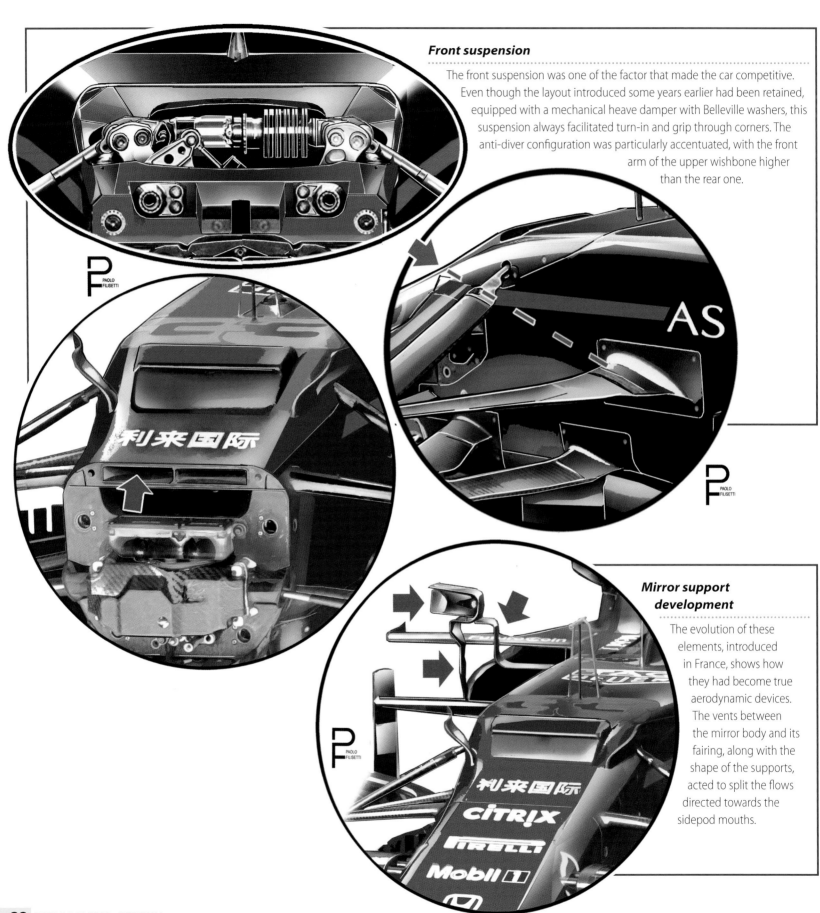

Front suspension

The front suspension was one of the factor that made the car competitive. Even though the layout introduced some years earlier had been retained, equipped with a mechanical heave damper with Belleville washers, this suspension always facilitated turn-in and grip through corners. The anti-diver configuration was particularly accentuated, with the front arm of the upper wishbone higher than the rear one.

Mirror support development

The evolution of these elements, introduced in France, shows how they had become true aerodynamic devices. The vents between the mirror body and its fairing, along with the shape of the supports, acted to split the flows directed towards the sidepod mouths.

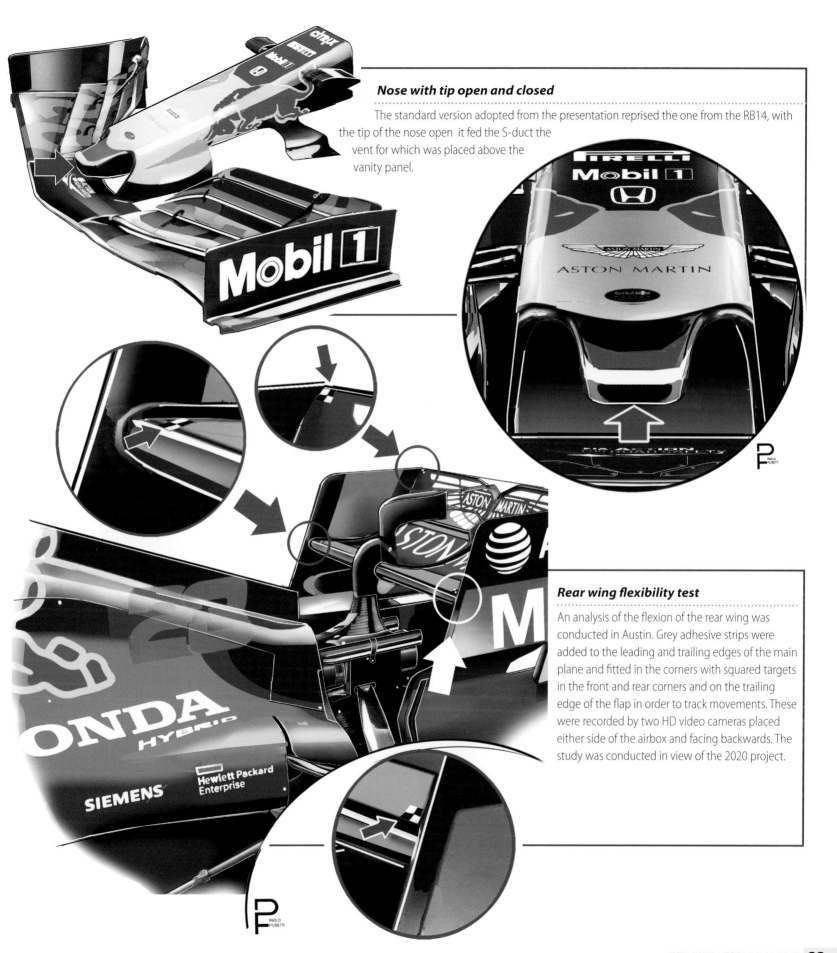

Nose with tip open and closed

The standard version adopted from the presentation reprised the one from the RB14, with the tip of the nose open it fed the S-duct the vent for which was placed above the vanity panel.

Rear wing flexibility test

An analysis of the flexion of the rear wing was conducted in Austin. Grey adhesive strips were added to the leading and trailing edges of the main plane and fitted in the corners with squared targets in the front and rear corners and on the trailing edge of the flap in order to track movements. These were recorded by two HD video cameras placed either side of the airbox and facing backwards. The study was conducted in view of the 2020 project.

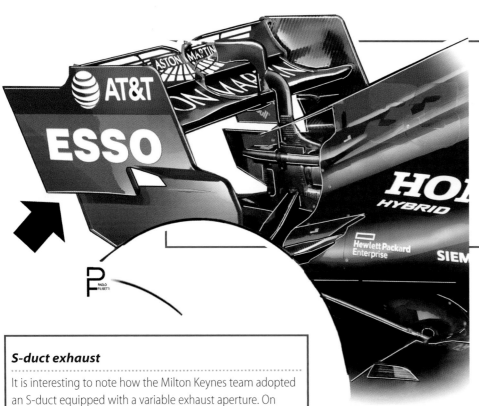

Rear wing comparison: Hungary and Singapore

At Marina Bay, along with a maximum downforce main plane, endplates with no vents in correspondence with the leading edge were adopted. In contrast, on the high downforce Budapest circuit the team adopted very similar wing profile but this time paired with endplates with a vertical slot.

S-duct exhaust

It is interesting to note how the Milton Keynes team adopted an S-duct equipped with a variable exhaust aperture. On certain tracks a version with a short slot was adopted and a wider one on others. The two configurations implied a variation in the pressure of the flow passing under the nose.

Vortex generators on the floor

Silverstone saw the introduction of four vortex generators on the footplate, at the base of the sidepods. In this way the air flow in this area was energized, increasing the efficiency of the longitudinal slots downstream.

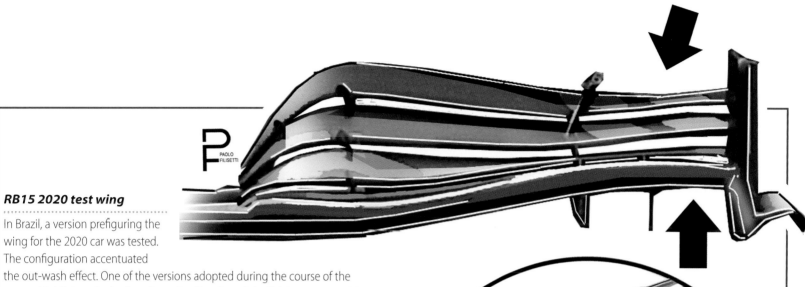

RB15 2020 test wing

In Brazil, a version prefiguring the wing for the 2020 car was tested. The configuration accentuated the out-wash effect. One of the versions adopted during the course of the season highlights, via the flow lines, the direction of the fluid streams, mainly concentrated towards the inside (in-wash).

Vanity panel winglets

The RB15 was one of the first cars to adopt the winglets directing the flow towards the sidepod intakes, located horizontally and high up thanks to the lowering of the crushable anti-intrusion cones.

McLAREN MCL 34

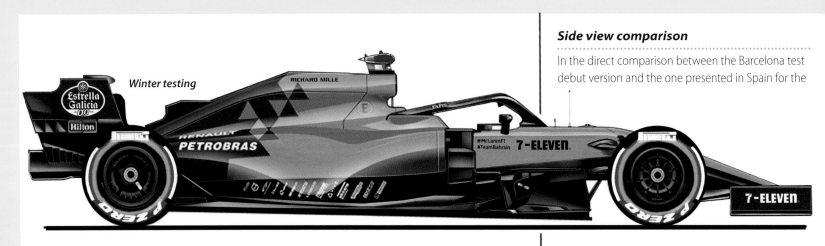

Winter testing

The MCL34 was the second McLaren powered by Renault. The project immediately appeared more mature, with more solid foundations than the previous year's car. It was well detailed, with an aerodynamic configuration featuring reduced and horizontal air intakes. Performance over the course of the season confirmed the sensations regarding the validity of the design gained in the early tests. The aerodynamic features adopted showed a certain originality, above all in the area ahead of the sidepods. Here, in fact, the MCL34 was the first car to present a kind of ring-like bargeboard that efficiently channelled the turbulence generated by the front wheels away from the body of the car.

Rear wing endplates Spain

In Barcelona, the development package was completed with the adoption of the front wing endplates characterised by a triple series of arching mini-profiles acting as vortex generators in the upper section, thereby increasing the efficiency of the wing.

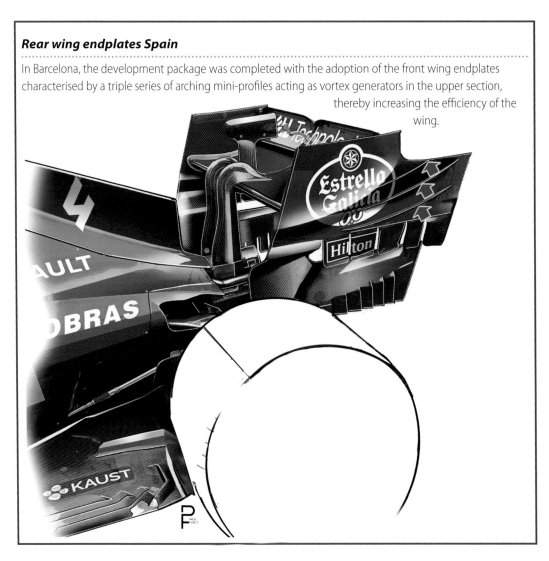

Grand Prix we can clearly see the different shape of the engine cover. In practice, in the first there is only a vestigial fin at the bottom, while in the second it is full length and faired into the upper edge of the bodywork. The second configuration determined a narrow yaw angle, making the car more reactive in changing direction. On the other hand, it had little negative effect on the rear wing.

Montmelò

Single or double front suspension brackets?

It was interesting to note over the course of the season how the team conducted numerous experiments on the front suspension, evaluating on various occasions the adoption of a bracket connected to the push-rod together with the pivot linking the upper wishbone to the hub-carrier. In the case of this last, it was also interesting to note that at Sochi the team tested a specific voluminous fairing that appeared above the wishbone fulcrum. Its aerodynamic function in the management of the airflows lapping the wheels was that of separating the turbulence from the flows directed towards the sidepods and the rear end.

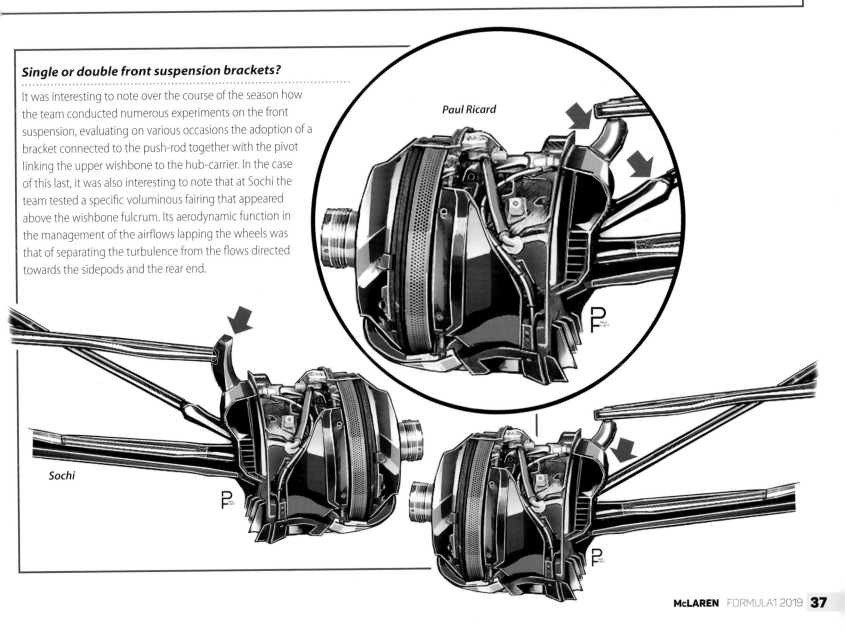

Paul Ricard

Sochi

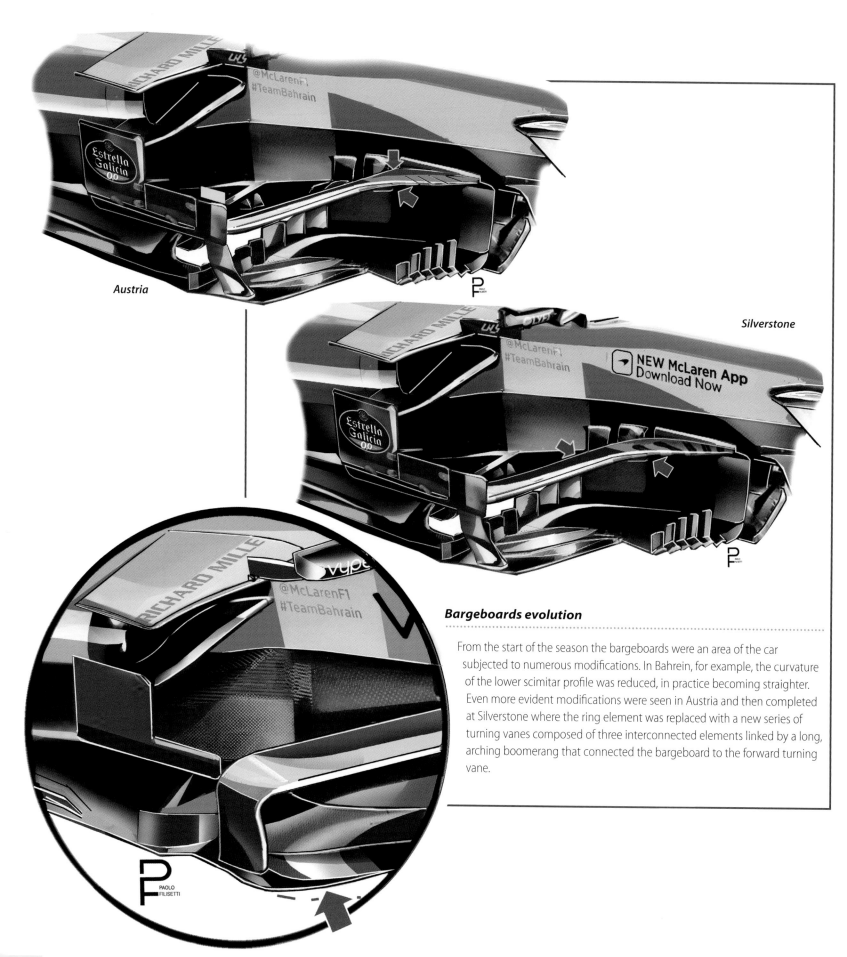

Austria

Silverstone

Bargeboards evolution

From the start of the season the bargeboards were an area of the car subjected to numerous modifications. In Bahrein, for example, the curvature of the lower scimitar profile was reduced, in practice becoming straighter. Even more evident modifications were seen in Austria and then completed at Silverstone where the ring element was replaced with a new series of turning vanes composed of three interconnected elements linked by a long, arching boomerang that connected the bargeboard to the forward turning vane.

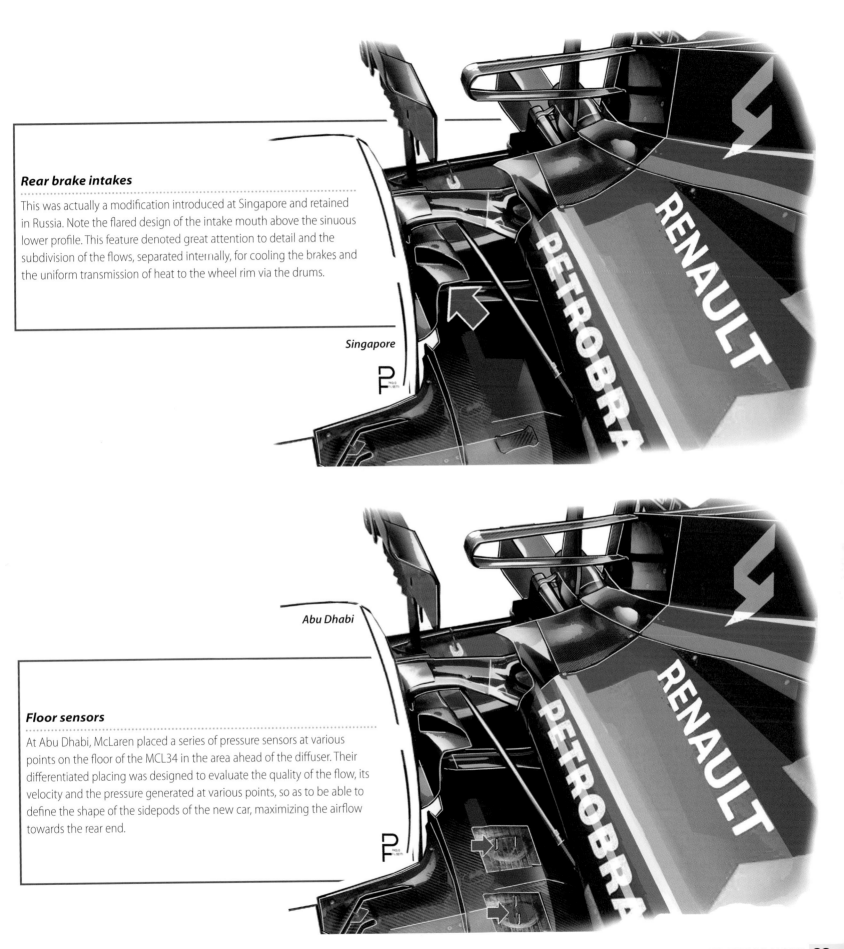

Rear brake intakes

This was actually a modification introduced at Singapore and retained in Russia. Note the flared design of the intake mouth above the sinuous lower profile. This feature denoted great attention to detail and the subdivision of the flows, separated internally, for cooling the brakes and the uniform transmission of heat to the wheel rim via the drums.

Singapore

Floor sensors

At Abu Dhabi, McLaren placed a series of pressure sensors at various points on the floor of the MCL34 in the area ahead of the diffuser. Their differentiated placing was designed to evaluate the quality of the flow, its velocity and the pressure generated at various points, so as to be able to define the shape of the sidepods of the new car, maximizing the airflow towards the rear end.

Abu Dhabi

RENAULT RS19

Sidepod inlet

The Renault RS19 was also characterised by high sidepod inlet's, a concept originally introduced by Ferrari in 2017.

On its presentation, the RS19 was something of a fake with respect to the actual car. Seen close up in testing at Barcelona it appeared to be a well-built single-seater with a number of original details, an excellent foundation. What we were able to note over the course of the season was the attention paid to details, along with the significantly reduced section of the sidepod area compared to the RS18. Like all the other teams, Renault also borrowed the concepts introduced by Ferrari with the SF70-H. Despite a number of development packages being introduced, the Enstone engineers proved unable to extract maximum performance from the car.

Renault rear aerodynamics

For Monaco the rear wing of the RS 19 was modified with a new high downforce profile and a T-wing characterised by a vent in the lower plane. A monkey seat was also fitted behind the support pylons.

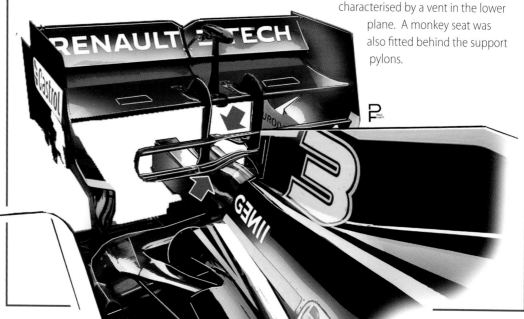

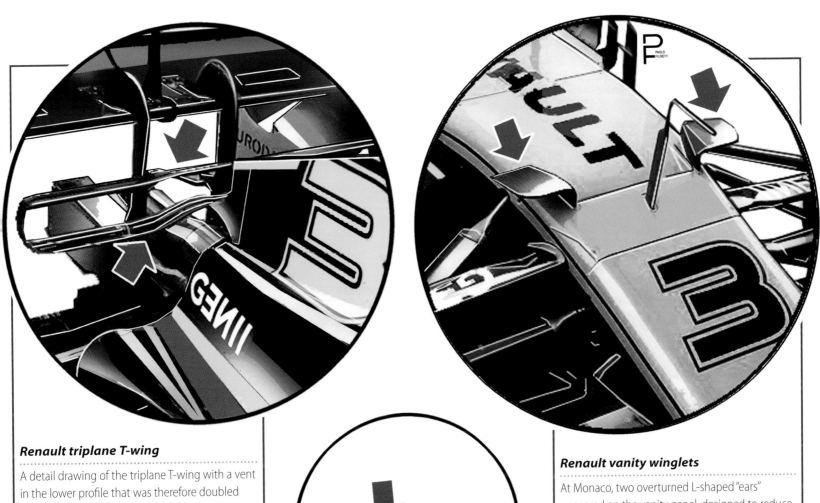

Renault triplane T-wing

A detail drawing of the triplane T-wing with a vent in the lower profile that was therefore doubled and a single upper profile. It was used on high-downforce circuits such as Monaco, Budapest and Singapore.

Renault vanity winglets

At Monaco, two overturned L-shaped "ears" appeared on the vanity panel, designed to reduce lift by deviating the flow of air exiting the front wing downwards.

Montreal

Renault: rear wing, DRS HUB and endplates

In Canada, the rear wing received revised endplates. Two profiles generating an up-wash effect were added and the DRS actuator was modified. A fairing now extended rearwards through to the upper edge of the wing. In the circle, the comparison with the previous version.

RS19: winglet in front of the rear wheels

In Montreal, in correspondence with the two longitudinal vents ahead of the diagonal ones managing tyre squirt, a winglet was added to the floor, curving outwards to augment the efficacy of the slots. The comparison shows the earlier version used through to Monaco.

Renault RS RS19: cape

In France, Renault introduced a Mercedes-style cape below the nose cone. It was the fifth team to adopt the feature following Mercedes, McLaren, Williams and Racing Point.

Renault RS19: rear vents

The Red Bull Ring constituted a particularly severe test due to the temperatures reached by the engines, the absence of long straights, along with a marginal rarefaction of the air being the principal causes. Renault adopted a megaphone-style rear bodywork vent to guarantee adequate heat dispersal for the RE19 power unit.

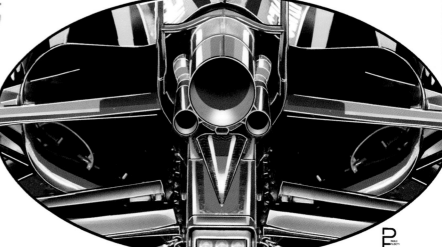

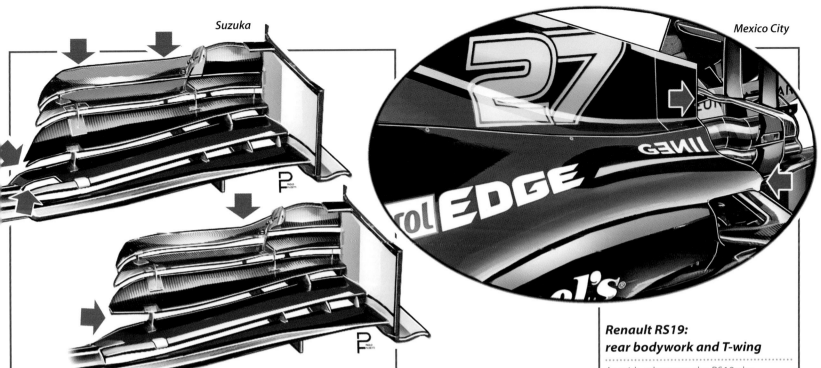

Suzuka

Mexico City

RS19 Front Wing

At Suzuka, Renault introduced an evolution of its front wing characterised by modifications to the main plane and the flaps. The internal portion of the first was characterised by a short but deep rectangular vent that effectively split it into two elements. The first flap had a leading edge that followed the line of the trailing edge of the main plane and had a small triangular cutaway at its lower internal extremity; the chord of the two adjustable flaps was also increased, in more tangible form on the last flap in the internal section with respect to the incidence adjustment mechanism. There were also visible differences with respect to the version used in Russia and the one from Italy, similar to the Sochi configuration.

Renault RS19: rear bodywork and T-wing

As with other cars, the RS19 also presented at Mexico with more voluminous rear bodywork. This ensured an increase in the thermal exchange otherwise penalised by the rarefaction of the air. There was also an interesting adoption of a monoplane T-wing with the extremities curving downwards. This feature was used in order to avoid excessive increases in the drag generated on the long straights despite the lower density of the air.

Baku

RS19 rear wing (low drag)

The low drag version of the RS 19's rear wing was characterised by a different configuration of the endplates in correspondence with the median vertical vents and of the main plane which featured a dished profile.

SPORT PESA RACING POINT RP 19

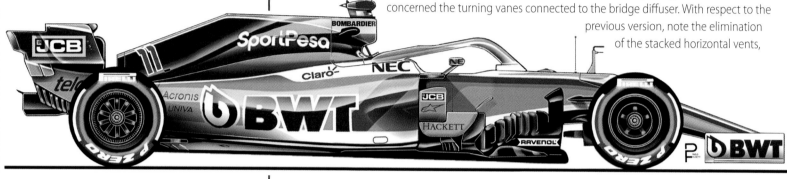

Side view comparison

The direct comparison between the initial version with which the Barcelona tests were conducted, the Melbourne car and the one seen in Canada highlight how the immature project was progressively developed over the course of the season. For Melbourne, in fact, a package was introduced that concerned the turning vanes connected to the bridge diffuser. With respect to the previous version, note the elimination of the stacked horizontal vents,

The RP19 was to all intents and purposes an evolution of the previous year's car. Over the course of the season there were frequent changes that gradually transformed what was a carbon copy of the VJM 11, albeit adapted to the new regulations, due to the transitional period between the previous ownership and that of Lawrence Stroll. The modifications that were introduced drew considerable inspiration from the Mercedes with which Racing Point shares its power unit. The Mercedes unit in fact represented the best part of the project.

Front wing endplate evolution

The footplate area of the front wing endplates was modified a number of occasions. In France the rear part was just shorter with respect to the length of the endplate. At Silverstone the shortening was even more evident, with a flared cutaway that considerably shortened the rear section of the footplate. In Singapore, paired with the nose introduced in Belgium, we saw a wing equipped with endplates with a lower hump in correspondence with the footplate cutaway.

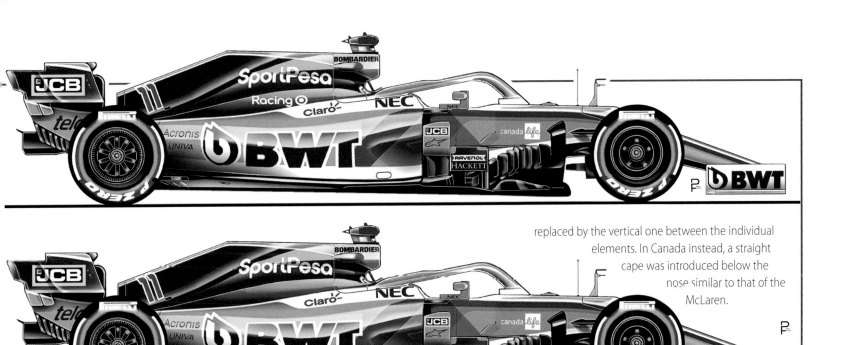

replaced by the vertical one between the individual elements. In Canada instead, a straight cape was introduced below the nose similar to that of the McLaren.

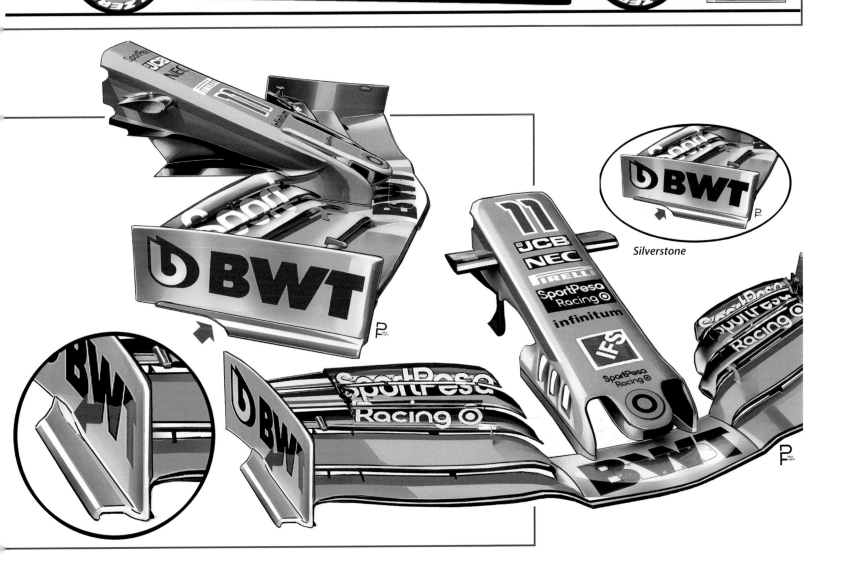

Silverstone

Adoption of the cape

In Canada, the RP19 was fitted with a cape similar to that of the McLaren, a feature retained for the following races with changes to the endplates as described above. In Montreal, the version used still had nostrils.

Heat dispersal rear end Austria

In order to facilitate heat dispersal, in Austria Racing Point increased the section of the rear megaphone thereby permitting the heat from the sidepods to be extracted efficiently.

Longitudinal vents on the floor

In Baku, it was interesting to note the appearance of a double series of three longitudinal vents designed to create a pneumatic seal below the car on the Azeri circuit's long straights.

Nose without nostrils

Spa saw the debut of a version of the nose without nostrils, characterised by large wing pylons with three vertical vents.

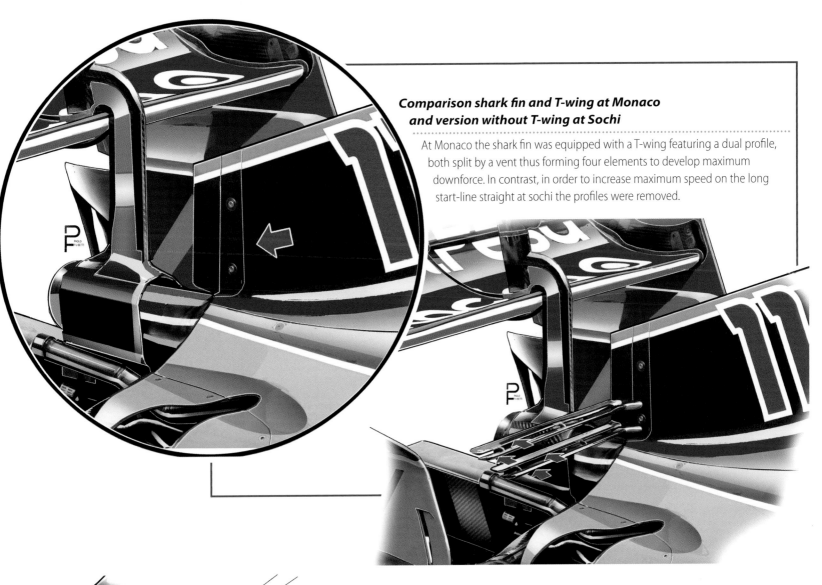

Comparison shark fin and T-wing at Monaco and version without T-wing at Sochi

At Monaco the shark fin was equipped with a T-wing featuring a dual profile, both split by a vent thus forming four elements to develop maximum downforce. In contrast, in order to increase maximum speed on the long start-line straight at sochi the profiles were removed.

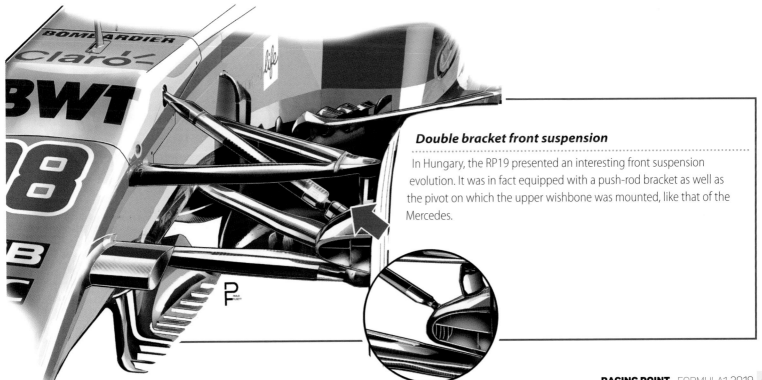

Double bracket front suspension

In Hungary, the RP19 presented an interesting front suspension evolution. It was in fact equipped with a push-rod bracket as well as the pivot on which the upper wishbone was mounted, like that of the Mercedes.

ALFA ROMEO RACING C38

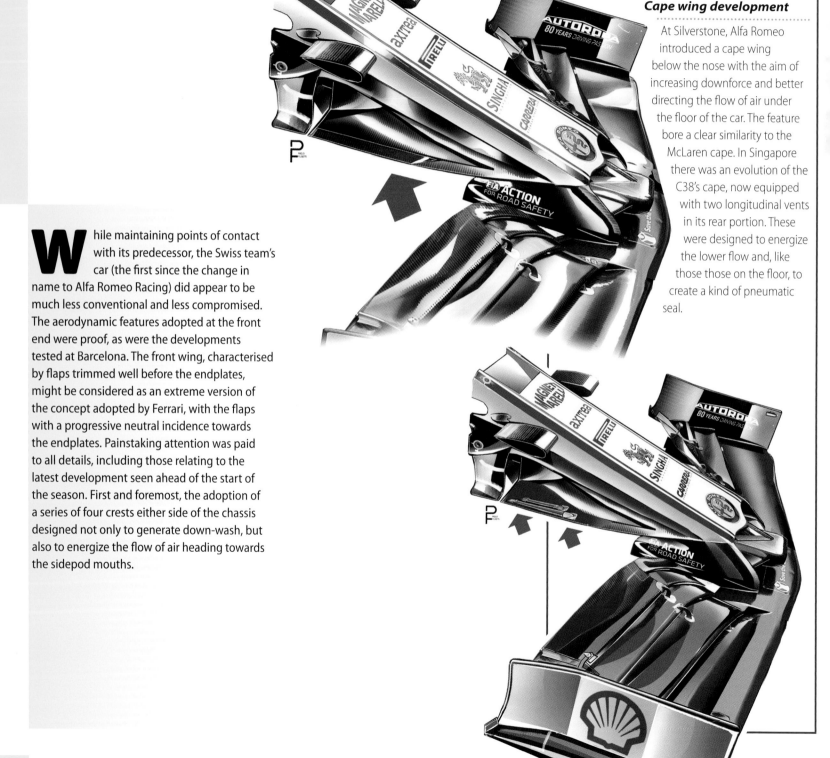

Cape wing development

At Silverstone, Alfa Romeo introduced a cape wing below the nose with the aim of increasing downforce and better directing the flow of air under the floor of the car. The feature bore a clear similarity to the McLaren cape. In Singapore there was an evolution of the C38's cape, now equipped with two longitudinal vents in its rear portion. These were designed to energize the lower flow and, like those those on the floor, to create a kind of pneumatic seal.

While maintaining points of contact with its predecessor, the Swiss team's car (the first since the change in name to Alfa Romeo Racing) did appear to be much less conventional and less compromised. The aerodynamic features adopted at the front end were proof, as were the developments tested at Barcelona. The front wing, characterised by flaps trimmed well before the endplates, might be considered as an extreme version of the concept adopted by Ferrari, with the flaps with a progressive neutral incidence towards the endplates. Painstaking attention was paid to all details, including those relating to the latest development seen ahead of the start of the season. First and foremost, the adoption of a series of four crests either side of the chassis designed not only to generate down-wash, but also to energize the flow of air heading towards the sidepod mouths.

Floor with 18 diagonal vents

Bahrain saw the debut of a floor equipped with 18 diagonal vents in correspondence with the outside edge, ahead of the rear wheels. These elements permitted the generation of a kind of pneumatic side skirt that would seal the floor, increasing the efficiency of the diffuser.

Monza and Singapore configurations compared

The Monza and Marina Bay circuits are poles apart. At the first, what counts is efficiency and the C38 adopted a particularly low downforce rear wing with a dished profile and particularly closed bodywork that was lower in the rearmost part that the upper wishbone. Moreover, T-wing was removed from the fin on the engine cover to reduce straight line drag. The Singapore configuration was quite the opposite. The T-wing in fact constituted a C-shaped profile doubled up by a full-length vent. The rear wing presented a very low main plane guaranteeing an elevated flap incidence.

Bargeboards with boomerang

In France, Alfa Romeo introduced a boomerang wing on the C38 that linked the vertical elements of the bargeboards with those of the turning vanes. This element separated the airflow into two superimposed portions, directed respectively to the sidepod mouths and the floor.

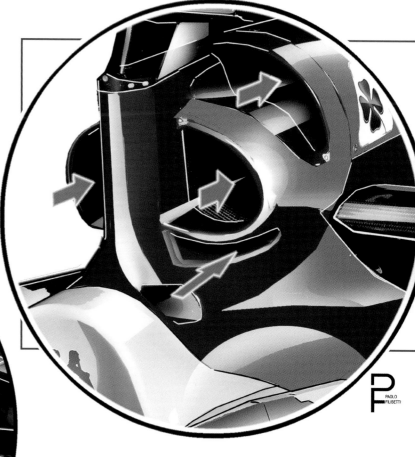

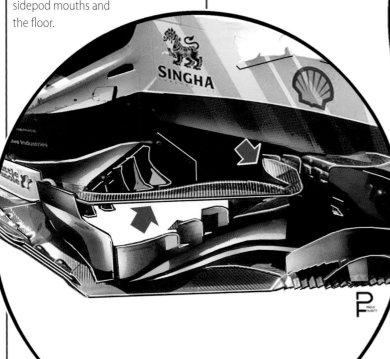

Winglets on the nose

From the winter tests onwards, the C38 was fitted with two series of winglets either side of the vanity panel. They were designed to deviate the airflow exiting the front wing downwards while directing a portion towards the sidepod mouths feeding the radiators.

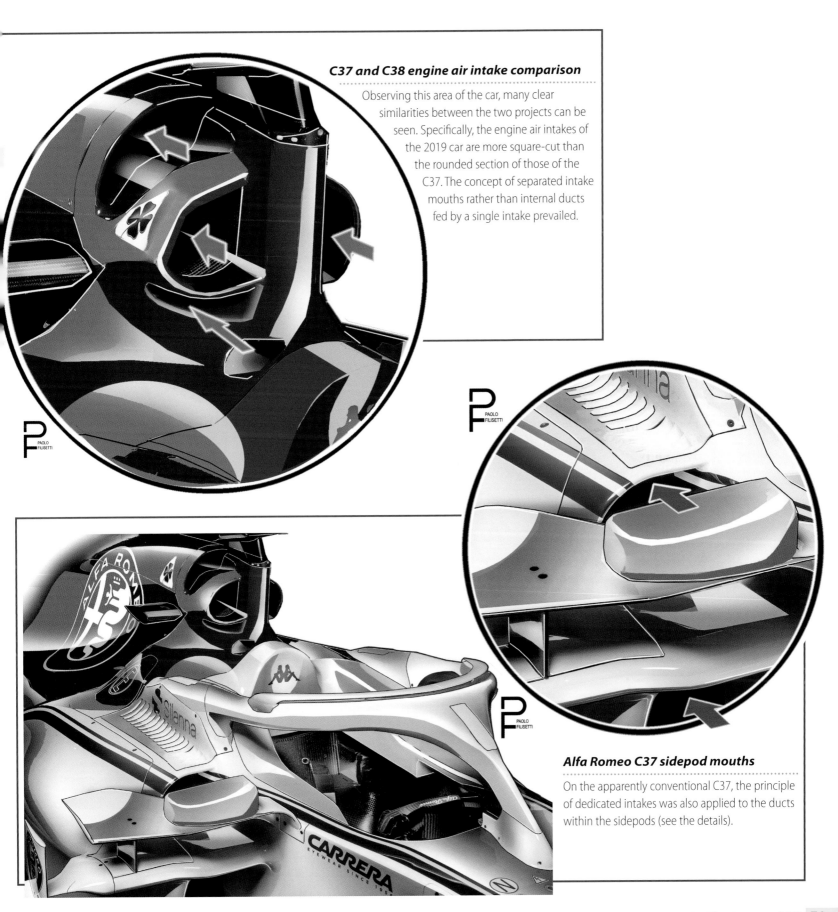

C37 and C38 engine air intake comparison

Observing this area of the car, many clear similarities between the two projects can be seen. Specifically, the engine air intakes of the 2019 car are more square-cut than the rounded section of those of the C37. The concept of separated intake mouths rather than internal ducts fed by a single intake prevailed.

Alfa Romeo C37 sidepod mouths

On the apparently conventional C37, the principle of dedicated intakes was also applied to the ducts within the sidepods (see the details).

TORO ROSSO STR14

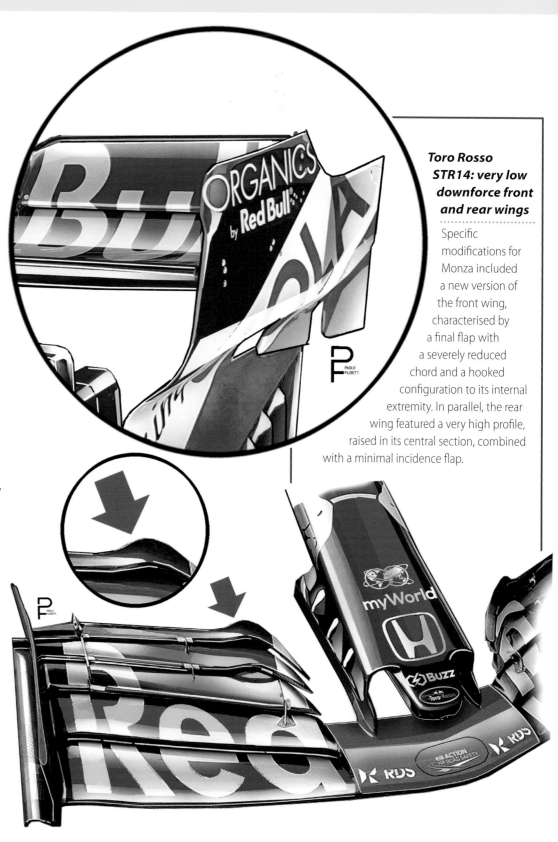

The Faenza-based team was in the second season of its partnership with Honda. The STR14 was a more "courageous" car, focussing less on a search for absolute reliability from the Japanese power unit than the STR13. It was no coincidence that the dimensions of the sidepods and the air intakes proved to be less generous. The car showed considerable potential with Albon and Kvyat. The team also showed that it had what it takes in terms of the capacity for developing the car. The STR14 was in fact the only car, apart from the Ferrari and Alfa Romeo, to be fitted from its debut with a front wing equipped with flaps chamfered towards the endplates.

Toro Rosso STR14: very low downforce front and rear wings

Specific modifications for Monza included a new version of the front wing, characterised by a final flap with a severely reduced chord and a hooked configuration to its internal extremity. In parallel, the rear wing featured a very high profile, raised in its central section, combined with a minimal incidence flap.

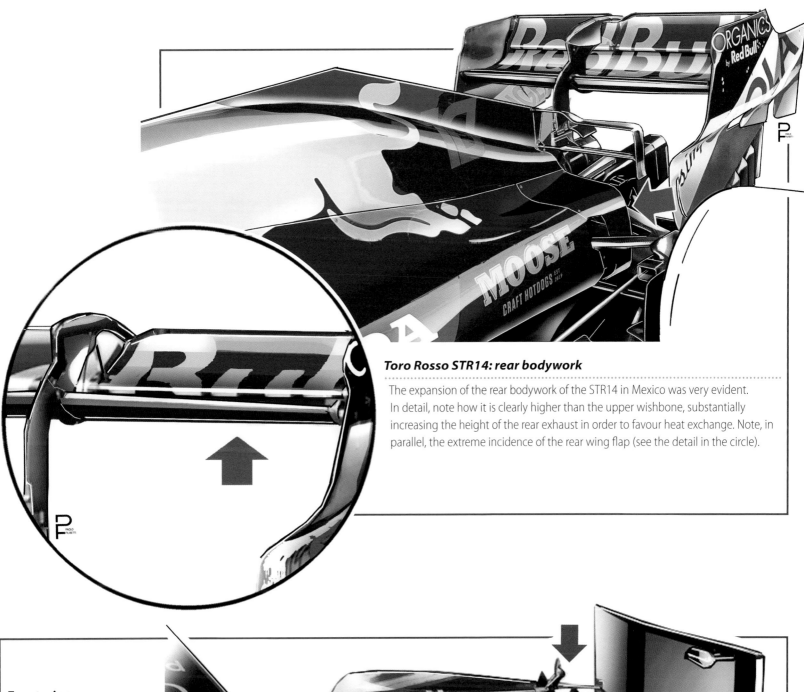

Toro Rosso STR14: rear bodywork

The expansion of the rear bodywork of the STR14 in Mexico was very evident. In detail, note how it is clearly higher than the upper wishbone, substantially increasing the height of the rear exhaust in order to favour heat exchange. Note, in parallel, the extreme incidence of the rear wing flap (see the detail in the circle).

Front wing

A new front wing was tested in Mexico and reprised at Austin that featured a different main plane, without the kink between the neutral central portion and the lateral sections and a revision of the out-wash flow management configuration.

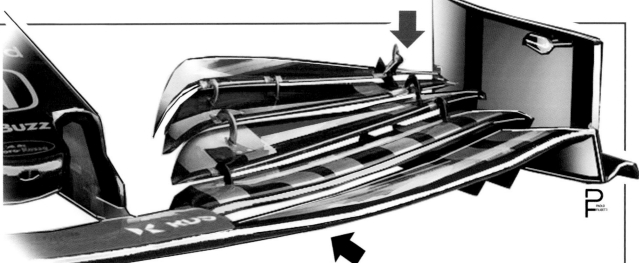

HAAS VF19

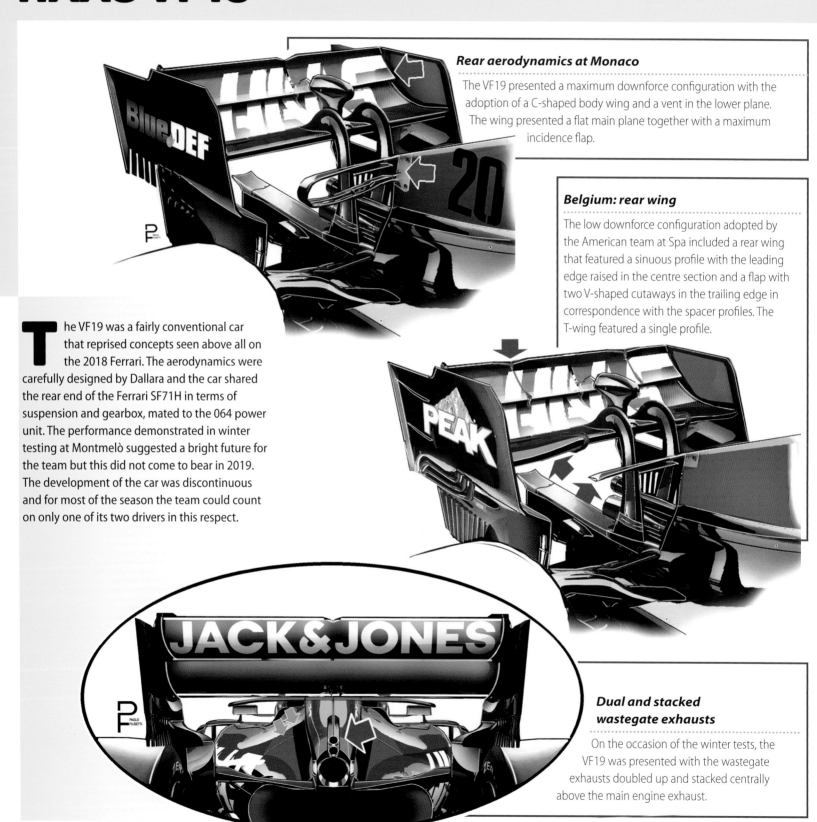

Rear aerodynamics at Monaco

The VF19 presented a maximum downforce configuration with the adoption of a C-shaped body wing and a vent in the lower plane. The wing presented a flat main plane together with a maximum incidence flap.

Belgium: rear wing

The low downforce configuration adopted by the American team at Spa included a rear wing that featured a sinuous profile with the leading edge raised in the centre section and a flap with two V-shaped cutaways in the trailing edge in correspondence with the spacer profiles. The T-wing featured a single profile.

T he VF19 was a fairly conventional car that reprised concepts seen above all on the 2018 Ferrari. The aerodynamics were carefully designed by Dallara and the car shared the rear end of the Ferrari SF71H in terms of suspension and gearbox, mated to the 064 power unit. The performance demonstrated in winter testing at Montmelò suggested a bright future for the team but this did not come to bear in 2019. The development of the car was discontinuous and for most of the season the team could count on only one of its two drivers in this respect.

Dual and stacked wastegate exhausts

On the occasion of the winter tests, the VF19 was presented with the wastegate exhausts doubled up and stacked centrally above the main engine exhaust.

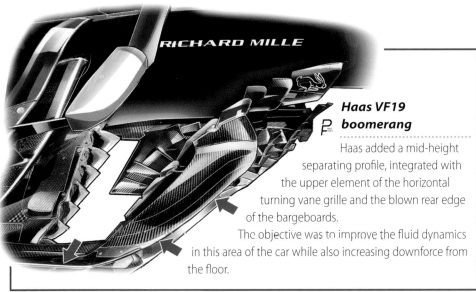

Haas VF19 boomerang

Haas added a mid-height separating profile, integrated with the upper element of the horizontal turning vane grille and the blown rear edge of the bargeboards.

The objective was to improve the fluid dynamics in this area of the car while also increasing downforce from the floor.

Haas rear wing endplates

In Germany sinuous vents resembling eyebrows were created in the transitional zone in the centre of the rear wing endplates that replaced the standard version with vertical vents used previously.

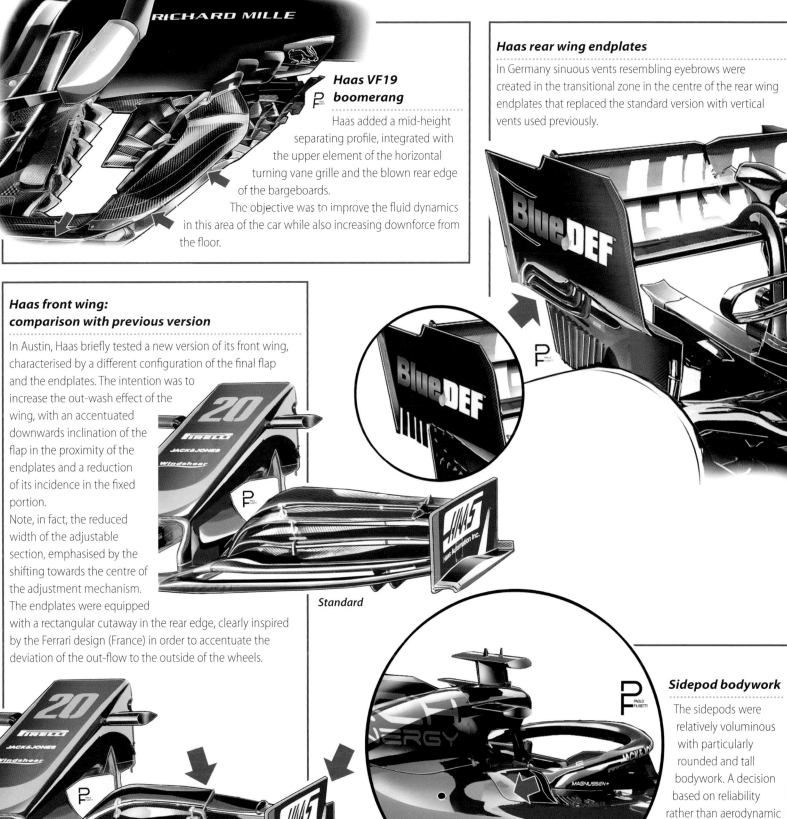

Haas front wing: comparison with previous version

In Austin, Haas briefly tested a new version of its front wing, characterised by a different configuration of the final flap and the endplates. The intention was to increase the out-wash effect of the wing, with an accentuated downwards inclination of the flap in the proximity of the endplates and a reduction of its incidence in the fixed portion.

Note, in fact, the reduced width of the adjustable section, emphasised by the shifting towards the centre of the adjustment mechanism. The endplates were equipped with a rectangular cutaway in the rear edge, clearly inspired by the Ferrari design (France) in order to accentuate the deviation of the out-flow to the outside of the wheels.

Standard

Sidepod bodywork

The sidepods were relatively voluminous with particularly rounded and tall bodywork. A decision based on reliability rather than aerodynamic efficiency.

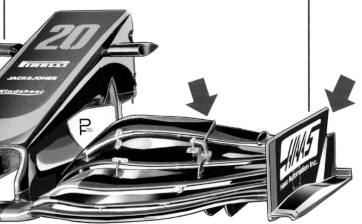

ROKIT WILLIAMS FW42

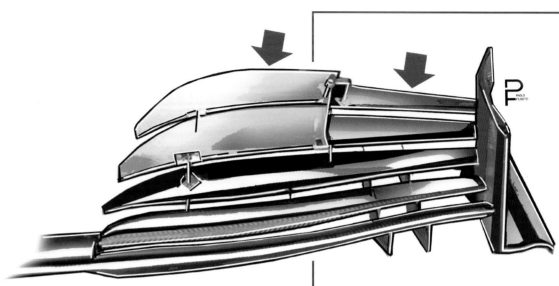

T he team from Grove trailed the pack. Not only did the FW42 arrive for the pre-season test three days late, but once it made it onto the track it was clearly far off the pace of the other cars. The project was a mere evolution of the previous car, adapted to meet the new regulations. Certain feature caused some perplexity with respect to those regulations, in particular the front suspension and the rear-view mirrors. These elements were later held to be non-compliant. Paddy Lowe leaving the team on the eve of the first race was another negative factor.

Front wing evolution

Williams took a profoundly revised version of its front wing to Japan that was designed to increase the out-wash effect. Available for George Russell only, the experimental version was characterised by an evident reduction in the width of the adjustable part of the last two flaps with respect to the standard configuration. The outermost portion was characterised by a clear downwards inclination in proximity to the endplates, accentuating the effect of deviating the turbulence to the outside of the wheels.

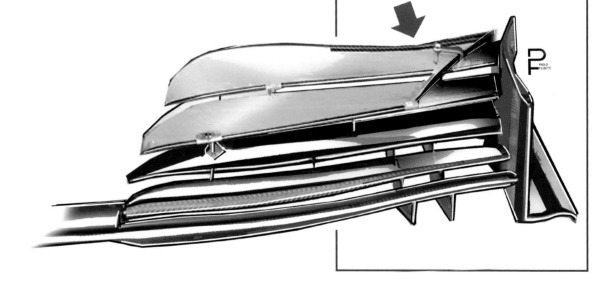

THE 2019 SEASON

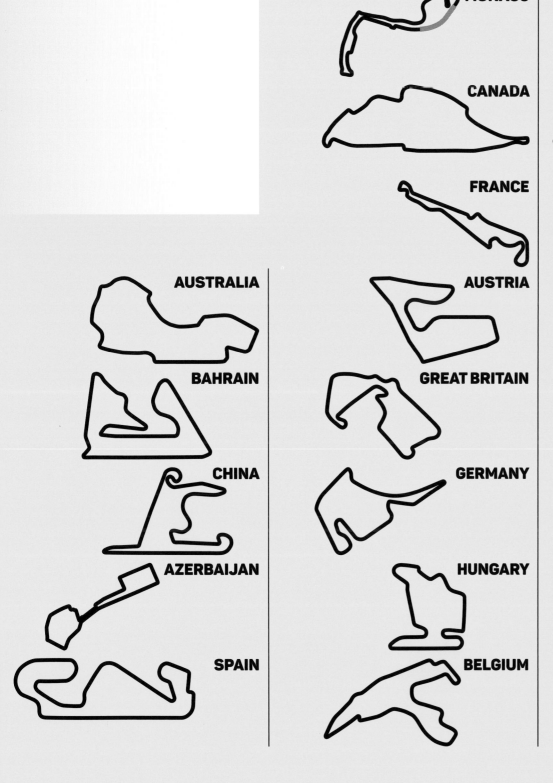

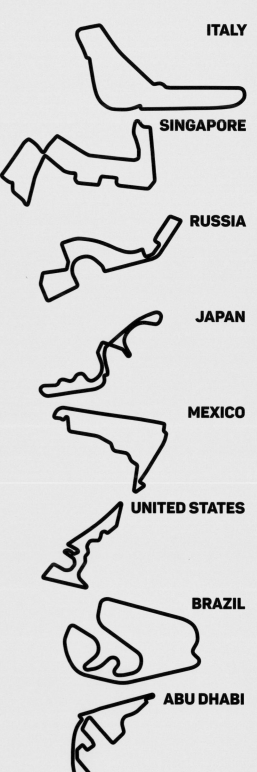

MONACO

CANADA

FRANCE

AUSTRALIA

BAHRAIN

CHINA

AZERBAIJAN

SPAIN

ITALY

SINGAPORE

RUSSIA

AUSTRIA

GREAT BRITAIN

GERMANY

HUNGARY

BELGIUM

JAPAN

MEXICO

UNITED STATES

BRAZIL

ABU DHABI

DEVELOPMENTAL MANOEUVRES...

AUSTRALIAN GRAND PRIX
MELBOURNE
ALBERT PARK
17 MARCH

The first GP of the season is always eagerly awaited from a technical point of view as at Melbourne the cars frequently present features that had yet to be signed off in time for the winter tests and to all intents and purposes represent the earliest versions. Generally speaking, rather than macroscopic modifications they tend to be tweaks to the aerodynamic configurations previously tested. While Mercedes had been the standout team at Montmelò, with the adoption in the second week of a revised package so extensive that the car could be considered as effectively a B version of the W10, in Melbourne the Brackley-based team fine-tuned the configuration of the car with less conspicuous detail changes. Specifically, small lower winglets appeared either side of the halo, designed to divert and energise the air flow heading towards the rear of the car while also optimizing the one towards the engine air intake.

The fine-tuning of the W10's aero package through these minor modifications would appear to indicate that Brackley was happy with the path followed during testing in Spain and had progressively adopted those changes that would optimize certain specific areas of the car. It is interesting to note that in Melbourne, following the multiple set-up tests focusing on rake angle that were undertaken in Barcelona, an inclination of around 1.4° was adopted, that is to say 0.2° more than the configuration in which the car was presented. We have often said and it is worth repeating here: in designing the W10, the Brackley engineers retained the DNA of the W09, but were well aware that the life cycle of the earlier car was effectively over in that it was itself an evolution of the 2017 design. In the case of the W10, a number of conceptual contaminations from rival cars (Red Bull, Ferrari) effectively made its development curve less restricted. The increment in the rake angle, as subtle as it may have been, is a clear example. While Mercedes showed an attention to micro-aerodynamics, Ferrari spared no efforts in terms of achieving reliability and aerodynamic efficiency. It was very interesting to see that asymmetric front brake drums were adopted. In this case, the asymmetry was not exclusively associated with the different thermal dumping between the right and left side of the car, but was rather indicative of particular attention paid to the flow of hot air generated under braking and the path it takes within the wheel rim. It can, in fact, be seen how the right-hand drum was characterised by two parallel vents along its circumference, in practice one more internal and the other more external, along with two small ducts in the lower part of the drum. The left-hand drum instead featured a deep groove with a sinuous profile that clearly revealed the direction of the flow that would pass through it, deviated towards the outside of the wheel after having run diagonally across the full width of the drum. There was, therefore, a clear intent to manage not only the tyre pressures through the dispersal of heat produced under braking, but also that of creating a vent, on the outer side with respect to the direction of the track that would disperse towards the outside the turbulence generated by the rotation of the front tyres. In this way the team attempted to favour the feeding of the rear diffuser with a flow under the car that was less disturbed. A further modification instead concerned the floor of the car, effectively an evolution of the one fitted during winter testing for a brief comparison test. The version adopted in Melbourne in fact lacked the three vertical flaps that had been introduced in Barcelona to act as turning vanes ahead of the rear wheels. Their elimination was not so much a rejection of the concept as due to the need to reduce the collecting of marbles and leaf fragments mixed up with them that could potentially have created a blockage in the area closest to the lateral channels of the diffuser. However, the attention paid to these details did not help the SF90 find the required balance on the Albert Park circuit. From the first free practice session, both drivers were complaining that they did not have the same confidence in the car they had enjoyed in Spain. Various modifications to the aerodynamic and suspension configurations only partly corrected a lack of balance that was particularly evident with the softer compounds. Qualifying and the race set the seal on an unexpectedly difficult weekend, with the SF90 reduced to a faded copy of the competitive "rossa" seen in Spain. As for Red Bull, the third force after testing, in Australia the team continued with the refinement of the RB15's aero package. A new version of the front wing was introduced characterised by a rectangular cutaway on the upper rear corner of the endplates. This was a feature shared by many cars and was designed to help drive the turbulence generated at the tips of the flaps towards the outside (out-wash). In parallel, the refinement of the turning vanes at the sides of the sidepods continued with the introduction of three shaped slits in the lower support of the vanes that extend forwards. They were designed to improve the management of the peripheral flow along the sidepods, keeping it attached to the bodywork and reducing interference with the flow under the car.

Main plane configuration

The overall front view of the RB15 highlights how this car was initially characterised by a wing with a main plane extending the full width to the endplates with a configuration that was only slightly sinuous. In substance it was a single profile in which there was an absence of a clear demarcation between the neutral central section and the lateral elements. In terms of flaps, the shaping indicates a principally in-wash configuration with the flows directed inside the wheels. From this race, however, modifications to the endplates were designed to facilitate partial out-washing.

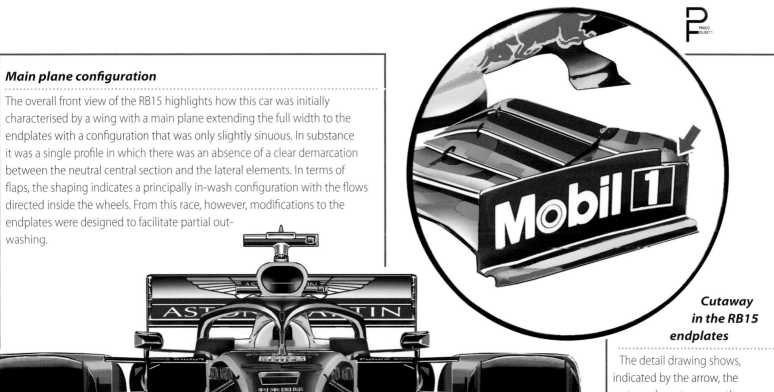

Cutaway in the RB15 endplates

The detail drawing shows, indicated by the arrow, the rectangular cutaway on the upper rear corner of the endplate. The tip of the upper flap can be seen, acting as an outboard "invitation" for that portion of the flow skimming the inner face of the endplates. The inner leading edge of the two upper flaps have a steep downturn with a very accentuated cusp.

Ferrari and Mercedes comparison

In the comparison between the main plane of the Ferrari SF90 front wing and that of the Mercedes W10 it can be seen that in both cases it is characterised by very sinuous lateral sections, with an accentuate central kink, despite the clear diversity of the general configurations: in-wash (Mercedes) out-wash (Ferrari).

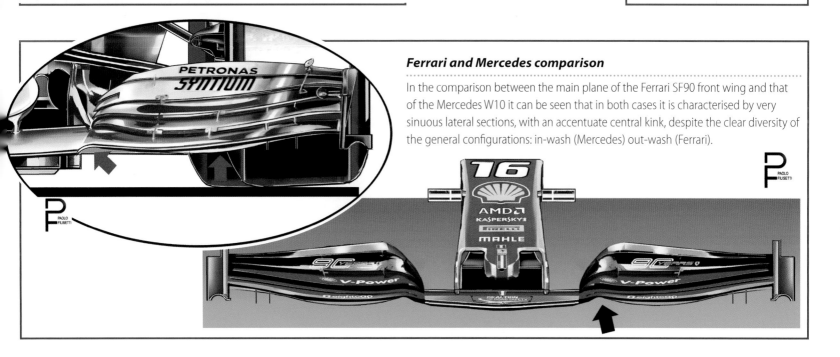

Mercedes W10 sidepod versions compared

In Melbourne Mercedes adopted, without variations, the configuration seen in the second Barcelona test session. It is interesting to compare it with the earlier version (seen at the presentation and the first test session at Montmelò) to see how the fine-tuning concerned above all the upper sidecut of the sidepods and the appearance on the footplate of a series of vortex generators to energize the air flow.

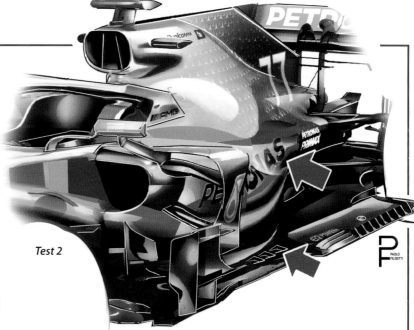

Test 2

Test 1

Mercedes W10: micro-aerodynamic developments on the halo

In Melbourne, the W10 differed with respect to the version seen in the second test session in Spain in a number of micro-aerodynamic developments. There was the very interesting, albeit difficult to detect, adoption of two small triangular fins on the lower part of the halo. These were micro vanes and vortex generators that energized the flow of air directed towards the rear of the car, while also improving that heading to the air-box thanks to a partial reduction in lift produced by the impact against the halo.

Micro-aerodynamics for the turning vanes

Micro-aerodynamic tweaks also affected the turning vanes ahead of the sidepods. In particular, there was an interesting introduction of vertical vents in the lower front turning vane support, integrated at the top with the lower lip of the intake mouths. These vents were designed to energize the flow over the lower part of the sidepods, ensuring that it remained attached.

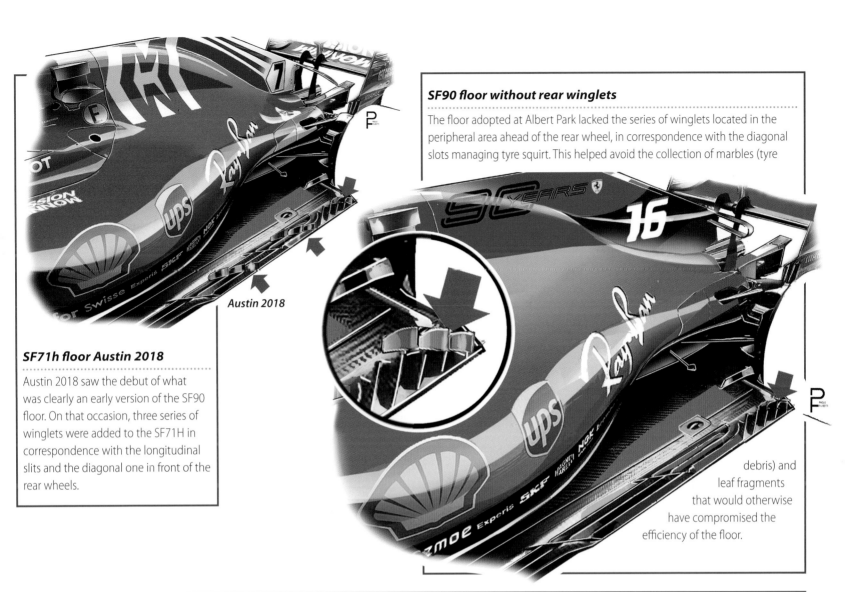

SF90 floor without rear winglets

The floor adopted at Albert Park lacked the series of winglets located in the peripheral area ahead of the rear wheel, in correspondence with the diagonal slots managing tyre squirt. This helped avoid the collection of marbles (tyre

Austin 2018

SF71h floor Austin 2018

Austin 2018 saw the debut of what was clearly an early version of the SF90 floor. On that occasion, three series of winglets were added to the SF71H in correspondence with the longitudinal slits and the diagonal one in front of the rear wheels.

debris) and leaf fragments that would otherwise have compromised the efficiency of the floor.

SF90: asymmetric front brake drums

The adoption of asymmetric front brake drums was interesting and designed to optimize differentiated cooling and distribution of heat to the wheels rims. The SF90 in fact presented a dual parallel vent along the circumference of the right-hand drum, with the exception of the lower part where the caliper was located. Moreover, we can also note two small channels in the lower part of the drum.

On upper part of the left-hand drum, we can see a deep groove that reveals the path taken by the air towards the outside of the wheel. This asymmetric configuration had a dual function: creating on the left-hand side a blow that directs the turbulence generated by the tyres outboard and managing the internal tyre pressures.

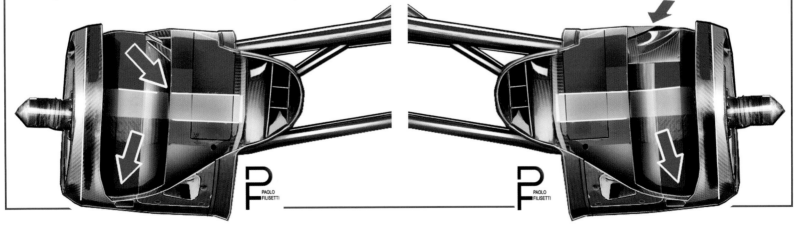

 # BAHRAIN(IAN) RHAPSODY

BAHRAIN GRAND PRIX

SAKHIR
MANAMA
31 MARCH

Sakhir, very different to Melbourne in being first and foremost a permanent track characterised by long straights and level but highly abrasive asphalt, was the ideal location to find answers to the questions certain teams were grappling with, especially Ferrari. The accentuated diversity with respect to Albert Park permitted the Scuderia, at least on paper, to verify the competitiveness of the SF90, or at least its design configuration. None of the cars were characterised by visually striking changes, the most obvious being restricted to modifications designed to facilitate heat exchange. Within a field of cars generally featuring expanded hot air vents on their sidepods, the Ferrari was distinguished by having adopted particularly closed bodywork with the addition, during free practice only, of three small gills either side of the cockpit that were not used for the race. This uniqueness attracted the attention of rival engineers and also permitted the Scuderia to demonstrate unequivocally that the problems it suffered in Australia were not caused by overheating of the power unit components. The smoothness of the track surface offered the possibility of adopting reduced ride heights and brought the best out of the

F90's aerodynamic configuration through fast corners and on the straights. In a head-to-head comparison of the Ferrari and the Mercedes it was clear that the two cars were complementary in terms of efficiency. In practice, the SF90 was uncatchable on the straights, almost as if it had a more aggressive default mode for its power unit (although this was not the case), while the W10 gained ground through the twisting sections, displaying remarkable precision and agility in changes of direction. That said, the answer the Maranello engineers were looking for was found in the first free practice session, with the SF90s monopolising the first two positions, which they were in fact to retain through to the end of qualifying. The area in front of the sidepods, characterised by a series of vanes and scimitar profiles on the SF90, was observed at length by numerous rival engineers, especially on the Thursday, every time the car was taken to the FIA pits for dimensional scrutineering (autonomous from 2019). In substance, among the rival engineers, it was clear that the aerodynamics of the "rosse" guaranteed a degree of balance on this track that was unmatched by any other car.

It is only right to point out that following the race there were word-of-mouth rumours doing the rounds whereby the problem that deprived Charles Leclerc of his first F1 victory was due to overheating that caused a failure of the MGU. For the sake of clarity, the issue that affected the motor generator unit attached to the turbo was not caused caused by overheating and thanks to the Recovery mode selected by the Monaco-born driver at the suggestion of his pit crew he was able to finish the race despite a significant loss of power (around 80 hp) and increased fuel consumption.

However, it is understandable that many outside observers may have considered Mercedes decision to "invest" in power unit reliability to have been a

winning strategy, with large vents being opened in the bodywork of the W10. Repeating that it was not reduced heat dispersal that crippled the first of the two Ferraris at the finish, it was clear that at Brackley they had tried to guarantee efficient heat exchanging, thanks in part to the advanced configuration of the sharply tapering sidepods (introduced in the second week of testing at Montmelò). It is also interesting to note how great attention was paid to the running temperatures of the internal combustion engine and those of the ERS components on the starting grid too. The fans attached to the sidepod mouths were used at the maximum setting, blowing air chilled via large containers of dry ice. However, Mercedes was not the only team to pay particular attention to sudden and damaging rises in internal engine temperatures.

Red Bull introduced (for the first time) a large vent on the RB15 behind the base of the halo, improving the heat exchanging effect. The Honda power unit, which had hitherto displayed an unprecedented reliability, nonetheless revealed clear performance limitations on the Sakhir straights. Aerodynamic efficiency, always a strong suit of Adrian Newey's cars, was partially sacrificed on the altar of reliability, successfully so it has to be said.

McLaren introduced a first evolution of the turning vanes in front of the sidepods. Specifically, the scimitar profile at the bottom was profoundly modified in shape, with a reduction in its chord at the outermost section. Various vortex generators and vertical winglets were added to the inboard section in order to manage the lower peripheral flow. There was also an interesting extension to the splitter, with a horizontal blade guiding the flow towards the leading edge of the floor. Toro Rosso also presented a first evolution of the bargeboards, characterised by an upper edge with three separated vertical elements in place of the earlier single one.

Mercedes heat dispersal grilles

In order to avoid possible problems associated with overheating given the elevated temperatures, Mercedes adopted a different configuration for the hot air dispersal grilles either side of the cockpit. Those seen at Sakhir were in fact more accentuated, with a more conspicuous duct than in Australia. In contrast, the vertical slot at the base of the halo present in Melbourne was eliminated.

Red Bull: hot air vents at the base of the halo

Like all the teams, Red Bull took counter-measures to avoid an excessive increase in the temperatures of the Honda power unit components. A triangular section vertical slot was therefore introduced at the base of the halo structure to guarantee adequate heat exchange.

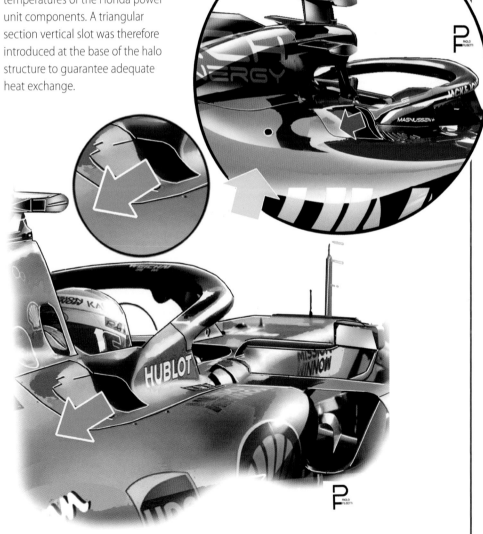

SF90 hot air vents at the base of the halo comparison with the Hass VF19

In contrast with other teams, Ferrari did not substantially increase the air vents for the dispersal of heat. The slots at the base of the halo were in fact a feature present on the SF90 from its debut; here they are flanked by horizontal grilles not increased in section. There is an interesting comparison with the Haas VF19 equipped with the same slots at the base of the halo, but also bodywork that was less pinched behind the radiators, with a more generous internal passage for the hot air.

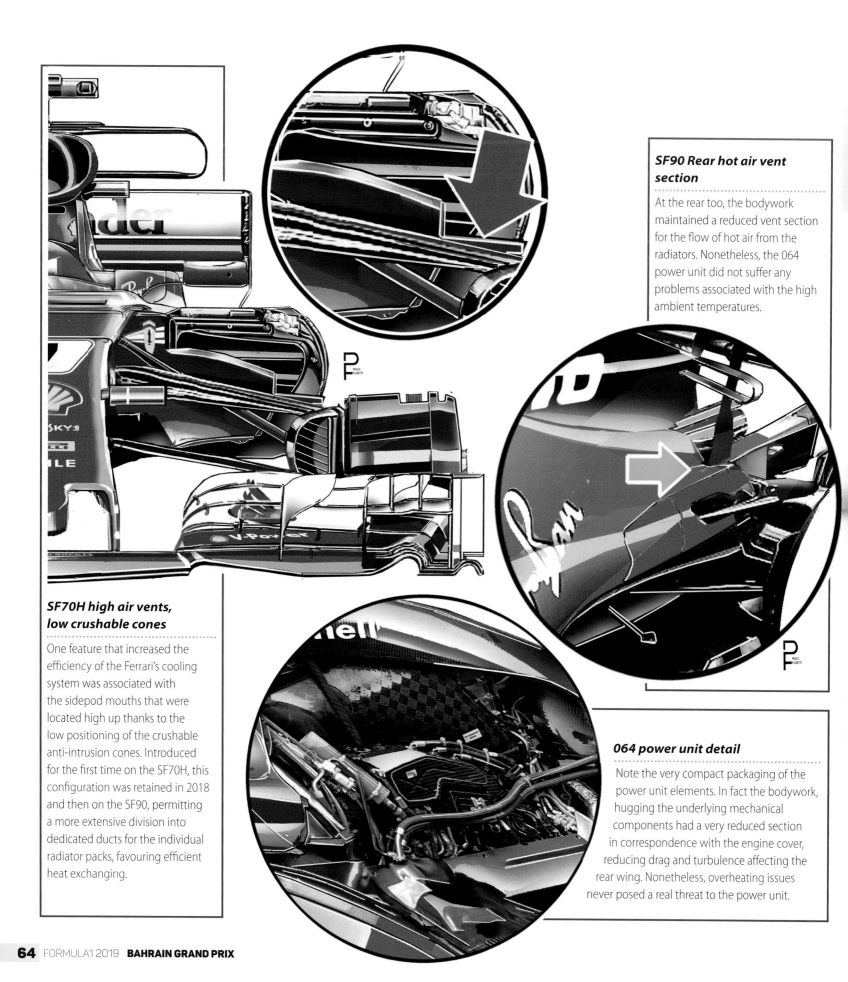

SF90 Rear hot air vent section

At the rear too, the bodywork maintained a reduced vent section for the flow of hot air from the radiators. Nonetheless, the 064 power unit did not suffer any problems associated with the high ambient temperatures.

SF70H high air vents, low crushable cones

One feature that increased the efficiency of the Ferrari's cooling system was associated with the sidepod mouths that were located high up thanks to the low positioning of the crushable anti-intrusion cones. Introduced for the first time on the SF70H, this configuration was retained in 2018 and then on the SF90, permitting a more extensive division into dedicated ducts for the individual radiator packs, favouring efficient heat exchanging.

064 power unit detail

Note the very compact packaging of the power unit elements. In fact the bodywork, hugging the underlying mechanical components had a very reduced section in correspondence with the engine cover, reducing drag and turbulence affecting the rear wing. Nonetheless, overheating issues never posed a real threat to the power unit.

Ferrari SF90 and Haas VF19 wastegate exhaust comparison

While not a true development, there is an interesting comparison to be made between the Ferrari and the Haas with regard to the wastegate valve exhausts. The SF90 featured a single large diameter terminal set above the principal exhaust, while on the VF19 there were two stacked wastegate exhausts, generating a different blow in the lower part of the wing and centrally above the diffuser. Note also the size of the rear vent in the bodywork of the American car with respect to the Ferrari.

Alfa Romeo C38 diagonal floor slits

A by no means secondary aerodynamic modification concerned the adoption of a new floor for the Alfa Romeo C38. The new version featured no less than 18 diagonal slits along the side edge so as to generate a pneumatic seal preventing the turbulent flows from wedging laterally under the car and reducing the downforce generated by the diffuser.

McLaren MCL 34 bargeboards development

McLaren presented a bargeboard development characterised above all by a different shape to the scimitar profile at the base of which can be seen the reduction in the curvature at the outermost point (dotted line).

Racing Point RP19 bargeboards

For Racing Point to note a revised version of the front vertical element, connected to the barge board vented shield via a boomerang shaped profile.

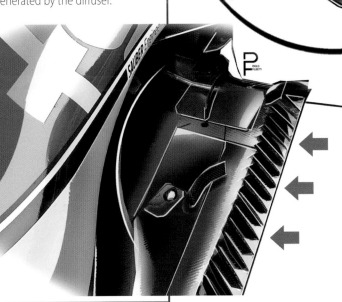

 # SHANGHAI NO SURPRISE

CHINESE GRAND PRIX

SHANGHAI
SHANGHAI CIRCUIT
14 APRIL

By the third race of the season, the standings were unequivocally evidence of Mercedes' domination the early stages of the championship, while Ferrari, despite the encouragement of the winter tests, had only managed to demonstrate the potential of the SF90 on the favourable Bahrain circuit, without managing to take Leclerc to the win due to a technical problem.

In China, the SF90 enjoyed a positive start to the weekend, demonstrating in the first two free practice sessions that it was faster than the Mercedes W10, especially in the final sector characterised by a long straight leading to corner 14. Toto Wolff himself repeatedly said during the course of the Shanghai weekend (even after the race when it may have seemed insensitive) that Ferrari shown that it had been able to get the best out of its power unit from the Friday sessions onwards, drawing on a calibration and operational mode that could not be compared with those available on the Brixworth-built engine. While on the Friday it was possible to find some basis for the Austrian team principal's declarations, while after the race it was legitimate to ask ourselves and ask him where he had found on Mercedes' behalf the power unit performance that before qualifying had appeared to be unattainable.

That said, it is undeniable that in this case in terms of development of the car taken to Shanghai, Mercedes had been profoundly influenced by its Italian rival, considered to be a point of reference in terms of certain aerodynamic features. In fact, paradoxically to some extent, after two races and two one-two finishes (going into Shanghai), Mercedes was leading the championship on maximum points but had proceeded to carefully "copy" the SF90. It is well known that the basic concepts underlying the two cars are profoundly different, with the W10 being a radical development of the 2018 car from which it inherited the wheelbase. Its aero package was characterised by the in-washing of the turbulence generated by the full-width front wing. However, the new version of this element actually followed the concepts of the SF90's front wing. Maranello's car, like the Alfa Romeo C38, had from its presentation caught the attention of rival designers thanks to its wing characterised by flaps with decreasing incidence, becoming neutral at the extremities, in proximity to the endplates curving outwards so as to create an out-wash, that is to say a deviation of the turbulence outside the wheels. This characteristic has an impact on the management of the flows over the central section of the car and those directed below the floor. In practice, a comparison of the central sections of the Mercedes and Ferrari shows how on the former the management of the flows and their breakdown was particularly complex. The elements making up the flow vanes ahead of the sidepods on the W10 and the vortex generators providing precise guidance of the airflow were particularly numerous and their interaction was complex. In contrast, the SF90's bargeboards were much simpler as they had to handle less congested fluid dynamics in this area. On the Ferrari, the outwash downstream of the front wing allowed the turbulence to be directed away from the body of the car immediately and more efficiently, without requiring any further

grooming by the turning vanes. It is legitimate to claim that the concept of the SF90 front wing was a trendsetter. Clearly, Mercedes could hardly adopt a photocopy of the Italian car's wing as the aerodynamic configuration underlying the feeding of air to the W10's underbody and the sidepod inlets was based, as mentioned, on a in-wash, that is to say the deviation of the flow towards the centre of the car. However, this factor further reinforced the perception that the Brackley engineers considered that there were tangible advantages to the configuration introduced by their rivals and tried to integrate the feature.

The FIA then judged that the modification made to the W10's front wing did not conform to the regulations as the cutaway on the flared cutaway on the upper rear edge exposed the end of the flap. In a directive sent to the teams during the week leading up to the GP, the separation of the flap from the endplate was outlawed as, in theory, it permitted flexing of the end of the profile no longer anchored to the endplate as the downforce increased. It is useful to note that the principal function of the new version was that of increasing the flow of air between endplate and flap to as to generate outwash. On the Saturday, in order for the team to be able to use the new version, the end of the flap was connected to the endplate with carbonfibre matting and the new wing was then used for the rest of the weekend. An almost identical episode involved the Red Bull RB15, which was also fitted with a new wing in an attempt to generate out-wash. In this case, the end part of the endplate presented a profile that was too thin and sharp and all that was required was for the upper and read edges to be thickened to allow it to be used. With regard to the SF90 instead, there were no modifications to the aerodynamic elements; instead, following the problem with the CPU on Leclerc's car in Bahrain, an earlier specification was fitted to both cars and was also used by Haas.

Mercedes W109 front wing and flow visualisation

In Shanghai Mercedes introduced a development of the front wing integrating it with the original concept of a partial out-wash. In detail, the endplates presented a sinuous cut-away of the rear corner. In effect, the cut-away initially left the end section of the flap exposed. In relation to a recent FIA directive, no part of the flap could extend laterally beyond the endplate

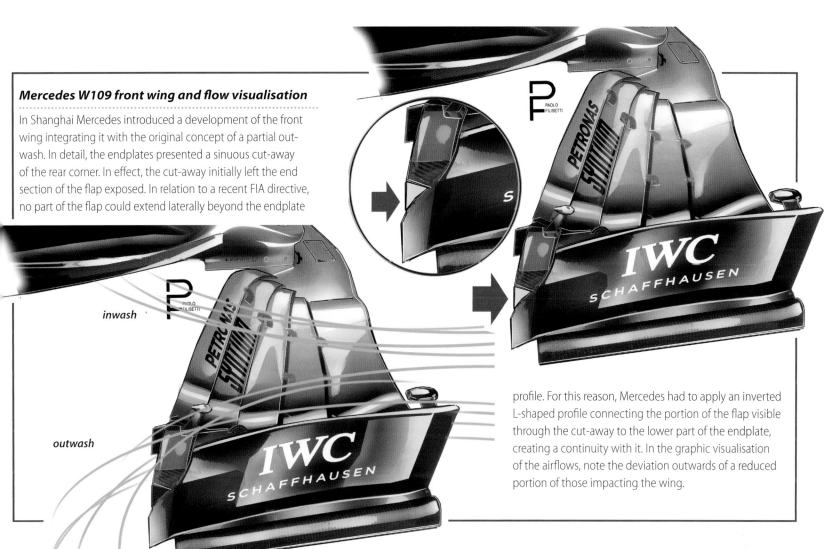

inwash

outwash

profile. For this reason, Mercedes had to apply an inverted L-shaped profile connecting the portion of the flap visible through the cut-away to the lower part of the endplate, creating a continuity with it. In the graphic visualisation of the airflows, note the deviation outwards of a reduced portion of those impacting the wing.

Mercedes W10 floor detail

While it was not a modification, it is interesting to observe close up the large central channels feeding the diffuser. In practice, they were fed by the airflow around the lower part of the sidepods which remained attached thanks to the action of the lateral turning vanes. The flow, accelerated through the progressively narrowing channel section towards the rear, incrementing the extraction of air from the diffuser and therefore the downforce generated. The concept was also present on other cars, including the Ferrari where it had been adopted some years earlier.

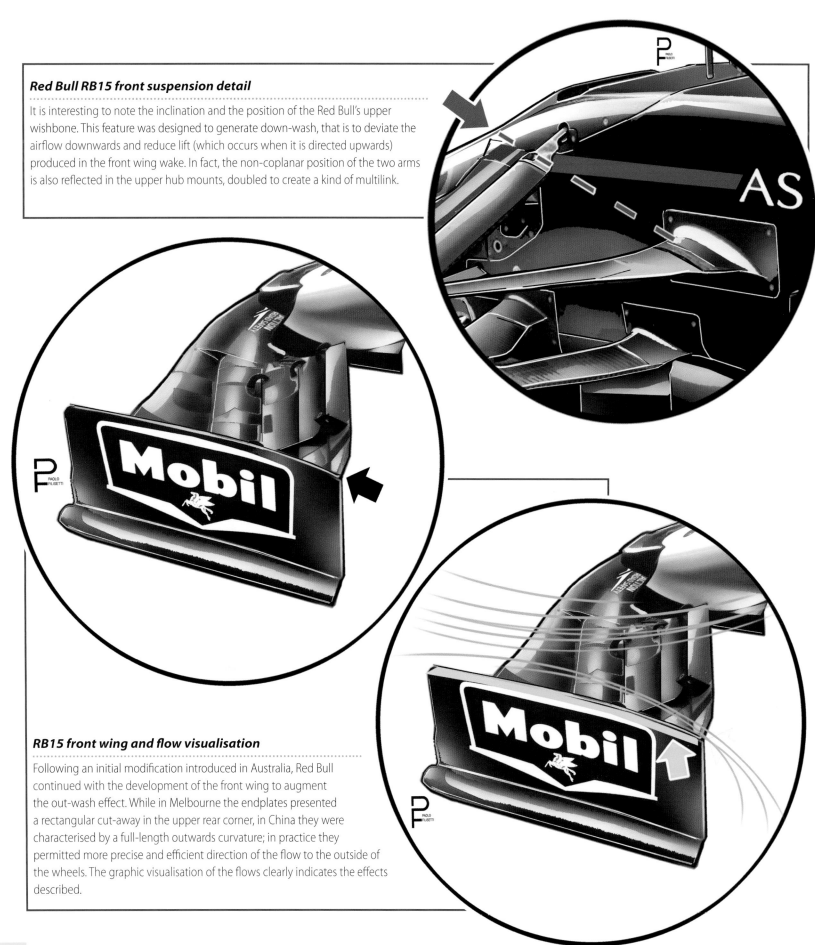

Red Bull RB15 front suspension detail

It is interesting to note the inclination and the position of the Red Bull's upper wishbone. This feature was designed to generate down-wash, that is to deviate the airflow downwards and reduce lift (which occurs when it is directed upwards) produced in the front wing wake. In fact, the non-coplanar position of the two arms is also reflected in the upper hub mounts, doubled to create a kind of multilink.

RB15 front wing and flow visualisation

Following an initial modification introduced in Australia, Red Bull continued with the development of the front wing to augment the out-wash effect. While in Melbourne the endplates presented a rectangular cut-away in the upper rear corner, in China they were characterised by a full-length outwards curvature; in practice they permitted more precise and efficient direction of the flow to the outside of the wheels. The graphic visualisation of the flows clearly indicates the effects described.

Racing Point RP19 floor

Racing Point brought an evolution of the RP19's floor characterised by the presence of a triple series of lateral and three diagonal grooves in proximity to the rear wheels. This was an evolution designed to increase the efficiency of the diffuser, attempting to recover downforce. The design of the car, which began very late and was very raw, was then subjected to significant development during the course of the season.

Position of the Ferrari ERS control unit

This detail shows the position of the ERS control unit on the Ferrari SF90. It was placed far from sources of heat and vibration produced by the engine. The problem suffered by Charles Leclerc in Bahrain had in fact been caused by issues associated with the last control unit iteration adopted. In China, both Ferrari and Haas used the earlier specification, while Alfa Romeo maintained the latest version, which in the event failed on Giovinazzi's car.

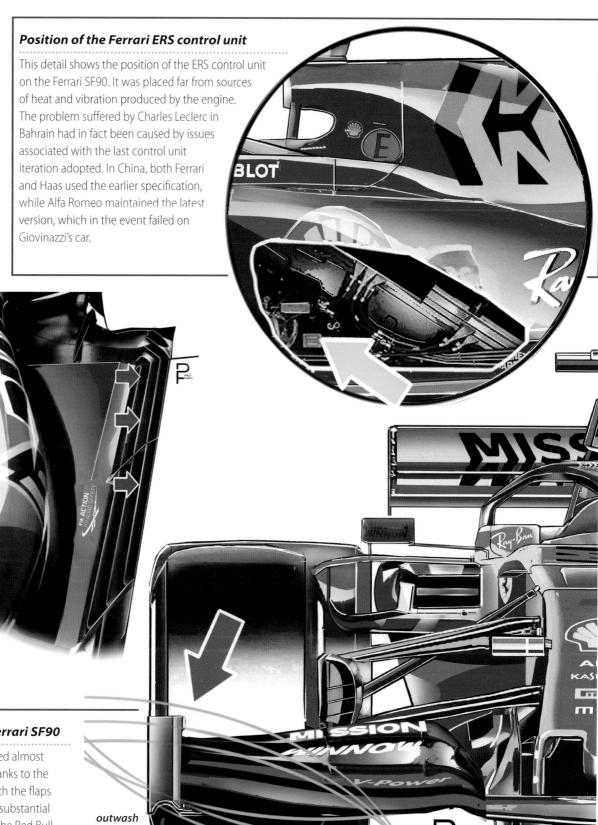

The extreme out-wash of the Ferrari SF90

The drawing visualises the flows deviated almost exclusively outside the front wheels, thanks to the particular configuration of the wing, with the flaps steeply inclined towards the outside. A substantial difference can be seen with respect to the Red Bull and the Mercedes where in-wash was prevalent.

outwash

EFFICIENCY THE WATCHWORD AT BAKU

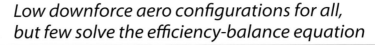

AZERBAIJAN GRAND PRIX

BAKU
BAKU CITY CIRCUIT
28 APRIL

The Baku circuit, characterised by long straights winding around the centre of the Azeri capital, requires a set-up exalting the aerodynamic efficiency of the cars, with a medium-low downforce configuration. These specific characteristics make it an atypical street circuit and inevitably inspired the majority of the developments introduced to the cars. In most cases, in fact, it would hardly seem right to consider the modifications seen in Baku as true evolutions of the designs, but rather adaptations to the characteristics of the circuit. It was in this vein that Renault introduced a low drag version of the RS 19's rear wing with a different configuration of the endplates and the main plane. Mercedes moved in this direction too, while also presenting a rear wing trailing edge with an adhesive saw tooth profile designed to energize the exiting air-flow, increase the efficiency of the wing and favour the extraction of air from the diffuser. Ferrari took to Baku what was effectively an aero package composed of simple adaptations to the circuit such as the rear wing equipped with a spoon profile (reducing drag) and others that can be seen as true evolutions of the SF90's aerodynamic design. These last were the most visually conspicuous and concerned the turning vanes in front of the sidepods and the floor in front of the rear wheels, equipped with three small vertical vanes, previously tested in Barcelona and still earlier in Austin (in 2018 on the SF71H). The turning vanes now had a different profile on the leading edge of the bargeboards and were equipped with new vortex generators in correspondence with the lower edge and over the scimitars that followed them. These were in fact set closer together and had a larger section; this from the forward one characterised by a fin shape with rounded edges in place of the earlier three vertical "fingers". The aim of this evolution was to generate efficient vortexes that would deviate the airflow outwards, far from the floor of the car. The small turning vanes ahead of the rear wheels instead deal with the turbulence, enhancing the efficiency of the diffuser. This last was significantly modified in the lateral sections now equipped with a sawtooth external profile so as to deviate the turbulence caused by the deformation of the tyre sidewalls. A note regarding reliability: the power unit control electronics on Antonio Giovinazzi's Alfa Romeo C38 were replaced in China after suffering problems that prevented him from taking to the track in qualifying and at Baku the car was equipped with the same specification unit as Ferrari and Haas (older than the one used through to Shanghai). As this was Giovinazzi's third CE unit, the Italian driver was given a 10-place grid penalty.

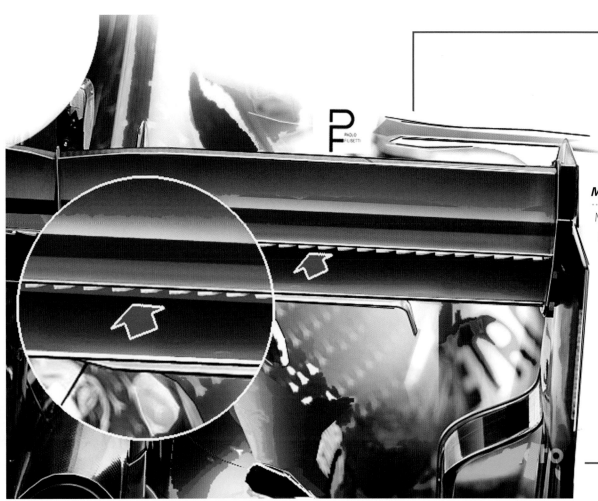

Mercedes W10 rear wing

Mercedes added an adhesive sawtooth profile to the trailing edge of the rear wing designed to energize the exiting air flow, increase the efficiency of the wing and favour the extraction of air from the diffuser.

RS19 rear wing

The low drag version of the RS 19's rear wing was characterised by a different configuration of the endplates in correspondence with the median vertical vents and of the main plane which featured a dished profile.

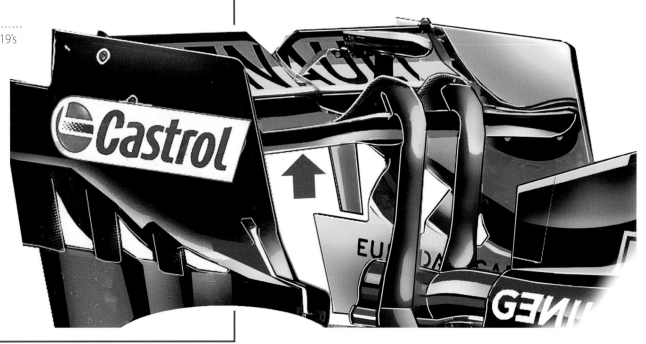

Ferrari rear wing

With regards to the rear wing, simple modifications were made to adapt it to the characteristics of the circuit. It was equipped with a dished profile that reduced drag, while the upper horizontal vents were eliminated from the endplates.

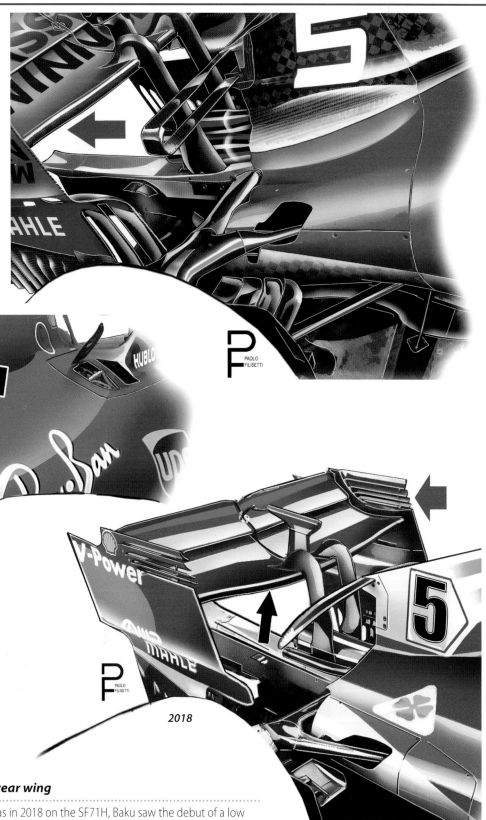

Ferrari SF71H rear wing

Note in the detail, as in 2018 on the SF71H, Baku saw the debut of a low drag version of the rear wing with a dished profile.

Ferrari SF90 floor

The floor ahead of the rear wheels was equipped with three small vertical turning vanes, a feature already tested a Barcelona and still earlier at Austin (in 2018, on the SF71H). The vanes groom the turbulence which is deviated towards the outside, improving the efficiency of the diffuser.

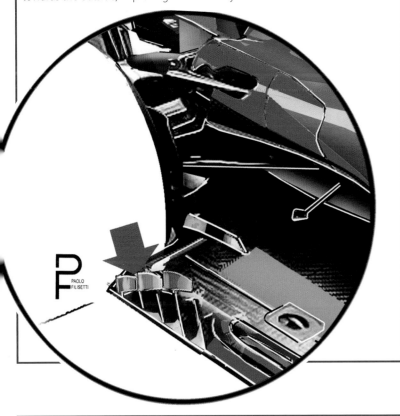

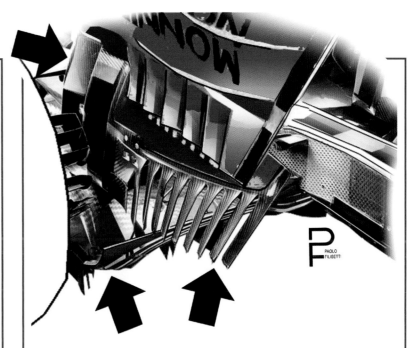

Ferrari diffuser

Important modifications were made to the lateral sections, now equipped with a sawtooth external profile so as to deviate the turbulence caused by the deformation of the tyre sidewalls (tyre squirt).

Red Bull RB15 rear wing

While many teams adopted rear wings with dished profiles, Red Bull instead opted to raise the main plane, significantly reducing the angle of incidence of the flaps. This decision significantly favoured efficiency on the long straights.

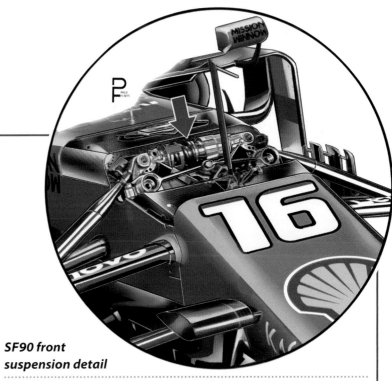

SF90 front suspension detail

The adjustment of the heave damper (the third damping element) controlling ride height played an important role in Baku. During the course of practice, in fact, multiple interventions were made in this respect and the anti-roll bar was also replaced.

Ferrari and Mercedes introduce their first evolutionary packages, but others such as McLaren also present interesting developments

(EUROPEAN) RE-ENTRY MANOEUVRES

SPANISH GRAND PRIX
BARCELONA
MONTMELÒ
12 MAY

As per F1 traditions, all the teams consider Barcelona to be the first race at which not only is it easier to introduce substantial developments to the cars, given the logistical advantages, but the results of the tests are also more valuable. The Montmelò circuit in fact includes long straights, fast curves and tight corners in which traction is fundamental. In substance, it is reasonable to say that a car that performs here can be considered to be competitive on most of the World Championship circuits. After having previewed the package of modifications originally intended for this race at Baku, Ferrari completed the first evolution of the SF90, introduced new elements to the wings and the engine cover and actually anticipated the debut of the evolution of the 064 power unit by two races with respect to the original programme. While we might consider tangible efforts to have been made to take part of the packet scheduled for Spain to Azerbaijan, it is equally important to underline the "titanic" efforts made on the production side, in particular on the power unit test benches. The team principal and technical director, Mattia Binotto, confirmed as much immediately after the Spanish race, emphasising in both cases the positive reactions of the team after having noted, as

early as the Melbourne GP, the SF90's performance deficit in terms of race pace.

The developments taken to Barcelona, part of a programme planned for some time, allowed the efficiency of the car to be increased while reducing certain detrimental factors such as turbulence generated by the upper edge of the fin over the engine cover and also improving the efficiency of the rear wing in terms of the downforce generated. This wing featured a new flat profile with a slightly reduced chord but above all endplates on which the section of the vent in correspondence with the leading edge (laminators) was increased. The rear fringes were also enlarged and now had seven elements rather than the six of the version seen in Azerbaijan. The front wing, while retaining the underlying out wash configuration (whereby the airflows are directed outside the front wheels), also presented new endplates, characterised by an accentuated outwards curvature and inclination with respect to the vertical, which visually increased the section of the lateral channel (footplate). All the modifications tested on both cars, at the same time as the adoption of brake drums with larger vents to enhance the dispersal of heat, led to an improvement in the handling of the car, even on the twisty sections, although in the third sector (the most complex), the SF90 did continue to suffer from a serious lack of mechanical grip, with evident understeer when turning in.

The power unit, with particular attention being paid to the combustion phase, deserves a chapter to itself. In parallel with its introduction, new fuel and lubricant formulae were signed off. Both were to have obtained, apart from the improved combustion of the first, a useful reduction in the heat produced in the cylinder heads, therefore guaranteeing less friction due to dilation and favouring the energy

balance with a reduction in consumption as well as enhanced guarantees of reliability.

Despite the lead in the standings it had accumulated in the first four races, in Spain Mercedes spared no effort with the introduction of an evolution of the W10's aero package. Specifically, the interventions concerned the turning vanes ahead of the sidepods, with an increase in the number of vertical elements from two to three. In parallel, new rear view mirrors were introduced, equipped with an aerodynamic profile above them that acted as a support and helped improve flow management. While these were not macroscopic modifications, they were significant in improving, in the first case, the management of the flows feeding the diffuser and those flanking the sidepods. The new version of the mirrors instead permitted a down-wash, incrementing the portion of the flow directed towards the sidepod inlets. In reality, they were only used in free practice and despite there being no formal protest by the FIA officials, they were removed on the Saturday. The suspicion that lingered in the paddock concerned the strong similarity of these elements, in particular the additional upper profile, to the mirrors introduced in Spain in 2018 on the SF71H, which were subsequently banned by the federation, the aerodynamic effect produced rather than the structural factor being considered primary. Last but not least, a new version of the front wing was characterised by the presence of a rectangular vent in correspondence to the internal extremity of the first of the two adjustable flaps. McLaren introduced an interesting new version of its front wing with a different curvature to the leading edge of the main plane, a new profile to the trailing edge of the last flap and a new position for the tyre temperature sensor. Minor changes were also made to the rear wing endplates.

SF90 engine cover

A new engine cover was introduced, characterised by a cutaway at the start of the vertical shark fin designed to reduce the turbulence produced by the previous version, joined horizontally, which damaged the quality of the air flow towards the rear wing.

Rear wing endplates

The section of the vent in correspondence with the leading edge was increased (hanging vanes). In parallel, the rear fringes were also increased, with seven elements instead of the six of the version seen in Azerbaijan.

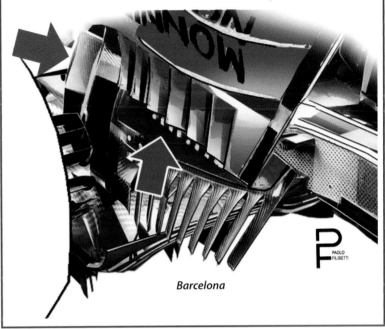

Barcelona

Front wing endplates

The front wing retained its out-wash configuration (with the air flows being directed outside the front wheels) and featured new endplates with an overt curvature towards the outside as well as a strong inclination with respect to the vertical axis. At a visual level at least, the section of the lateral channel (footplate) was also accentuated and terminated at the rear with a low vertical flip-up.

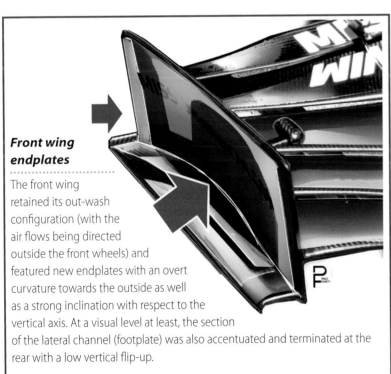

Red Bull RB15: multilink front suspension

This was not strictly a novelty. In reality, at Barcelona were able to inspect close up the separate mounting points for the upper wishbone (1-2) on the wheel hub. Note the angle formed with respect to the vertical passing along the axis of the wheel thus permitting an increase in the tyre footprint when steering.

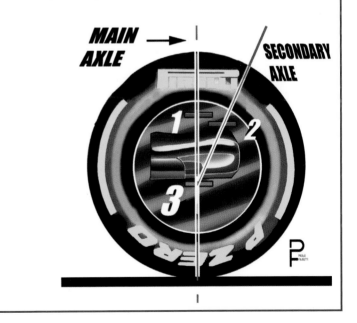

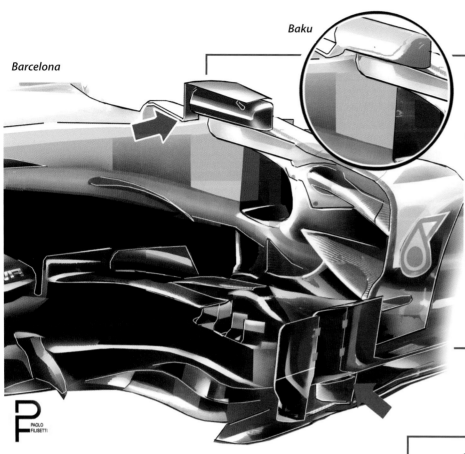

Baku

Barcelona

Evolution of bargeboards and mirrors

The bargeboards ahead of the sidepods saw an increase in the number of vertical vanes from two to three. In parallel, new rear view mirrors were introduced, equipped with an aerodynamic profile above them that had a secondary support function while improving flow management. The first of these modifications improved the efficiency of the diffuser management while the new mirrors created a downwash in the direction of the sidepod mouths.

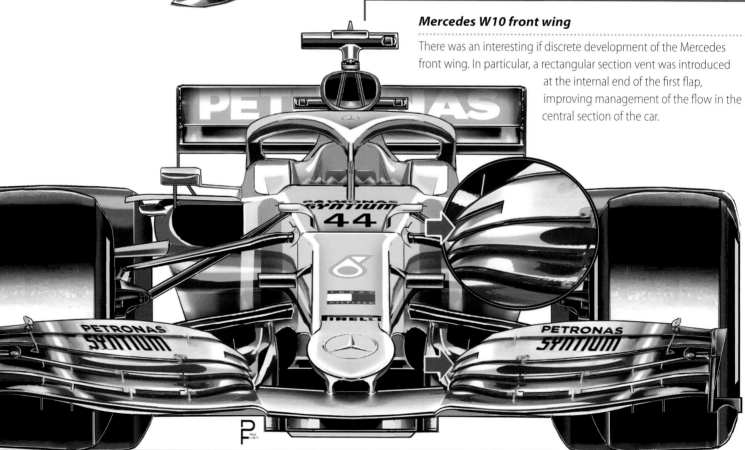

Mercedes W10 front wing

There was an interesting if discrete development of the Mercedes front wing. In particular, a rectangular section vent was introduced at the internal end of the first flap, improving management of the flow in the central section of the car.

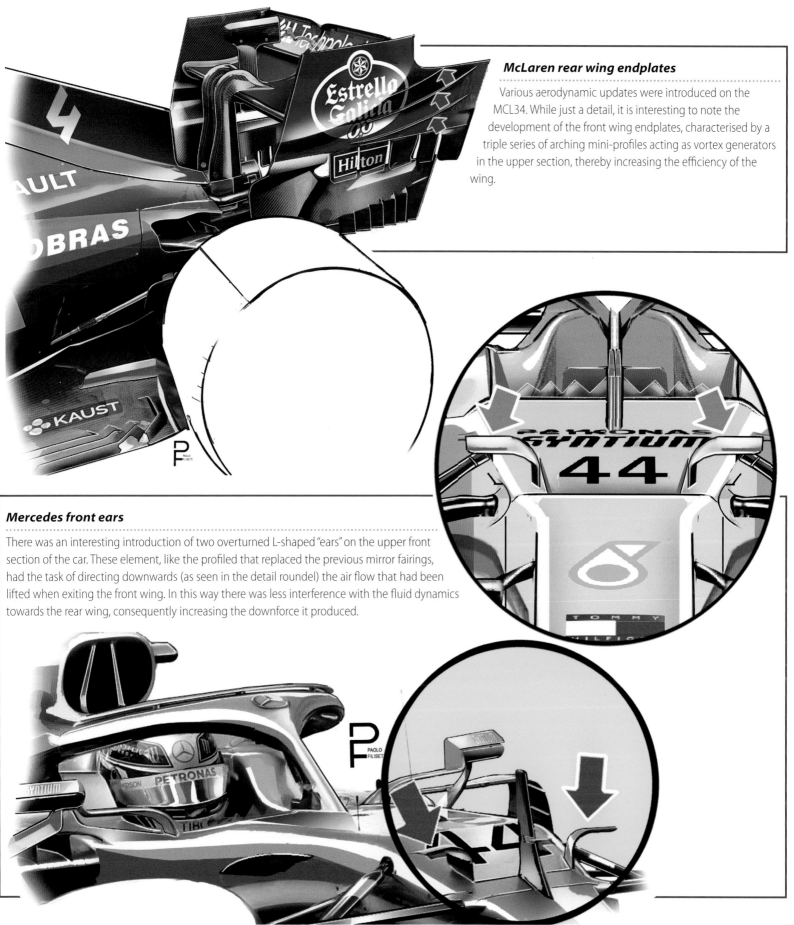

McLaren rear wing endplates

Various aerodynamic updates were introduced on the MCL34. While just a detail, it is interesting to note the development of the front wing endplates, characterised by a triple series of arching mini-profiles acting as vortex generators in the upper section, thereby increasing the efficiency of the wing.

Mercedes front ears

There was an interesting introduction of two overturned L-shaped "ears" on the upper front section of the car. These element, like the profiled that replaced the previous mirror fairings, had the task of directing downwards (as seen in the detail roundel) the air flow that had been lifted when exiting the front wing. In this way there was less interference with the fluid dynamics towards the rear wing, consequently increasing the downforce it produced.

Maximum downforce, and more besides on the streets of the Principality

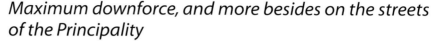

YOU DON'T WIN ANYTHING WITH ALGORITHMS

MONACO GRAND PRIX
PRINCIPATO DI MONACO
MONTE CARLO
26 MAY

The Monaco circuit presents a unique challenge in the F1 World Championship, with features that are only partially comparable to the Hungaroring. The set-ups adopted here are therefore exclusive due the peculiarities of the Principality's toboggan run. Although this is undeniable, in reality, for a few years now there have been no displays of original features designed exclusively for this round of the World Championship. Nonetheless, a recipe followed by all the teams was that of increased ride heights to respond to the irregularities of the asphalt, combined with a greater steering angle and a clear increase in the incidence of the flaps. No substantial novelties were introduced by the top teams with the exception of that represented by the adoption of the new nose by Red Bull. The RB15, in fact, presented the extremity of the nose cone characterised by the closure of the S-duct intake. This modification was introduced because at Monte Carlo, due to the low average speeds and the low downforce generated by the floor of the car, the functionality of the S-duct was significantly reduced. With regard to Mercedes, the adaptation of the W10 to the principality's street circuit saw the adoption of a double T-wing stacked profiles and augmented vents for heat dispersal. This configuration could actually be seen

on many cars., Renault was very active, with most of the modifications being adaptations to the circuit. The rear wing of the RS 19 was modified, while two aerodynamic "ears" with an inverted "L" shape appeared on the front part of the chassis, designed above all to direct the airflow leaving the front wing downwards. One element that is not particularly stressed at Monaco was instead the object of a specific evolution. This concerned the monoblock Brembo calipers which the Curno-based company supplied to its client teams. The evolution of the calipers introduced at the start of the season was characterised here by a trapezoidal version having its corners chamfered at 45 degrees. The modification not only permitted a slight reduction in weight, maintaining unaltered the standard version's mechanical rigidity characteristics, but also provided for improved dispersal of the heat generated and, up stream, a reduction of its peak under braking. An unusual feature was the angle of attack of the pads with respect to the disc. In detail, the contact area between disc and pad was reduced as elevated braking torque is not required at Monaco. The result consisted in improved brake modulation, especially when releasing the pedal, along with the aforementioned reduction in the heat generated. This feature was adopted by Alfa Romeo, Red Bull and Mercedes.

Vortex generators on the floor of the RB15

Also of interest was the addition of a series of four vortex generators at the base of the sidepods, on the footplate in the area of the forward knife-like profiles. They permitted improved management of the flow over the lower part of the sidepods.

RB15 closed nose cone

The RB15 presented a nose cone with the frontal intake feeding the S-duct blanked off. This was because the low speeds at Monaco and the greater ride heights considerably reduced its efficiency.

RB15 Rear Wing

The wing presented a main plane arching slightly in the central section and a flap with a pronounced incidence, capable of generating as much downforce as possible. Note instead the absence of a body wing at the rear extremity of the fin on the engine cover.

Renault rear aerodynamics

The rear wing of the RS 19 adopted a new high downforce profile together with a T-wing characterised by a slit in the lower plane. Also of interest was the small monkey seat behind the support pylons.

Vanity winglets Renault

Above the front part of the chassis, on the vanity panel, appeared two overturned L-shaped "ears" which were designed to reduce lift, deviating downwards the flow of air exiting the front wing.

Haas rear aerodynamics

The VF19 presented a maximum downforce configuration with the adopted of a C-shaped body wing and a slit in the lower plane. The wing presented a flat main plane together with a maximum incidence flap

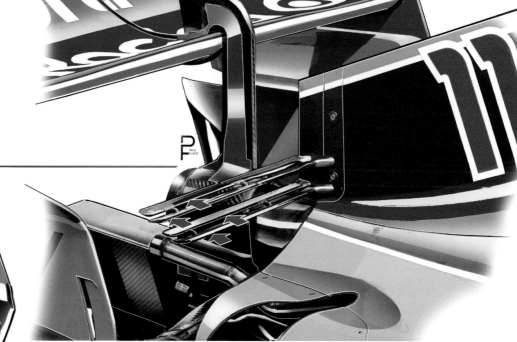

Racing Point RP19 multiple body wing

The configuration adopted by Racing Point on the RP19 was very unusual and particularly sophisticated. It was composed of two straight profile, each split by a full length slot, open at the extremities. The function of these elements was to direct with precision and to laminate the flow heading towards the rear wing, increasing the downforce produced.

Trapezoidal-section lightweight Brembo caliper

The evolution of the Brembo calipers was characterised here by a trapezoidal version with the corners chamfered at 45°. This permitted a slight reduction in weight while maintaining unaltered the mechanical stiffness values. Heat dispersal was improved. There was different angle of attack for the pads, with a smaller area in contact with the disc. The new version was used by Alfa Romeo, Red Bull and Mercedes.

Ferrari SF90: front suspension detail

Higher ride heights with respect to the traditional circuits and a generally softer suspension configuration characterised the typical Monaco set-up. Ferrari tested diverse ratings for the third front damper in search of the best compromise for the three track sectors.

EFFICIENCY POWER AND TRACTION

CANADIAN GRAND PRIX
MONTRÉAL
GILLES VILLENEUVE CIRCUIT
9 JUNE

The Gilles Villeneuve circuit has been defined as a "stop and go" track, with sharp acceleration and hard braking but no fast corners, the quickest section being characterised by the long straight flanking the rowing basin ahead of the chicane leading to the finish line. These characteristics make it a difficult circuit to set up for as optimum configurations and adjustments can be found by both privileging efficiency – and in any case the performance of the power unit – or by going the opposite way and focusing on manoeuvrability and traction in the more tortuous section. This was particularly evident in 2019 if we consider the choices made by and the respective performance of Ferrari and Mercedes. The SF90 was perfectly suited to the specific characteristics of this track. It was the power unit rather than aerodynamics that had the greater influence on performance. This is hardly surprising if we consider that Montreal is the venue at which the power unit, above all in terms of acceleration, counts most in the entire championship (hence Mercedes introducing here the evolution of its own PU). While the qualities of the Ferrari power unit emerged clearly on the straight, the same was true of the SF90's aerodynamic efficiency with respect to the Mercedes W10. Thanks to the car's greater adaptability to the circuit, the Italian team did not introduce any significant changes. In reality, Montreal did see the completion of the evolution of the power unit in that the second step of the internal combustion engine first seen in Spain was flanked in Canada by the introduction of the second example of the ERS turbocharger and motor-generators (Mgu-H and Mgu-K). Thanks to the new components, the potential of the internal combustion engine appeared significantly greater. A significant, if not decisive, role was also played by the engine mapping, configured to provide highly efficient power delivery out of corners. A contribution was also made by the decision to use the highest downforce configuration of the two available (tested on the simulator at Maranello). During free practice, in fact, both he "Baku" version of the rear wing and the standard one with a flat profile were tested. The choice rapidly fell on this last, capable of producing higher downforce at the expense of a slight increase in drag. No less important were the brakes, which in Canada are subject to particularly high mechanical and thermal stress. During the course of the first two free practice sessions, both drivers carried out a comparison of the front brake drums. The team eventually opted for the ones equipped with a double vent (already used previously) to ensure more efficient heat dispersal. It should be emphasised that among the primary objectives of the comparison was that of evaluating which of the two options facilitated rapid tyre warming. This is, in fact, a very pertinent factor here due to the low abrasiveness of the asphalt, which makes the warm up phase allowing the tyres to reach optimum running temperatures longer and more complex. Few significant modifications were seen among the various teams, the exception being Racing Point which introduced a new nose cone equipped with a under-nose "cape" as well as a rear wing characterised by a dished profile. This said, it was interesting to note how Red Bull retained the nose cone that had debuted in the Principality, characterised by the absence of the S-duct intake on the tip. In parallel, from the second free practice session, winglets appeared in correspondence with the S-duct vent that recalled similar elements introduced at the start of the season on the Alfa Romeo. These elements were designed to generate down wash, that is to say, to deviate downwards the airflow leaving the front wing, improving the quantity and quality of the flow heading to the sidepod mouths. Renault instead introduced a rear wing with revised endplates and DRS control. On the floor, in correspondence with the longitudinal slits in front of those managing tyre squirt appeared a conspicuous turning vane curving outwards to increase its efficiency.

RS 19: winglet in front of the rear wheels

In correspondence with the two longitudinal slits ahead of the diagonal ones managing tyre squirt, a conspicuous winglet was added to the floor, curving outwards to augment the efficacy of the slots themselves. In this way the flow was significantly deviated outwards, reducing turbulence. The comparison drawing shows the earlier version used through to Monaco.

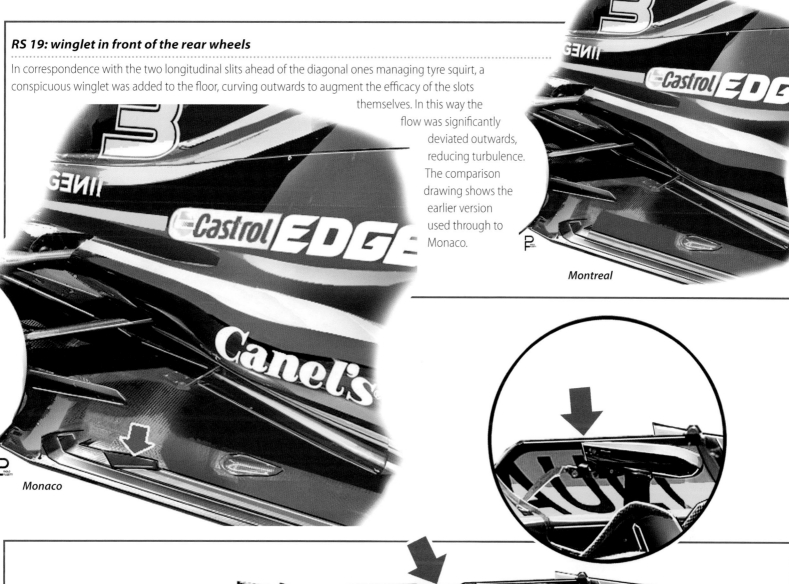

Montreal

Monaco

Renault: rear wing, DRS and endplates

The rear wing endplates were revised, now being equipped with two side strakes generating up-wash, while the DRS pod was also new. This last was characterised by a fairing that extended rearwards through to the upper edge of the wing. In the circle, the comparison with the previous version.

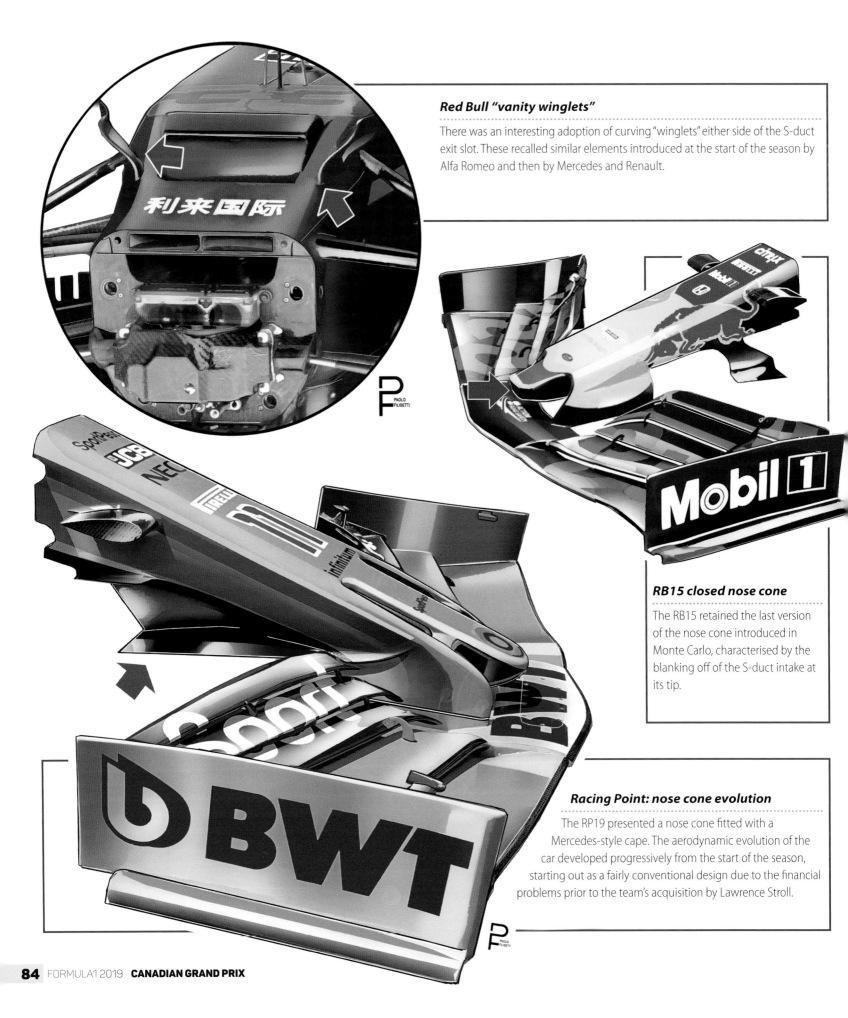

Red Bull "vanity winglets"

There was an interesting adoption of curving "winglets" either side of the S-duct exit slot. These recalled similar elements introduced at the start of the season by Alfa Romeo and then by Mercedes and Renault.

RB15 closed nose cone

The RB15 retained the last version of the nose cone introduced in Monte Carlo, characterised by the blanking off of the S-duct intake at its tip.

Racing Point: nose cone evolution

The RP19 presented a nose cone fitted with a Mercedes-style cape. The aerodynamic evolution of the car developed progressively from the start of the season, starting out as a fairly conventional design due to the financial problems prior to the team's acquisition by Lawrence Stroll.

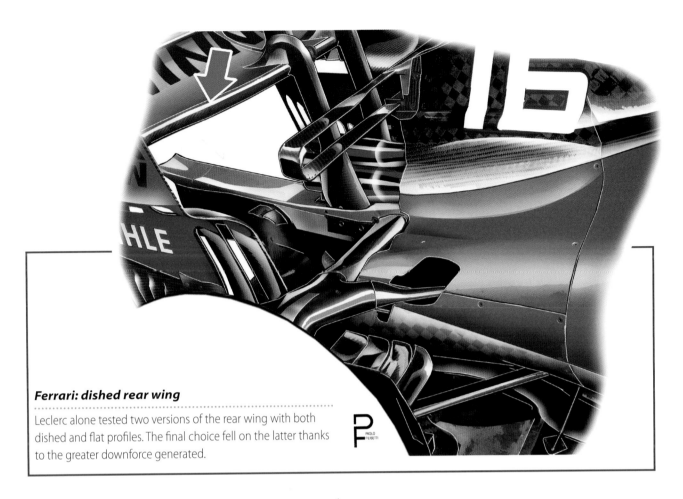

Ferrari: dished rear wing

Leclerc alone tested two versions of the rear wing with both dished and flat profiles. The final choice fell on the latter thanks to the greater downforce generated.

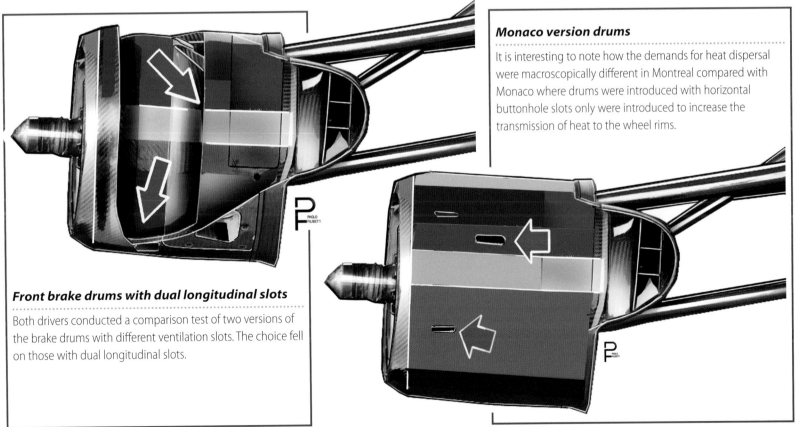

Monaco version drums

It is interesting to note how the demands for heat dispersal were macroscopically different in Montreal compared with Monaco where drums were introduced with horizontal buttonhole slots only were introduced to increase the transmission of heat to the wheel rims.

Front brake drums with dual longitudinal slots

Both drivers conducted a comparison test of two versions of the brake drums with different ventilation slots. The choice fell on those with dual longitudinal slots.

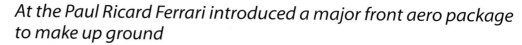

At the Paul Ricard Ferrari introduced a major front aero package to make up ground

■■ FRENCH EVOLUTION

FRENCH GRAND PRIX
LE CASTELLET
PAUL RICARD CIRCUIT
23 JUNE

That Ferrari had planned a development for France, focusing above all on the evolution of the front wing was well-known. Along with the wing, an evolution focusing on the front part of the floor was also in the air, but in reality the scope of the package brought to the Paul Ricard surprised in one way or another those working for the Scuderia's rivals. Front wing, front brake air intakes, floor and rear wing were the principal components involved. We can confidently state that it was the most extensive development introduced to the SF90 from the beginning of the season, even more important that the one that appeared in Spain. At first sight, this immediately suggested that after the first part of the season (with the exception of Barcelona of course) in which, effectively, the car had not presented significant modifications, this package had been signed off as a kind of revision of the development programme initially planned. In substance, at Ferrari, following the problems that had emerged in Melbourne, it was as if they had reset the development plan, firstly trying to understand the direction to take in order to correct the SF90's weaknesses. As we know, one of the main problems, or rather the main problem, resolvable with interventions restricted to the aerodynamics, was the lack of downforce being generated. Immediately after the race in France, Binotto was at pains

to emphasise that the direction taken was and of course would continue to be at the forthcoming races that of increasing downforce, even at the expense of straight line efficiency. Going back to the analysis of the modifications introduced, on the basis of the words of the team principal it is clear that the only not to have convinced the engineers from the first two free practice sessions, was the floor which was compared with the old version on the two cars. This element, at least on the visual plane, displayed a close relationship to the previous one but was differentiated in the upper part by the appearance of a double series of vortex generators, set diagonally in correspondence to the longitudinal slits. These were the visible characteristics, but were also accompanied by a different profile to the rear diffuser channels. It should be underlined that the new floor was not dispensed with outright, but was tested again in Austria a week later. In this case, it would not be right to talk about a lack of correlation between the simulator, the wind tunnel and the track, something that Binotto himself was keen to emphasise. Nonetheless, it was evident, albeit less clearly so than in Spain, that for the second time the new developments were not wholly convincing. Looking in detail at the new components tested and retained on the cars throughout the weekend, the new front wing, as mentioned, conserved at least in appearance strong links to the preceding version, but actually represented a radical evolution. While, in fact the out-wash concept (directing the airflows outside the front wheels) was retained, it was equally clear that it had been significantly revised. The principal differences concerned the main plane which had a more accentuated downwards curvature in proximity to the endplates, the flaps, which no longer had the torsion that produced a progressive reduction in incidence towards the outside and, lastly, the endplates, equipped with a rectangular cutaway in correspondence with the upper rear corner. On the external footplate instead,

a triangular section vortex generator was added to increase lateral extraction of the fluid streams deviated towards the outside. The interventions on the rear wing instead focused on the endplates. These elements were in fact revised in their lower section, both at the leading edge – where the large vertical vents (rectifiers) were eliminated, along with a reduction in the number of vertical fringes deviating the flow towards the outside – and above the diffuser; it appears that they actually produced a marginal blockage and it was decided to eliminate them. While Ferrari had in fact attracted the attention of the media and fans thanks to the breadth of the package introduced, another team, Red Bull, did so for the type of development adopted, in correspondence with the rear view mirrors. It had already been noted in the earlier races how these elements played an important role in the management of the flows heading to the rear and the sidepod intakes. In this case, the RB15 presented a complex evolution of the support struts of these elements. In detail, not only was the inboard support characterised by an angular S-profile, incorporating the upper fairing of the mirrors, but the outboard support also acted as a turning vane so as to increase the pressure of the incoming flow at the sidepod inlets, while an external portion was deviated thanks to the generation of small vortices distancing the turbulence generated by the elements. Clearly, this was an example of micro-aerodynamics but also evidence of the painstaking research of the Milton Keynes aerodynamicists as they attempted to optimize the particularly strategic zone ahead of the sidepods. In addition, Red Bull also presented new front wheels without the circular vortex generating profile design to deviate towards the outside the heat produced under braking. Renault also decided to update the RS19 for its home GP: a cape profile characterised the area of the front wing pylons while there was also a significant evolution of the turning vanes ahead of the sidepods.

SF90 Front Wing

This new version differs from the preceding one in the main plane with a more extreme downwards curvature (1) in the proximity of the endplates. The flaps (2) lost the torsion that reduced their incidence in the proximity of the endplates, now equipped with a rectangular cutaway (3) in correspondence with the upper rear corner. A triangular vortex generator was added to the footplate (4) in order to increase the deviation of the flow to the outside.

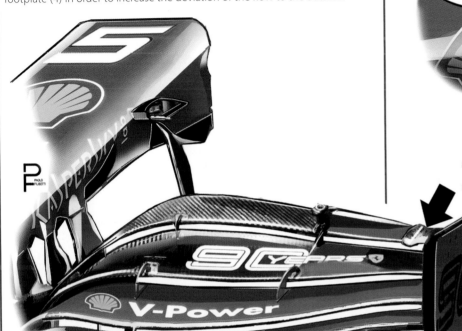

Comparison test modified floor

A test was run comparing the original floor and a new version, which was used in neither qualifying nor the race. This element differed only in the addition of a double series of vortex generators set diagonally, in correspondence with the longitudinal slits.

RB15 front wheel comparison

New front wheel rims were introduced permitting a diverse management of the outflow of hot air. In practice, the earlier version was characterised by a circular profile set in the middle of the spokes. This was missing from the new version, permitting a slight weight saving and a reduction in turbulence.

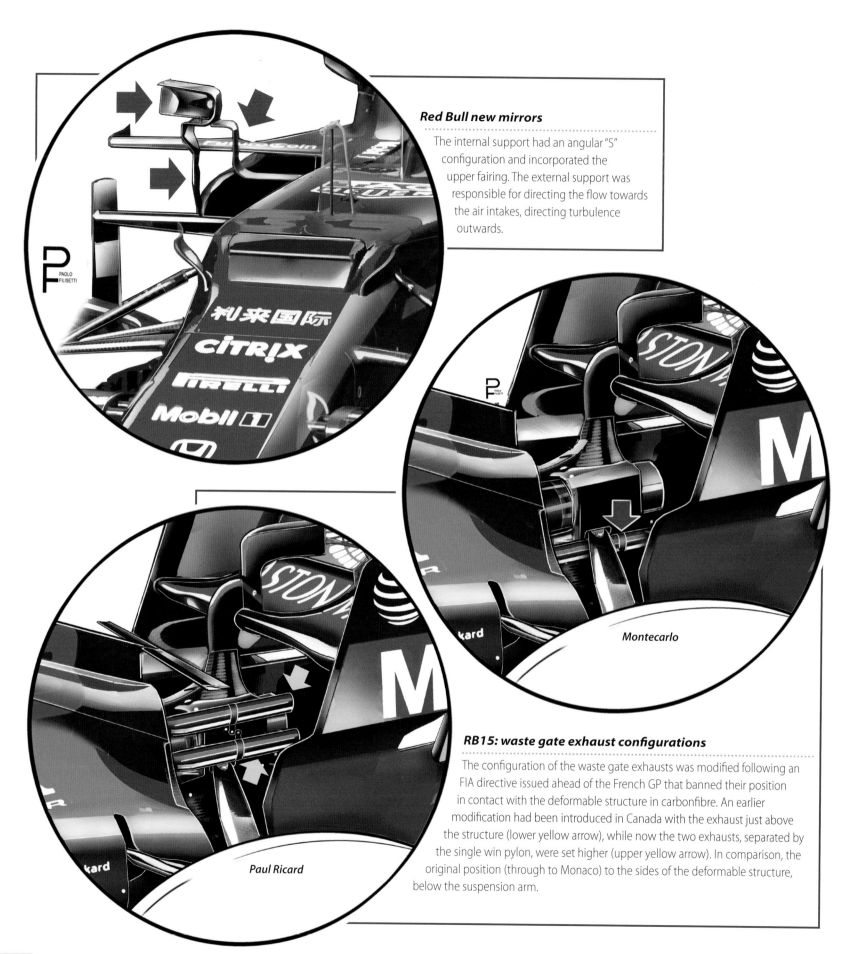

Red Bull new mirrors

The internal support had an angular "S" configuration and incorporated the upper fairing. The external support was responsible for directing the flow towards the air intakes, directing turbulence outwards.

Montecarlo

Paul Ricard

RB15: waste gate exhaust configurations

The configuration of the waste gate exhausts was modified following an FIA directive issued ahead of the French GP that banned their position in contact with the deformable structure in carbonfibre. An earlier modification had been introduced in Canada with the exhaust just above the structure (lower yellow arrow), while now the two exhausts, separated by the single win pylon, were set higher (upper yellow arrow). In comparison, the original position (through to Monaco) to the sides of the deformable structure, below the suspension arm.

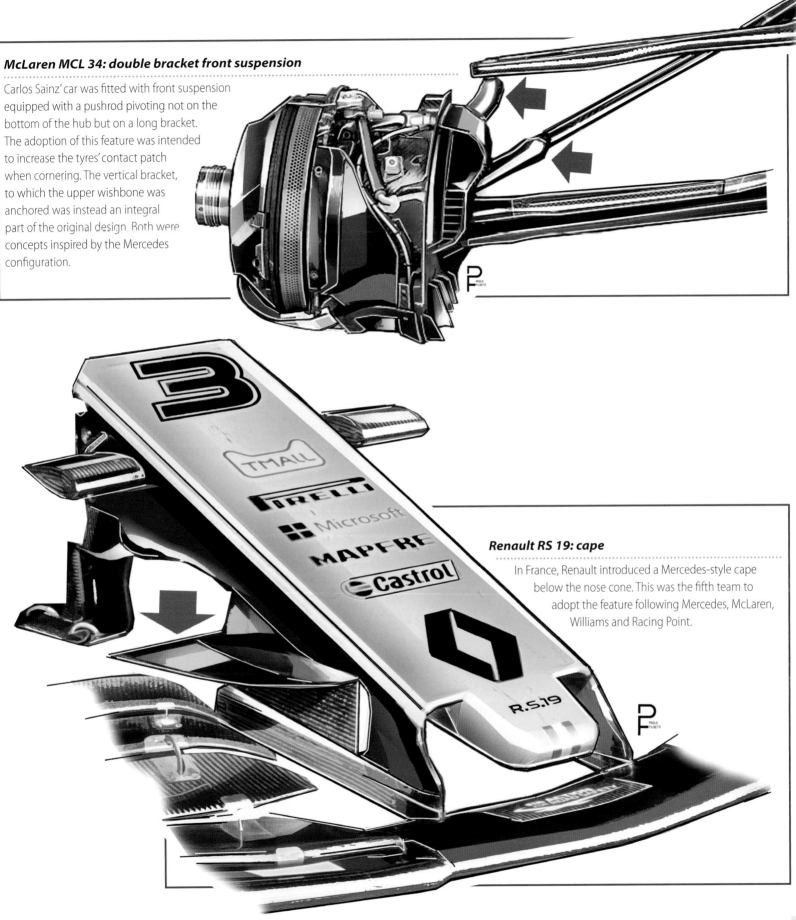

McLaren MCL 34: double bracket front suspension

Carlos Sainz' car was fitted with front suspension equipped with a pushrod pivoting not on the bottom of the hub but on a long bracket. The adoption of this feature was intended to increase the tyres' contact patch when cornering. The vertical bracket, to which the upper wishbone was anchored was instead an integral part of the original design. Both were concepts inspired by the Mercedes configuration.

Renault RS 19: cape

In France, Renault introduced a Mercedes-style cape below the nose cone. This was the fifth team to adopt the feature following Mercedes, McLaren, Williams and Racing Point.

AUSTRIAN GP, MERCEDES: HOT SHIVERS AND MORE...

AUSTRIAN GRAND PRIX
SPIELBERG
RED BULL RING
30 JUNE

From the beginning of the season the Mercedes W10 showed itself to be capable of generating very high downforce in fast corners, albeit at the expense of straight-line efficiency, with a DNA that allowed it to achieve peak performance on circuits such as Silverstone. These characteristics contrasted with those of the Ferrari SF90, which up until the Austrian GP had been characterised by excellent straight-line efficiency that dropped off when turning in to and negotiating corners. At the Red Bull Ring it was clear how the Italian car was immediately at home from Friday free practice sessions, while the Mercedes displayed a certain incompatibility with the stop-and-go nature of the Austrian circuit, highlighted by failing to claim pole position and then by an anonymous race. That the DNA of the W10 struggled to adapt to this kind of track was well-known, but the problems faced by the team from Brackley were exacerbated by the high ambient temperatures, combined with a marginal rarefaction of the air, which made cooling less effective. Toto Wolff himself had declared as much on the Saturday, repeating himself post-race: "Ferrari significantly increased the performance of its power unit. It's clearly the most powerful, of that I've no doubt. We saw this advantage in qualifying, but I have to say that the Ferrari also went well in terms of cornering speed and cooling this weekend. Instead we had to open up the bodywork to favour reliability."

In fact, it seems that further confirmation came after the race: the Mercedes Phase 2 Power Unit (which had debuted in Canada), struggles with ambient temperatures over 30° and a high humidity. In substance, it seems, on the basis of observation and certain indiscretions, that in the definition of the new specification, the primary objective of the Brixworth engineers was thermodynamic efficiency (consumption) and improvement in the performance of the internal combustion engine. In Austria, these two objectives clashed with the reduced efficiency of the cooling system and put the engineers on red alert. Hence the need to instruct the drivers during the race to undertake multiple prolonged stints in which in certain sections a "lift-and-coast" mode was prevalent, together with a blander electronic throttle management mode aiming at fuel-saving and reduced thermal stress. This had a significant impact on Hamilton and Bottas's races, as the British driver himself admitted later: "We had serious overheating problems. Ferrari and Red Bull didn't. We weren't able to exploit the full potential of the car and this was clearly a limitation, associated with the conditions we found here." In Austria, therefore, the Anglo-German behemoth displayed a vulnerability that clashed with its absolute dominance in terms of performance. For Ferrari instead, in spite of everything, there were signs that the SF90 project was not beyond redemption and that it was worth making further efforts, as late as the may have been, to introduce developments to correct its chronic defects.

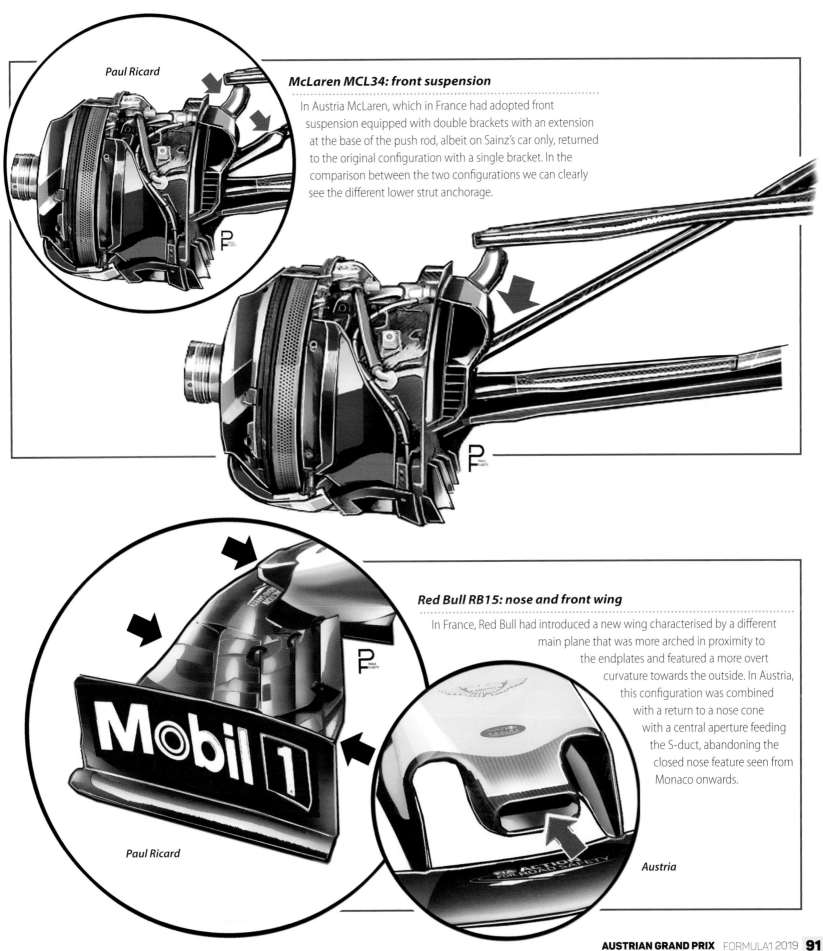

Paul Ricard

McLaren MCL34: front suspension

In Austria McLaren, which in France had adopted front suspension equipped with double brackets with an extension at the base of the push rod, albeit on Sainz's car only, returned to the original configuration with a single bracket. In the comparison between the two configurations we can clearly see the different lower strut anchorage.

Red Bull RB15: nose and front wing

In France, Red Bull had introduced a new wing characterised by a different main plane that was more arched in proximity to the endplates and featured a more overt curvature towards the outside. In Austria, this configuration was combined with a return to a nose cone with a central aperture feeding the S-duct, abandoning the closed nose feature seen from Monaco onwards.

Paul Ricard

Austria

Mercedes: front brake drum comparison

At the Spielberg the W10s were equipped with an evolution of the front brake drums. They were characterised by an increase in the external channelling which was designed not for cooling

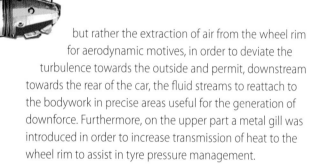

but rather the extraction of air from the wheel rim for aerodynamic motives, in order to deviate the turbulence towards the outside and permit, downstream towards the rear of the car, the fluid streams to reattach to the bodywork in precise areas useful for the generation of downforce. Furthermore, on the upper part a metal gill was introduced in order to increase transmission of heat to the wheel rim to assist in tyre pressure management.

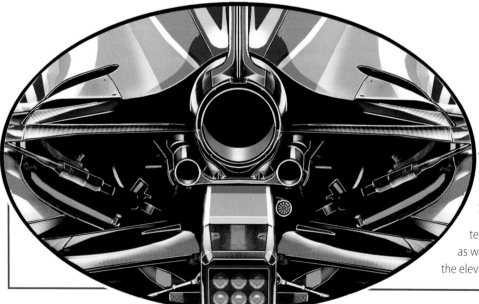

Renault RS19 and Racing Point Rp19: rear heat dispersal vent comparison

The Red Bull Ring constituted a particularly severe test due to the temperatures reached by the engines. The absence of long straights, as well as a marginal rarefaction of the air, highlighted the problem of the elevated ambient temperatures encountered during the weekend. It is

Ferrari SF90: nose evolution with new pylons and turning vanes

The Paul Ricard circuit saw the debut of a new version of the front wing, characterised by endplates no longer inclined like those introduced in Spain with a vortex generator on the footplate and new flaps. At the Red Bull Ring, the evolution was completed with addition of a nose with different wing pylons featuring much larger venting. At the base, moreover, was a horizontal knife-edge profile running the full length. The turning vanes below the nose were also new, now characterised by a dual rather than single element.

interesting to note how Renault equipped the rear bodywork with a "megaphone" vent to ensure adequate thermal exchange for the RE19 power unit. The Racing Point rear vent was large but far less accentuated, evidence of better internal fluid dynamics and radiator pack efficiency.

Balance pays: a perfect blend of downforce, efficiency and…
tyres subjected to enormous lateral accelerations

SILVERSTONE: AN AERODYNAMIC TEST BENCH FOR MANY TEAMS

BRITISH GRAND PRIX
SILVERSTONE
SILVERSTONE CIRCUIT
14 JULY

In England, on a demanding circuit in terms of aerodynamics, many teams introduced significant modifications. The leading teams did not make major changes to their cars, although the evolutions adopted undoubtedly improved the performance of both the Mercedes W10 and the Ferrari SF90 and in their respective areas reached the objectives that had been set for these admittedly marginal evolutions. It had been known since prior to the race that Silverstone, in contrast with the Red Bull Ring, was on paper at least anything but favourable to the SF90. Nonetheless, the Maranello engineers continued to work on those evolutions that would allow the SF90 to continue (albeit slowly) to close the performance gap on the Mercedes. The series of minor modifications made to specific areas of the car is to be seen in this light; crucial to its adaptation to this track and also a possible, albeit partial, solution to the issue of the downforce generation by the floor of the car in the fast corners typical of the circuit. While the floor that had been tested in FP 1 in France and then shelved did not reappear, it was in any case interesting to note that a version of this element was introduced, with stiffening in correspondence with the longitudinal lateral vents and the extremities ahead of the rear wheels. In detail, shaped metal reinforcements were applied that

prevented the deformation of the elements delimiting the horizontal slots. The aim therefore was to maintain unaltered the profile of these elements to guarantee their utmost efficiency. It is well that the function of the lateral vents is that of producing a kind of pneumatic side-skirt effect sealing the floor and enhancing the downforce generated by the diffuser. It was interesting to discover that the deformation of these carbonfibre "blades" altered the section of the vents, reducing their through-flow and efficiency. Along with the lateral stiffening of floor, the rear bodywork was also widely modified. It was now in a single piece rather than separate, modular elements. In this way marginal weight saving was achieved, while the different configuration of the Coke bottle area was designed to improve downforce, as above.

With Silverstone being so close to its Brackley headquarters, Mercedes was also able to take advantage of the favourable logistics to try to optimize the aerodynamic performance of the W10 on its home track. The performance of the car in Austria was below par due to the well known overheating problems induced by the high ambient temperatures and the layout of the circuit with no long straights. At Silverstone, in contrast, the conditions were diametrically opposite on both counts, allowing the W10 to adopt a more "closed" rear aero

configuration, with a reduced section for the hot air dispersal vent. With an eye to greater aerodynamic efficiency on the straights, the rear bodywork of the W10 featured a sinuous trailing edge, visibly lower than the rear arm of the upper suspension wishbone. Also visible was the straight profile concealed by the suspension element that effectively created a double blow. Despite the reduced section of the vent, thanks to the acceleration of the flow of air passing through the dual blow, the configuration adopted permitted the flow from the radiator packs to be extracted more efficiently. Despite the apparent marginality of these modifications, on this track, and specifically in the Hangar Straight area that follows the three fast corners, Maggots, Becketts and Chapel, the adoption of more closed bodywork paid off in terms of a tangible increase in speed, exploiting the floor of the car more efficiently. Among the midfield teams, Alfa Romeo introduced an interesting evolution of the nose of the C38 with the fitting of a front wing cape, similar in shape to that of the McLaren. The presence of this element should, on paper, have guaranteed great downforce on the front axle, thus mitigating a shortcoming which the extreme outwash configuration of the front wing, similar to that of the Ferrari, created from the outset. The management of the airflow under the car was also improved.

Mercedes W10 rear bodywork

At Silverstone, the W10 adopted a more "closed" rear bodywork configuration, with the hot air vent having a smaller section. With an eye to greater aerodynamic efficiency on the straights, the rear bodywork of the W10 featured a sinuous trailing edge, visibly lower than the rear arm of the upper suspension wishbone. Also visible was the straight profile concealed by the suspension element that effectively created a double blow.

Ferrari: metal inserts on the floor of the SF90

A stiffened version of the floor was introduced, with reinforced longitudinal side vents and trailing edges ahead of the rear wheels. Shaped metal reinforcements were applied to prevent the elements of the longitudinal slots from deforming, guaranteeing maximum venting efficiency which created a pneumatic seal between floor and track.

Alfa Romeo C38: nose cone evolution

Alfa Romeo equipped the nose of the C38 with a cape similar in shape to that of the McLaren. This feature was introduced to provide greater downforce on the front axle, originally a weakness of the design due to its extreme front wing outwash configuration, and to improve flow management beneath the car.

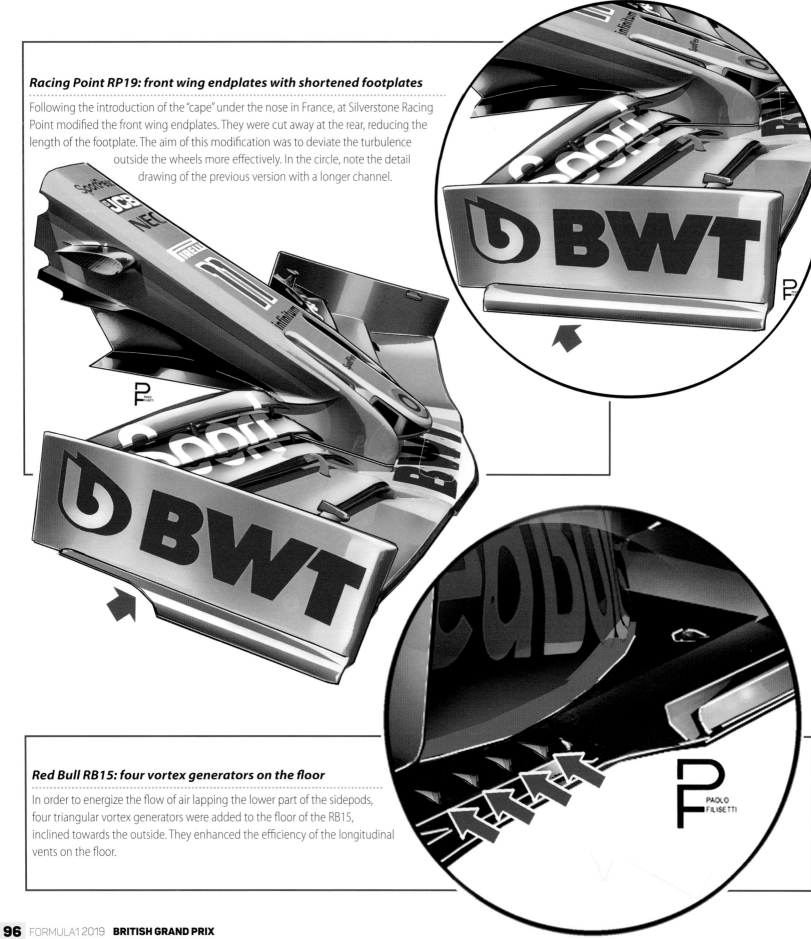

Racing Point RP19: front wing endplates with shortened footplates

Following the introduction of the "cape" under the nose in France, at Silverstone Racing Point modified the front wing endplates. They were cut away at the rear, reducing the length of the footplate. The aim of this modification was to deviate the turbulence outside the wheels more effectively. In the circle, note the detail drawing of the previous version with a longer channel.

Red Bull RB15: four vortex generators on the floor

In order to energize the flow of air lapping the lower part of the sidepods, four triangular vortex generators were added to the floor of the RB15, inclined towards the outside. They enhanced the efficiency of the longitudinal vents on the floor.

McLaren MCL34: new boomerang on the bargeboards

The Woking-based team introduced a series of aerodynamic modifications to the MCL34 for its home race. The reworking of the bargeboards was very interesting. These elements, already the object of development in previous races, presented a wide boomerang between the vertical vanes. In particular, the chord and the depth were increased with respect to the previous version. Set above the series of saw-tooth profiles, it was designed to generate downwash, deviating downwards the flow of air exiting the front wing towards the car's floor. In the comparison note the difference in the chord of the boomerang profile and the width of the external vertical element, greater than the version used in Austria.

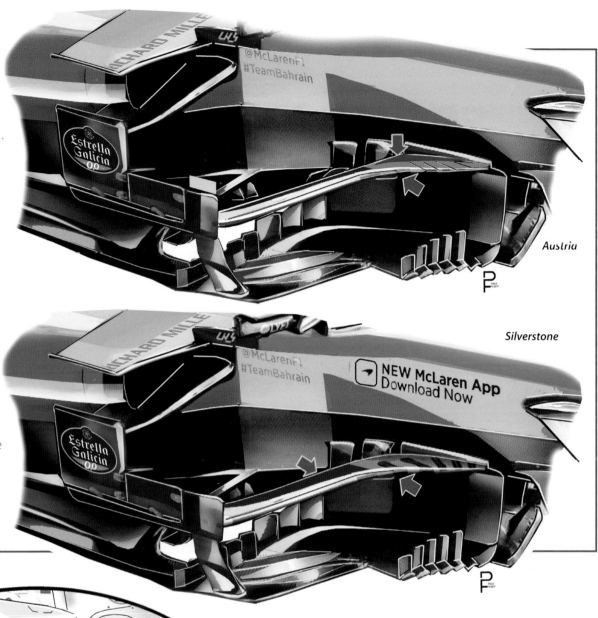

Austria

Silverstone

Williams FW42: turning vane evolution

Williams too introduced an interesting evolution of its FW42 at Silverstone. In practice, the horizontal bridging vane above the sidepod mouths were replaced with two separate elements. The mirror support were very complex, with the lower one anchored to the horizontal profile arching upwards that acted as a flow separator.

An anniversary without celebrations for the "Three-Pointed Star" despite the introduction of an extensive aero package

MERCEDES: ALMOST A B-VERSION OF THE W10

GERMAN GRAND PRIX
HOCKENHEIM
HOCKENHEIM RING
28 JULY

Curiously enough, in Formula 1 the adoption of extensive developments does not necessarily pay off on the macroscopic level. Or rather, it would perhaps be more correct to say that positive results do not always coincide with the introduction of the new features. At Hockenheim, it might be said that this "tradition" was maintained, almost as if it were a rule of counterpoint that no one can avoid, not even the world champion team, currently leading both championship standings. In Germany, in fact, Mercedes, which was celebrating 125 years in motorsport and its 200th Formula 1 GP as a constructor, by no means restricted itself to an elegant new celebratory livery in white and silver for the W10. The team from Brackley in fact took to what was effectively its second home circuit after Silverstone, a profoundly revised car. Specifically, great efforts were made with a radical intervention that extended from the front wing to the rear wing. This development package had two main thrusts concerning the management of two air flows: the external one running along the bodywork, starting with the impact against the front wing elements, and the one passing through the sidepods and exiting via the radiators. The optimization of the former aimed at increasing the efficiency of the W10, reducing drag thanks to more effective management of the turbulence generated by the front wing and the flows lapping the area ahead of the sidepods. The second instead concerned the revision of the cooling system. Included in the first group were the modifications to the front wing endplates, lengthened at the back to increase the out-wash effect (deviating the flow outside the wheels). With regard to the bargeboards and turning vanes alongside the sidepods, the interventions were decidedly radical. The earlier vertical elements were in fact replaced by fairly complex horizontal grilles (resembling venetian blinds), inspired by those used by Haas and Toro Rosso. The development in this particularly strategic zone in term of the downforce developed by the car's floor, the Mercedes aero engineers also worked on the peripheral area of the floor itself, with three superimposed vents in correspondence with the leading edge flare. There were also interesting modifications to the rear wing endplates. These were characterised by the stepped profile of the upper trailing edge. Visible modifications were also made to the lateral sections of the diffuser. The majority of the modifications that concerned the revision of the cooling system were instead concentrated laterally, towards the rear end. Although concealed, the position of the radiator packs was different, as was their surface areas, permitting enhanced thermal exchange. Looking at the bodywork, we could also see a less tapering configuration that allowed a great internal section to the advantage of heat extraction. This clearly had the aim of reducing the running temperatures of the components located in both the upper and lower parts of the power unit. It is interesting to see how the planning of this development dated back to the Bahrain GP when, for the first time, the W10 had clearly suffered from inadequate thermal exchange, due in part to the high ambient temperatures. The situation was repeated at the Austrian GP, highlighting the need for modifications in view of the potentially even hotter summer races in Germany and Hungary, Contradictory rumours did the rounds in the paddock at Hockenheim throughout the weekend, regarding the suggestion that a new version of the monocoque had been introduced with modifications around the fuel tank to permit a diversification of the radiator installations. The team subsequently clarified that the chassis taken to Hockenheim were standard, as used from the start of the season.

Mercedes W10: front wing development

In Germany we saw modifications to the front wing endplates, lengthened at the back to increase the outwash effect (deviating the flow outside the wheels). In the comparison with the previous version, introduced in China, note how the new endplate completely covers the profile of the last flap, while previously it protruded in the side view.

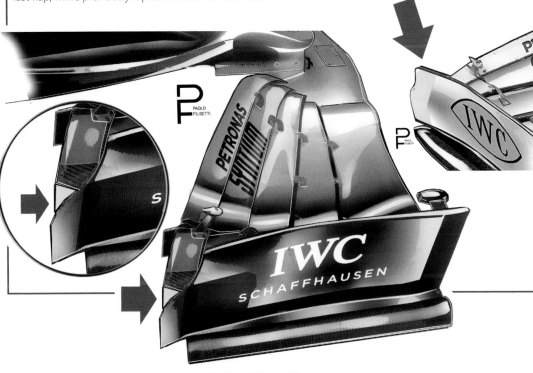

W10: bargeboards and turning vanes evolution

The turning vanes to the sides of the sidepods and the bargeboards were revised. The earlier vertical elements were in fact replaced by fairly complex horizontal grilles (resembling venetian blinds), inspired by those used by Haas and Toro Rosso. The evolution was completed in this zone of strategic importance for the downforce generated by the floor with modifications to the peripheral area, equipping it with three superimposed profiles separated by vents, in correspondence with the leading edge kink. The rear view mirror supports were new and a triangular profile was added downstream of the upper wishbone.

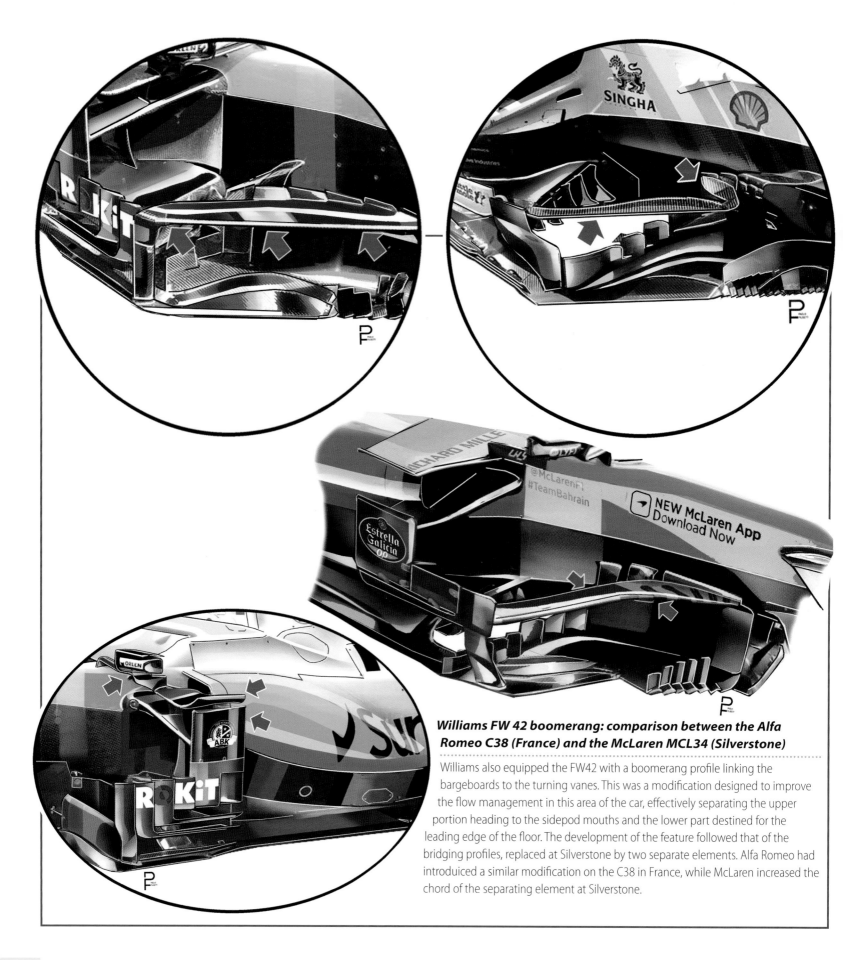

Williams FW 42 boomerang: comparison between the Alfa Romeo C38 (France) and the McLaren MCL34 (Silverstone)

Williams also equipped the FW42 with a boomerang profile linking the bargeboards to the turning vanes. This was a modification designed to improve the flow management in this area of the car, effectively separating the upper portion heading to the sidepod mouths and the lower part destined for the leading edge of the floor. The development of the feature followed that of the bridging profiles, replaced at Silverstone by two separate elements. Alfa Romeo had introduced a similar modification on the C38 in France, while McLaren increased the chord of the separating element at Silverstone.

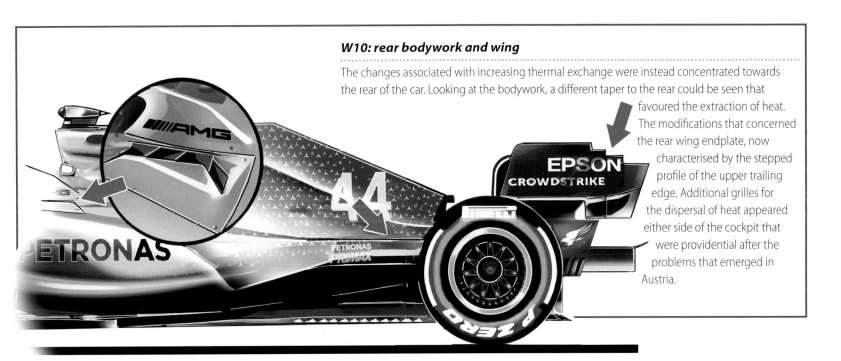

W10: rear bodywork and wing

The changes associated with increasing thermal exchange were instead concentrated towards the rear of the car. Looking at the bodywork, a different taper to the rear could be seen that favoured the extraction of heat. The modifications that concerned the rear wing endplate, now characterised by the stepped profile of the upper trailing edge. Additional grilles for the dispersal of heat appeared either side of the cockpit that were providential after the problems that emerged in Austria.

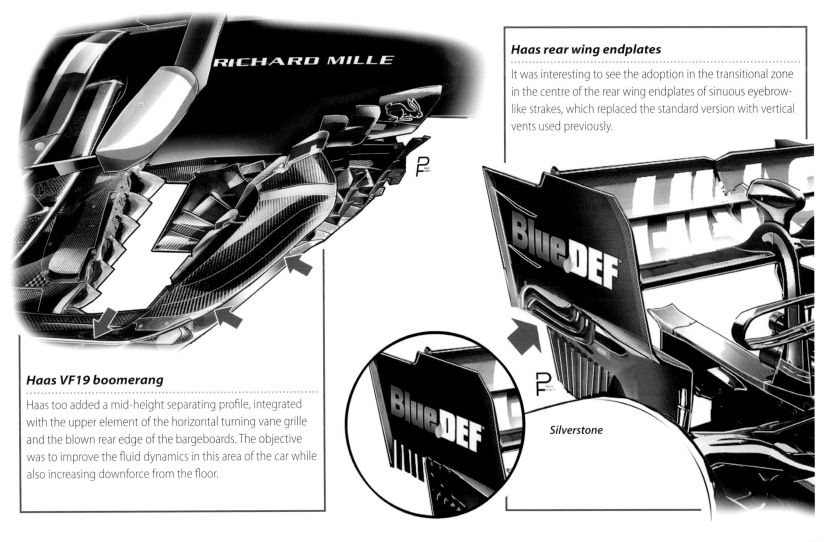

Haas VF19 boomerang

Haas too added a mid-height separating profile, integrated with the upper element of the horizontal turning vane grille and the blown rear edge of the bargeboards. The objective was to improve the fluid dynamics in this area of the car while also increasing downforce from the floor.

Haas rear wing endplates

It was interesting to see the adoption in the transitional zone in the centre of the rear wing endplates of sinuous eyebrow-like strakes, which replaced the standard version with vertical vents used previously.

Silverstone

MAXIMUS DOWNFORCE LEVEL AND MORE

HUNGARIAN GRAND PRIX
BUDAPEST
HUNGARORING
4 AUGUST

The Hungaroring is notoriously a circuit where the fundamental factor is represented the downforce generated. The characteristics of the track in fact correspond largely to those of Monaco, even though it is not actually a street circuit. To these are added the elevated lateral accelerations that place great stress on the tyres which, even with the hardest compound, go off very rapidly if they are not very well managed, within around 20 laps. As this race was staged just a week after the German GP, we could hardly expect significant modifications to the cars, although as things turned out this was only partially confirmed. In fact, while at Hockenheim Ferrari had avoided introducing aerodynamic developments, there was a clearly visible evolution of the bargeboards on the SF90 at the Hungaroring. Specifically, the upper sections of these elements were modified, while the lower one remained unchanged. In detail, two long, superimposed and interconnected "boomerangs" were added just below the upper edge. The first long and sinuous, the second shorter. The upper one was also characterised by a sinuous leading edged, equipped with curving transverse micro-vents (permitted by the regulations) and a sawtooth trailing edge. The two elements were connected and stiffened via central

and lateral metal inserts that prevented them from deforming. This was effectively to prevent any deformation of the boomerangs from reducing the transverse section of the vent between the two elements that in turn acted as a flow accelerator at that point.

These elements were clearly the inspiration for similar components introduced by Red Bull at the Spanish GP. It is curious to note that on that occasion the bargeboards on the team from Milton Keynes' car were also clearly inspired by those of the SF90. This can be seen in particular in the lower section where the "scimitar" profiles were located. At Montmelò a "boomerang" was added below the main profile to increase the downwash of the flow towards the leading edge. Moreover, in the case of both the RB15 and the SF90, this configuration also served to distance the turbulence generated by the front wheels. The coherence of the objectives associated with this development between the two cars confirms that the Red Bull and the Ferrari share a similar "DNA" also seen in the adoption of a high rake configuration.

However, Ferrari was not the only team to introduce interesting developments. Racing Point in fact continued with its extensive evolution of the RP19. The benefits deriving from the consolidated link with Mercedes were increasingly visible through

developments progressively adopted from race to race. While previously, this had mainly entailed aero packages affected the nose, the front and rear wings and the rear bodywork, in Hungary it was interesting to note an evolution of the front suspension. This was in fact now equipped with a pivot as well as the push-rod bracket similar to that of the Mercedes. While not a true novelty, it was possible to examine in detail the Mercedes W10's front brake drums. Apart from the adoption of asymmetric elements, as did almost all the cars (due to the prevalence of right-hand turns), we were able to note that the latest version featured an additional duct, below the principal air intake. This duct had a vertical development with four horizontal divisions. With the left-hand drum dismantled during free practice, we could see how this duct developed internally, "dragging" the flow of air towards the outside of the wheels. In this way the team obtain a "legal" effect similar to that produced by the blown front hubs (introduced by Red Bull a couple of seasons earlier and now banned). It is reasonable to suggest that this modification, in parallel with the turning vanes flanking the sidepods, introduced in Germany, were designed principally to increase aerodynamic efficiency, an area in which the W10 was lacking compared to the Red Bull and above all the Ferrari.

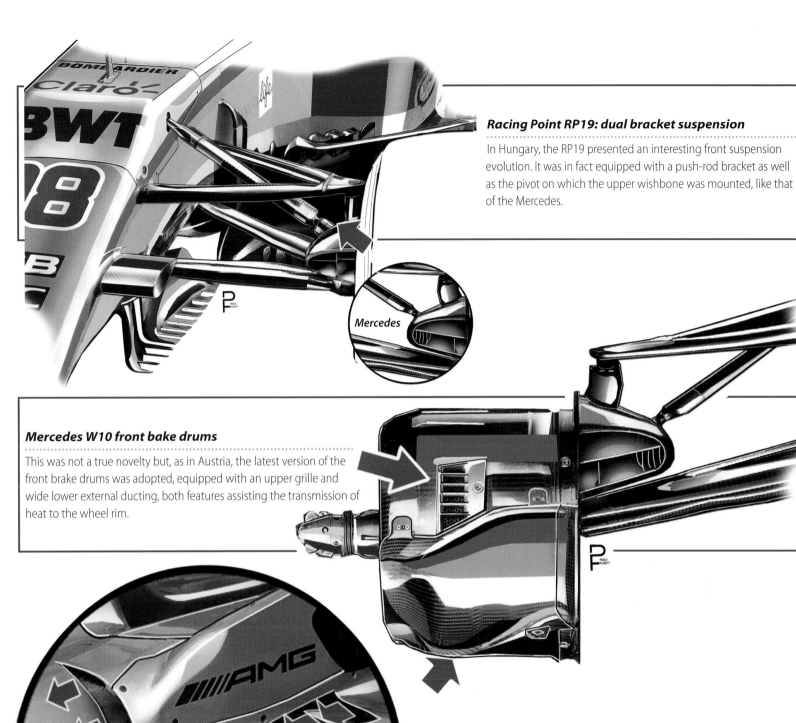

Racing Point RP19: dual bracket suspension

In Hungary, the RP19 presented an interesting front suspension evolution. It was in fact equipped with a push-rod bracket as well as the pivot on which the upper wishbone was mounted, like that of the Mercedes.

Mercedes

Mercedes W10 front bake drums

This was not a true novelty but, as in Austria, the latest version of the front brake drums was adopted, equipped with an upper grille and wide lower external ducting, both features assisting the transmission of heat to the wheel rim.

Mercedes W10: cooling grilles

At Budapest we saw the same combination of hot air vents either side of the cockpit and the gills at the base of the halo support adopted in Germany. This was the maximum "open" configuration for the bodywork, designed to increase thermal exchange considering the torrid temperatures that usually characterise the Hungarian weekend.

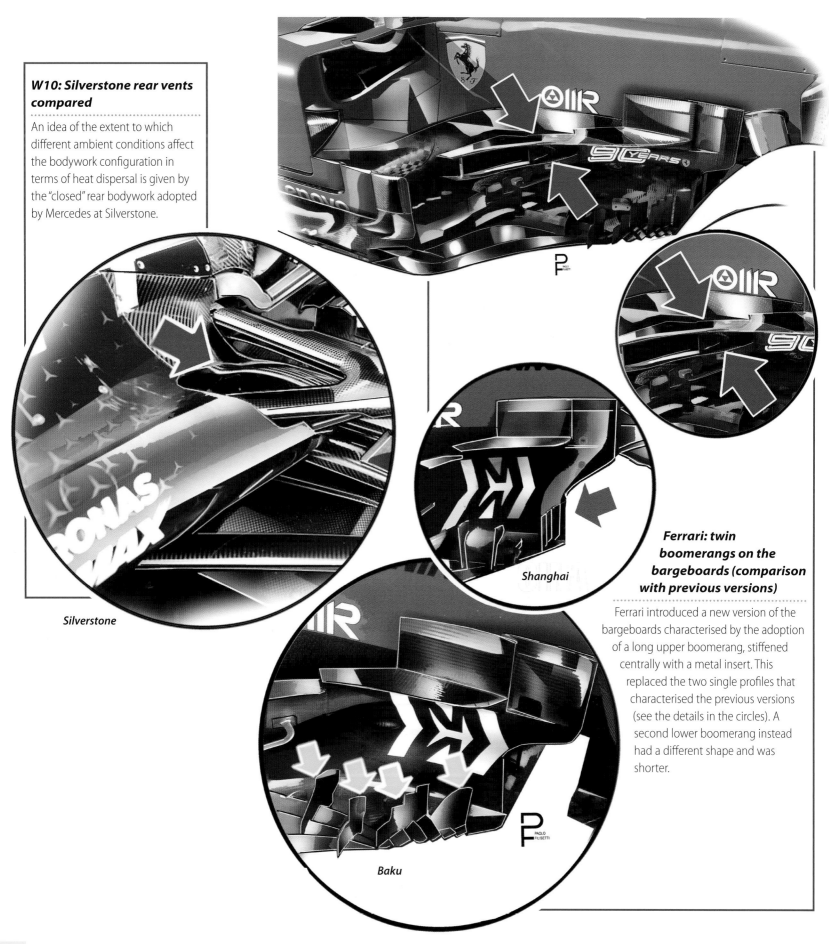

W10: Silverstone rear vents compared

An idea of the extent to which different ambient conditions affect the bodywork configuration in terms of heat dispersal is given by the "closed" rear bodywork adopted by Mercedes at Silverstone.

Silverstone

Shanghai

Baku

Ferrari: twin boomerangs on the bargeboards (comparison with previous versions)

Ferrari introduced a new version of the bargeboards characterised by the adoption of a long upper boomerang, stiffened centrally with a metal insert. This replaced the two single profiles that characterised the previous versions (see the details in the circles). A second lower boomerang instead had a different shape and was shorter.

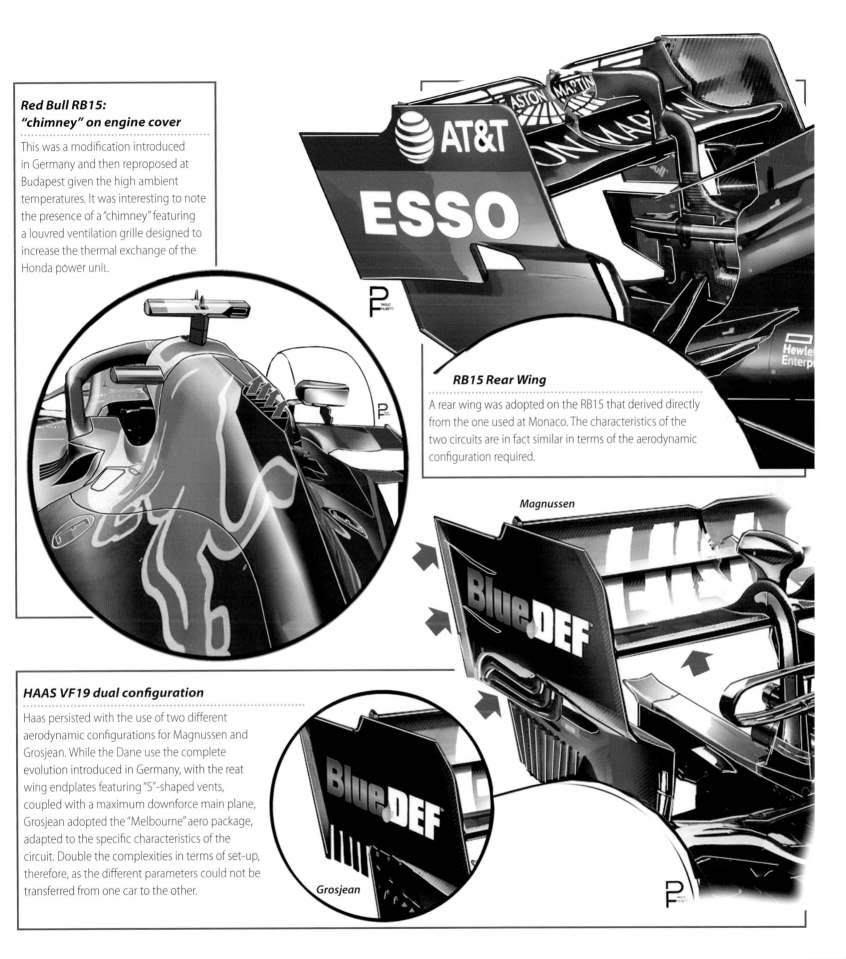

Red Bull RB15: "chimney" on engine cover

This was a modification introduced in Germany and then reproposed at Budapest given the high ambient temperatures. It was interesting to note the presence of a "chimney" featuring a louvred ventilation grille designed to increase the thermal exchange of the Honda power unit.

RB15 Rear Wing

A rear wing was adopted on the RB15 that derived directly from the one used at Monaco. The characteristics of the two circuits are in fact similar in terms of the aerodynamic configuration required.

Magnussen

HAAS VF19 dual configuration

Haas persisted with the use of two different aerodynamic configurations for Magnussen and Grosjean. While the Dane use the complete evolution introduced in Germany, with the reat wing endplates featuring "S"-shaped vents, coupled with a maximum downforce main plane, Grosjean adopted the "Melbourne" aero package, adapted to the specific characteristics of the circuit. Double the complexities in terms of set-up, therefore, as the different parameters could not be transferred from one car to the other.

Grosjean

◼◼ AERO DEVELOPMENTS ONLY FOR FERRARI

BELGIAN GRAND PRIX

FRANCORCHAMPS
SPA-FRANCORCHAMPS
1 SEPTEMBER

While the Belgian GP represents the start of the second half of the season, almost like the return to school in September, it is equally true that the evolutions introduced at this race generally do not entail particularly extensive development packages. In order to better define the breadth of the area of intervention it is worth pointing out that the proximity of this race to the one at Monza the following week substantially reduced the utility of introducing specific packages for Spa, including the debut of new iterations of the power unit. Ferrari in fact decided to postpone the introduction of its Evo 3 Power Unit until the Italian GP, restricting itself in Belgium to adopting a different aerodynamic configuration. Specifically, an engine cover without the T-wing at its rear end was introduced, coupled with a rear wing equipped with a new main plane capable of producing little drag in relation to the downforce generated. Considering the Belgian circuit's long straights, which effectively represent the distinguishing elements of the first and third sectors of the track, along with the presence of a twistier T2 section, the configuration of this element could hardly be an extreme reduction of drag to the detriment of downforce. In short, the version for Monza would, at least on paper, have been more radical in this sense, comparable to the one introduced in Baku (characterised by a dished main plane), decidedly more favourable in terms of drag. At the front, the wing presented a final flap with a significantly reduced chord, which increased only in proximity to the endplates. As mentioned previously, this was without doubt a low downforce configuration, with little drag being produced, but capable of generating sufficient downforce in the twistier intermediate section of the circuit.

The rival teams, especially Mercedes, did not present any novelties of note, preferring to rely on fine tuning of the aerodynamic, ride height and yaw sensitivity adjustments. Obviously, all teams tried to privilege penetration and reduce the negative influence of certain areas of their cars. In this sense, the W10 presented the same rear bodywork configuration introduced at Silverstone, characterised by a much reduced section, in particular its upper profile, in proximity to the upper wishbone.

It might be said that instead Red Bull was braver with the RB15, specifically in terms of the adoption of a low downforce rear wing, with the main plane rising at the centre and a reduced flap incidence. In this case the feature recalled the version introduced at Baku, albeit not taken to the same extremes, above all in terms of the main plane chord and the configuration of the endplates. In parallel, the team used the nose without the S-duct intake, favouring the penetration privileged by the overall configuration.

While as mentioned earlier Ferrari preferred to postpone the debut of the final iteration of its power unit, Mercedes decided otherwise and brought it to this race, in contrast with the schedule hypothesised prior to the summer break. The Phase 3 version of the unit manufactured at Brixworth and developed and tested throughout August, the obligatory shutdown for the Brackley-based team not applying (the same conditions were also enjoyed by the engine departments of the rival constructors), should on paper have represented tangible progress with respect to the Phase 2. There was talk of an increase in power output in the order of 20 hp, which should have served in Belgium to counter the greater aerodynamic efficiency of the Ferrari SF90. Despite the increase in power, it should be point out that while the benefits were clear at Spa, they were not sufficient to annul the advantage associated with the greater aerodynamic efficiency of the team's adversaries. This said, it is possible that the engine mode was less extreme than the one that was later to be employed at Monza, where the maximum throttle opening accounted for 75% of the full lap against 62% at Spa. The final iteration was adopted by the client teams at the same time. It is interesting to note that the Ferrari client teams (Alfa Romeo and Haas) used this final specification in contrast with the "mother company". Racing Point introduced a new version of its nose without nostrils and in addition new winglets on the upper part. The evolution of the RP19 had continued incessantly from Silverstone onwards. The very close collaboration with Mercedes will be very tangible from 2020.

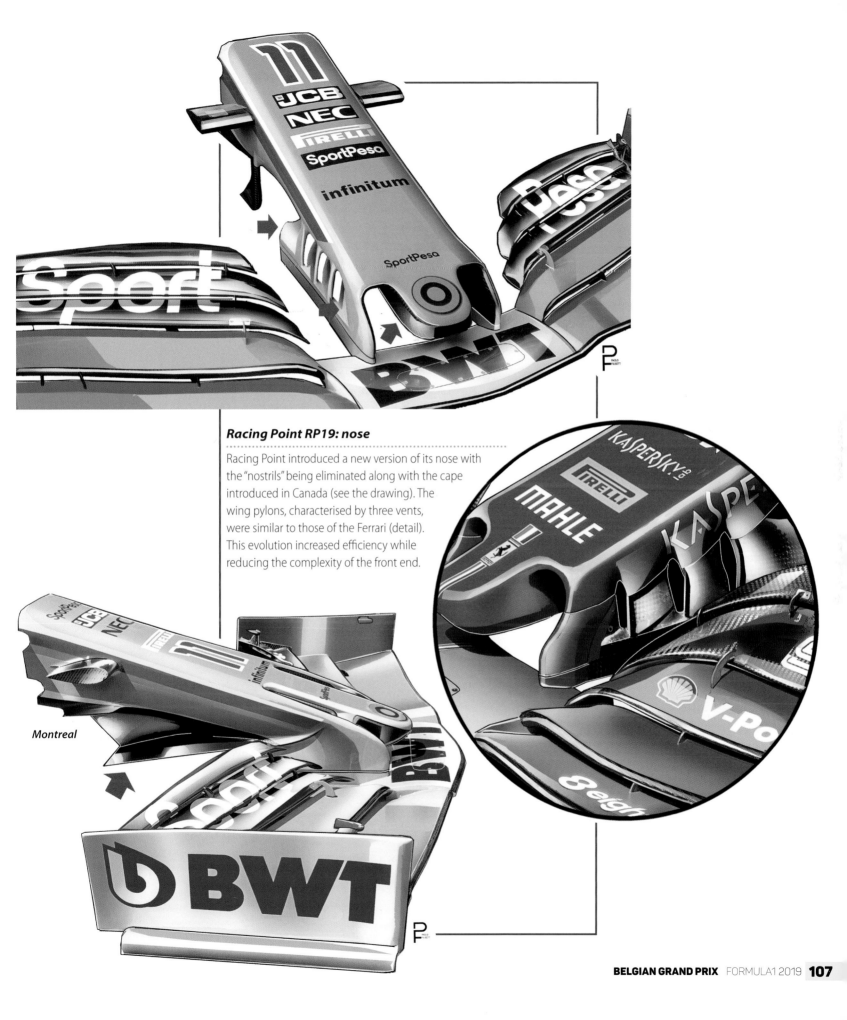

Racing Point RP19: nose

Racing Point introduced a new version of its nose with the "nostrils" being eliminated along with the cape introduced in Canada (see the drawing). The wing pylons, characterised by three vents, were similar to those of the Ferrari (detail). This evolution increased efficiency while reducing the complexity of the front end.

Montreal

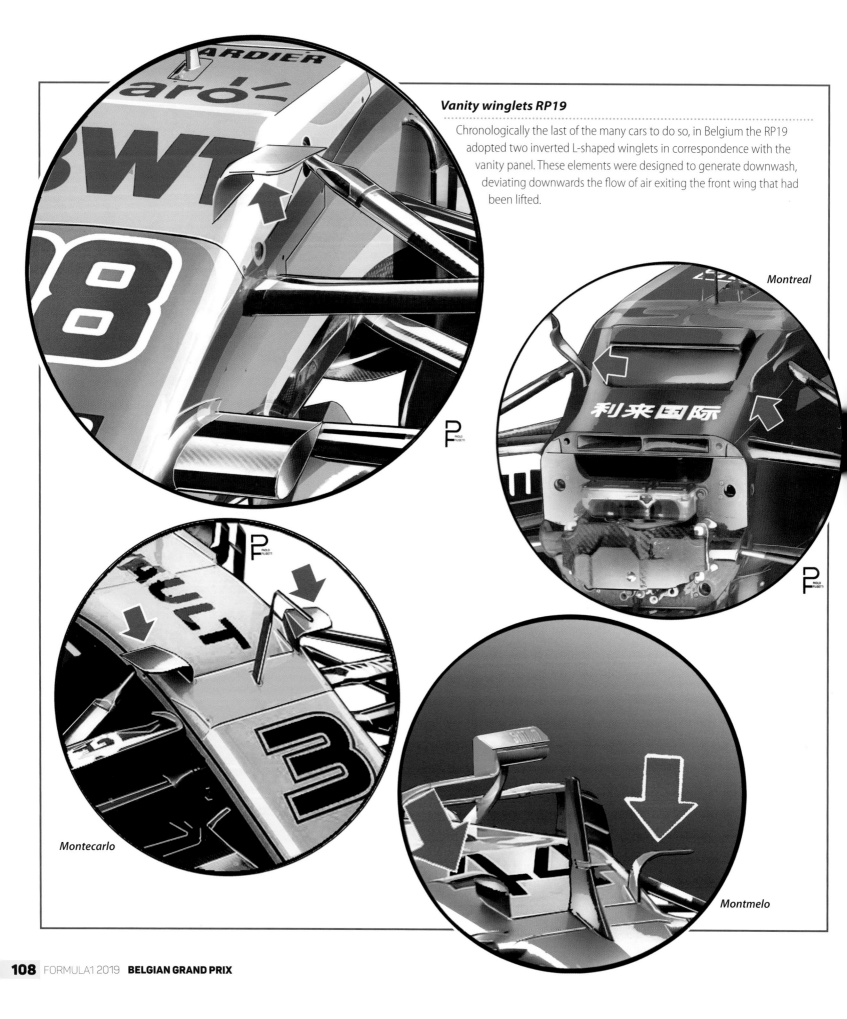

Vanity winglets RP19

Chronologically the last of the many cars to do so, in Belgium the RP19 adopted two inverted L-shaped winglets in correspondence with the vanity panel. These elements were designed to generate downwash, deviating downwards the flow of air exiting the front wing that had been lifted.

Montreal

Montecarlo

Montmelo

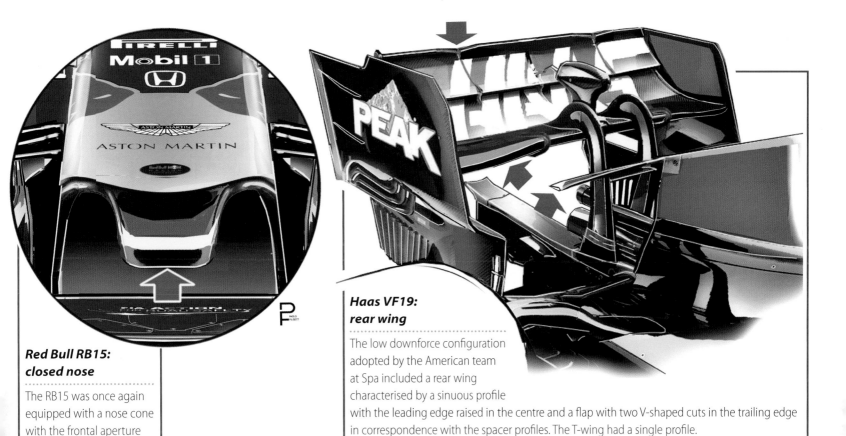

Red Bull RB15: closed nose

The RB15 was once again equipped with a nose cone with the frontal aperture feeding the SD-duct blanked off.

Haas VF19: rear wing

The low downforce configuration adopted by the American team at Spa included a rear wing characterised by a sinuous profile with the leading edge raised in the centre and a flap with two V-shaped cuts in the trailing edge in correspondence with the spacer profiles. The T-wing had a single profile.

SF90: low downforce front wing

At Spa Ferrari adopted a low downforce configuration in order to adapt to the characteristics of the track. Specifically, a version of the front wing developed for Canada was used. The last flap was characterised by a very reduced chord and a different curvature to the external part which modified slightly the outwash effect given to the air-flow.

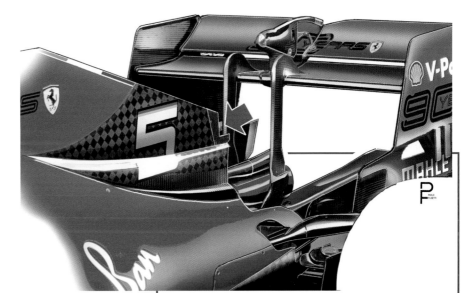

SF90: rear wing

In view of a possible use at Monza, Ferrari brought a very low downforce rear wing to Belgium, with the main plane set very high, coupled with a minimal incidence flap. Note, furthermore, the absence of the T-wing in order to reduce straight-line drag.

Ferrari wins at the Temple of Speed thanks to traction, aerodynamics, power and the talent of Leclerc

FERRARI AND CHARLES... A SHOW OF STRENGHT

ITALIAN GRAND PRIX

MONZA
AUTODROMO NAZIONALE DI MONZA
8 SEPTEMBER

Usually when a race is held just a week after the previous one, we can hardly expect particularly significant modifications to the cars. In this specific case, the two races in question were the Belgian GP at Spa and the Italian GP at Monza. Even though both can be considered as fast circuits, there are differences that place the second in a category of its own, thereby justifying the adoption of more extreme aerodynamic configurations than those seen in Belgium. Moreover, it should be remembered that these specific features, which justify the Brianza track's reputation as the "Temple of Speed", did not only have a tangible influence on aerodynamic choices but, in the case of Honda and Ferrari, also justified the debut of the first of the fourth generation power units used by Max Verstappen and, for the Maranello team, the introduction of the third iteration of the season.

The significance in terms of performance of even a minimal increase in power justified the decision of both constructors to fit fresh engines for Monza to ensure that they would be at their very best. The two power units were apparently both accredited with an increase of around 20 hp even though, obviously, these were paddock rumours circulating at Spa and Monza and therefore have no official blessing. For Ferrari, along with the Belgian track, Monza was the second in the World Championship calendar that was clearly tailor made for the SF90's aerodynamics. Leclerc's victory confirmed these characteristics, but the 53 race laps also highlighted the specific factors that allowed the Monaco driver to win again, just a week after his maiden F1 victory. While, as mentioned earlier, it was clear that the aerodynamic efficiency of the SF90 could guarantee significant maximum speed at the end of the long straights, it was equally true that traction out of corners was the most significant element in the success of the Italian car. It was in fact capital that was wisely invested by Leclerc as he successfully attempted to retain leadership in the race, defending himself from the Hamilton's attacks or at least mitigating them. The set-up of the SF90, in fact, guaranteed adequate grip from the rear tyres, even with the hard compound fitted by Leclerc at the pit stop, to allow all the power from the engine to be transmitted to the asphalt from the very first metres coming out of the chicanes. In this way a certain "cushion" was created in terms of the gap between Charles and Hamilton, an advantage which Leclerc was then able to manage in the sections when his adversary was able to activate the DRS, something he was unable to do while leading the race (except when lapping backmarkers). The increase in power, as previously mentioned quantifiable at around 20 hp, was therefore exploited to best effect, without generating the excessive wheel spin which would have triggered a premature drop-off in tyre performance. The blend of penetration and power was also reinforced by a third element – traction – which had hitherto rarely been seen as a strong suit of the SF90.

Specific modifications for this circuit included a new version of the Toro Rosso front wing, characterised by a final flap with a particularly reduced chord and a hooked configuration of its internal extremity. Ferrari and Red Bull instead both introduced a low downforce version of their rear wings. In the case of the RB15, the main plane was significantly raised, with a reduction in the incidence of the flap. Renault also adapted the RS 19 to the demands of the Monza circuit, with a front wing similar to that of the Red Bull.

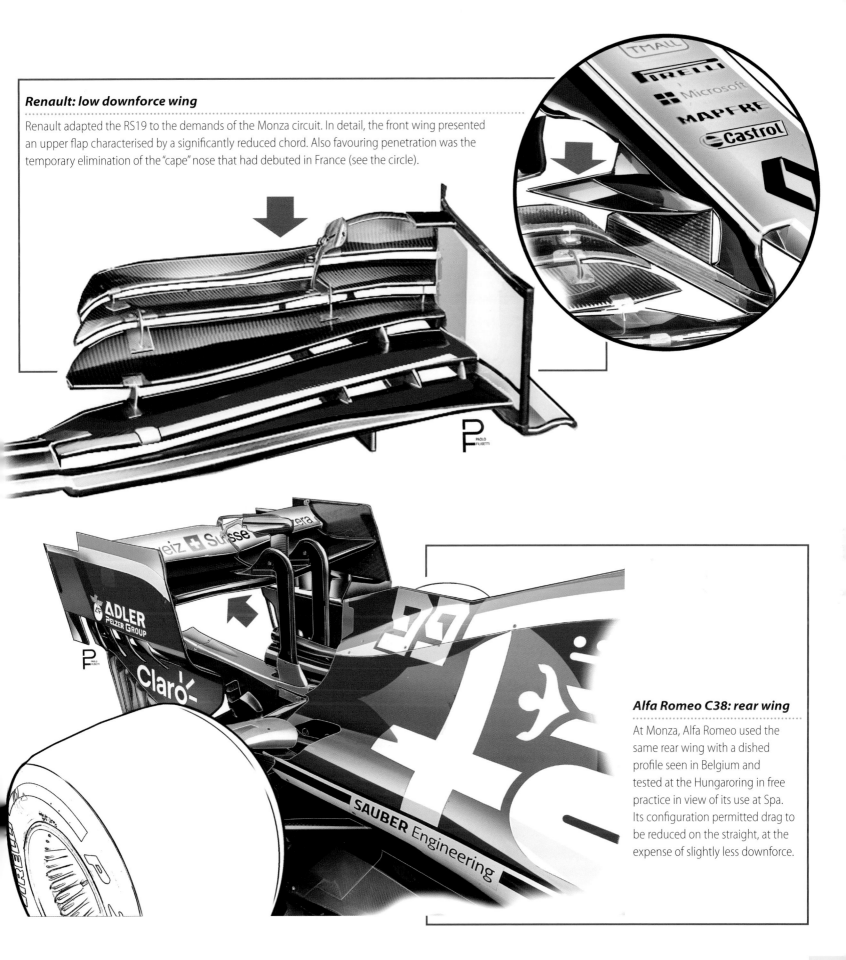

Renault: low downforce wing

Renault adapted the RS19 to the demands of the Monza circuit. In detail, the front wing presented an upper flap characterised by a significantly reduced chord. Also favouring penetration was the temporary elimination of the "cape" nose that had debuted in France (see the circle).

Alfa Romeo C38: rear wing

At Monza, Alfa Romeo used the same rear wing with a dished profile seen in Belgium and tested at the Hungaroring in free practice in view of its use at Spa. Its configuration permitted drag to be reduced on the straight, at the expense of slightly less downforce.

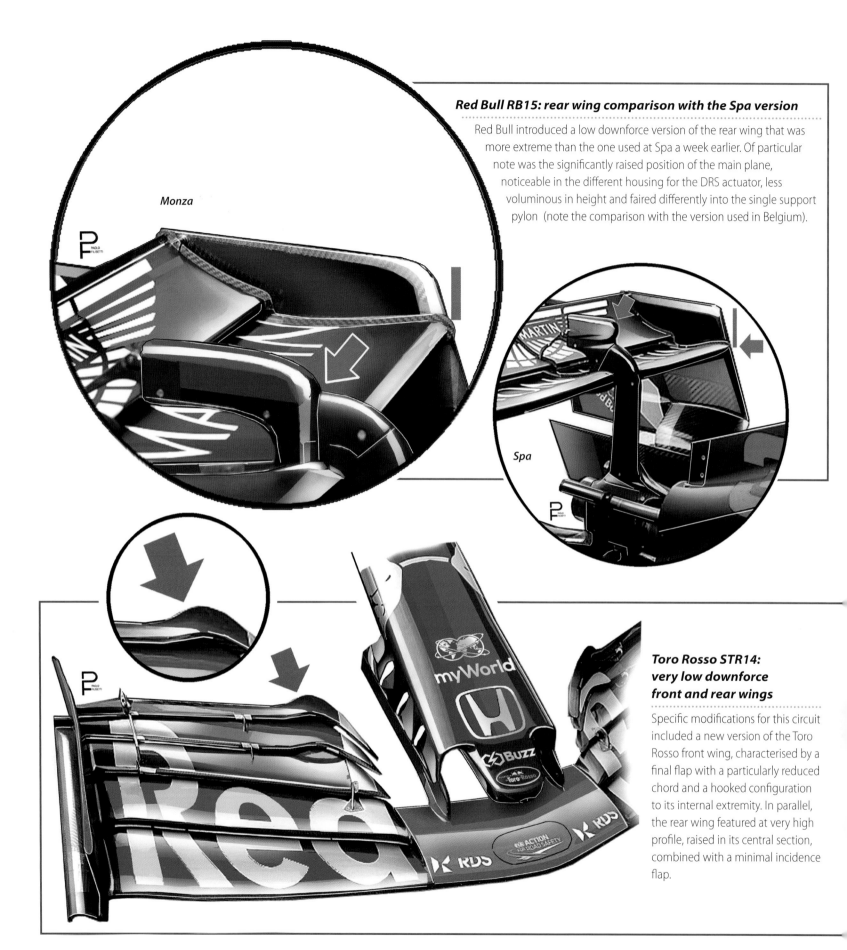

Red Bull RB15: rear wing comparison with the Spa version

Red Bull introduced a low downforce version of the rear wing that was more extreme than the one used at Spa a week earlier. Of particular note was the significantly raised position of the main plane, noticeable in the different housing for the DRS actuator, less voluminous in height and faired differently into the single support pylon (note the comparison with the version used in Belgium).

Monza

Spa

Toro Rosso STR14: very low downforce front and rear wings

Specific modifications for this circuit included a new version of the Toro Rosso front wing, characterised by a final flap with a particularly reduced chord and a hooked configuration to its internal extremity. In parallel, the rear wing featured at very high profile, raised in its central section, combined with a minimal incidence flap.

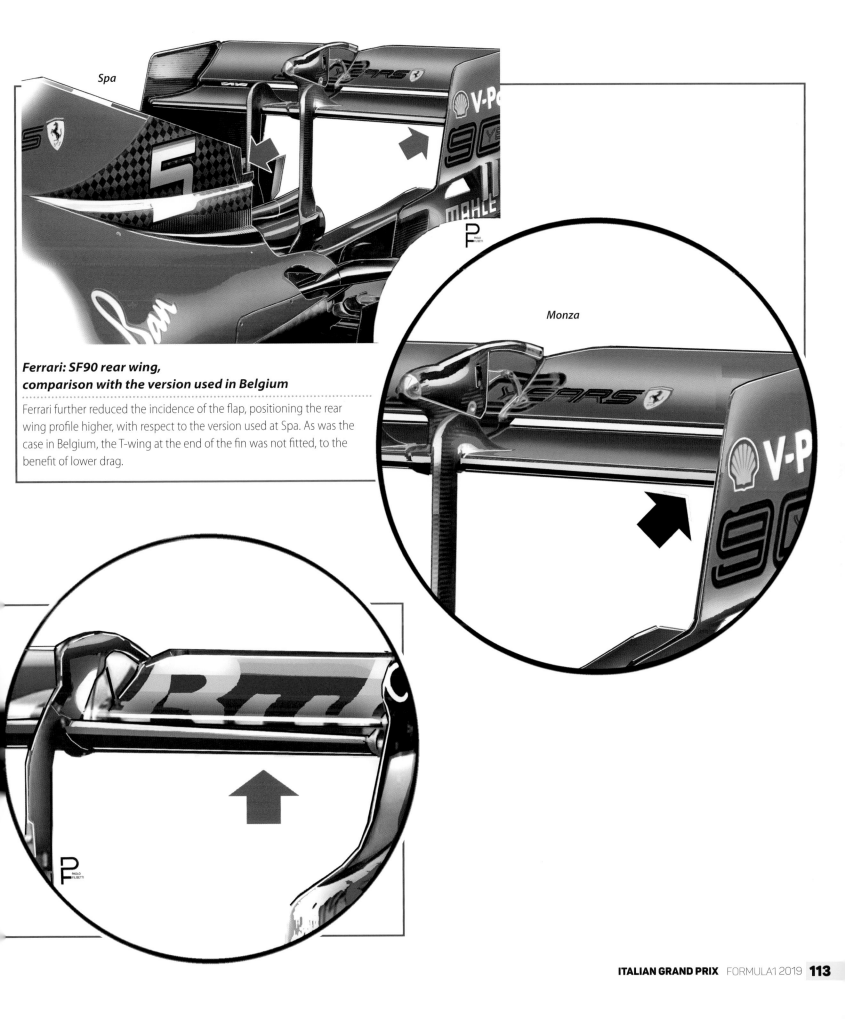

Spa

Monza

Ferrari: SF90 rear wing, comparison with the version used in Belgium

Ferrari further reduced the incidence of the flap, positioning the rear wing profile higher, with respect to the version used at Spa. As was the case in Belgium, the T-wing at the end of the fin was not fitted, to the benefit of lower drag.

The aero package introduced by Ferrari was strikingly effective in correcting the Rossa's chronic lack of downforce

LOWER AERODYNAMIC REVOLUTION FOR THE SF90

SINGAPORE GRAND PRIX

SINGAPORE
SINGAPORE STREET CIRCUIT
22 SEPTEMBER

Singapore has features similar to those of the Budapest circuit and traditionally has only rarely seen the introduction of extensive development packages. Generally, the modifications seen here are simply updates or adaptations of the configurations already adopted on the cars in Hungary. Without doubt, Ferrari represented an exception to this rule in 2019, having introduced an extensive aero package. The modifications were not confined to a single area of the car, but extended from the front to the rear wing, effectively involving the entire lower aerodynamic configuration of the SF90. Clearly, the efforts expended by the aerodynamics department directed by David Sanchez were titanic and might be said to be unprecedented in such an advanced stage of the season, were it not for Mercedes' feat last season in revising the internal kinematics of its car's rear suspension.

The modifications in question concerned the debut of a new version of the nose, characterised in the lower part by the presence of a cape, clearly inspired by the Mercedes school. The profile was located practically half way up the wing pylons. It was in the details, however, that the element differed from that adopted on the rival car, starting with the airflow feeding it. This flow was, in fact, channelled at the front via the "nostrils" that it forms along with the wing pylons and the lower part of the nose. It was also significantly shorter than that of the W10, extending only as far as the S-duct intake in the lower section of the nose cone. This modification was accompanied by an extensive revision of the floor, specifically its lateral peripheral sections, in correspondence with the longitudinal vents and ahead of the rear wheels. In practice, as well as the addition of vortex generators along the edge of the longitudinal vents, the profile of those placed diagonally, in proximity to the rear wheels, was modified. It was interesting to note that they were stiffened with very long metal inserts. These inserts had the crucial task of preventing the profile of the vents deforming irrespective of the loads to which they were subjected. In this way the pneumatic seal it produces is guaranteed thereby enhancing the efficiency of the diffuser. This last element also presented a different shape to the central section, which was no longer straight but rather curved, while in parallel there were tangible differences in the expansion zone. The rear wing was also revised, although the differences between the old and new profile could be defined as millimetric and very difficult to spot. With these changes, the team achieved its objective of generating more downforce, which was also better distributed with respect to the previous configuration. Considering the result obtained, which went beyond the rosiest expectation, it is important to note how complex the operation was, integrating a truly extensive series of modifications into what was already a mature design, without losing, as so often happens, the positive characteristics of the car. The balance displayed by the SF90 on the Marina Bay circuit drastically reduced the problem of tyre decay, which on this kind of circuit had afflicted the Ferraris early in the season. What emerged, therefore provided a valid roadmap for 2020. In terms of overall performance, the contribution of the power unit should not be overlooked on a circuit where power was not crucial in absolute terms but represented a resource that countered the greater drag produced by the maximum downforce configuration. Thanks to the traction that was already excellent when exiting the Monza chicanes, the cars were able to exit the right-angle corners at Marina Bay rapidly. Apart from the Ferrari aero package, among the top teams of particular interest was Red Bull's interpretation of the maximum downforce configuration with the rear wing of the RB15. The endplates were monolithic, with neither horizontal vents in the upper part nor fringes in the mid-section. In this way the team sought the maximum increase in downforce, obtained via the wing profile with a strongly curved section and a leading edge that was thicker at the centre and thinner to the sides.

Racing Point, continued with the development of the RP19 in the second half of the season and presented a new front wing with different endplates. Alfa Romeo instead adopted a multi-profile T-wing in order to increase downforce on the rear axle. In parallel, the cape on the C38 was developed with the addition of dual longitudinal vents. Renault instead employed a T-wing with a C-shaped profile in which the lower element was sinuous and traversed by a lengthy longitudinal vent.

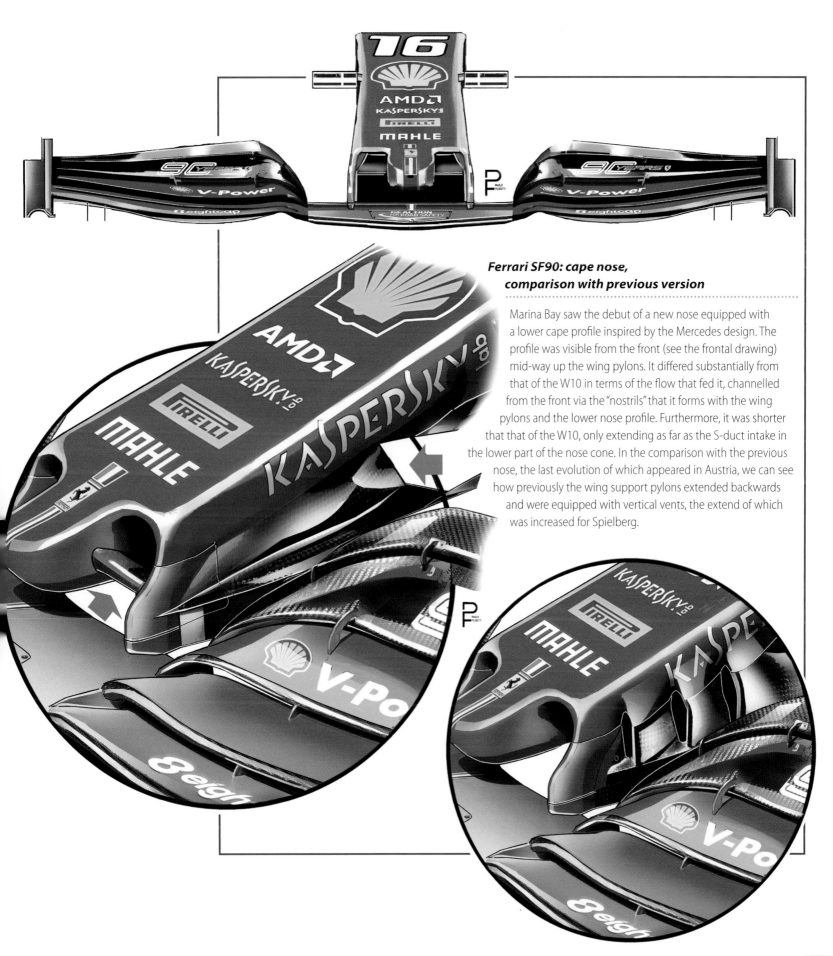

Ferrari SF90: cape nose, comparison with previous version

Marina Bay saw the debut of a new nose equipped with a lower cape profile inspired by the Mercedes design. The profile was visible from the front (see the frontal drawing) mid-way up the wing pylons. It differed substantially from that of the W10 in terms of the flow that fed it, channelled from the front via the "nostrils" that it forms with the wing pylons and the lower nose profile. Furthermore, it was shorter that that of the W10, only extending as far as the S-duct intake in the lower part of the nose cone. In the comparison with the previous nose, the last evolution of which appeared in Austria, we can see how previously the wing support pylons extended backwards and were equipped with vertical vents, the extend of which was increased for Spielberg.

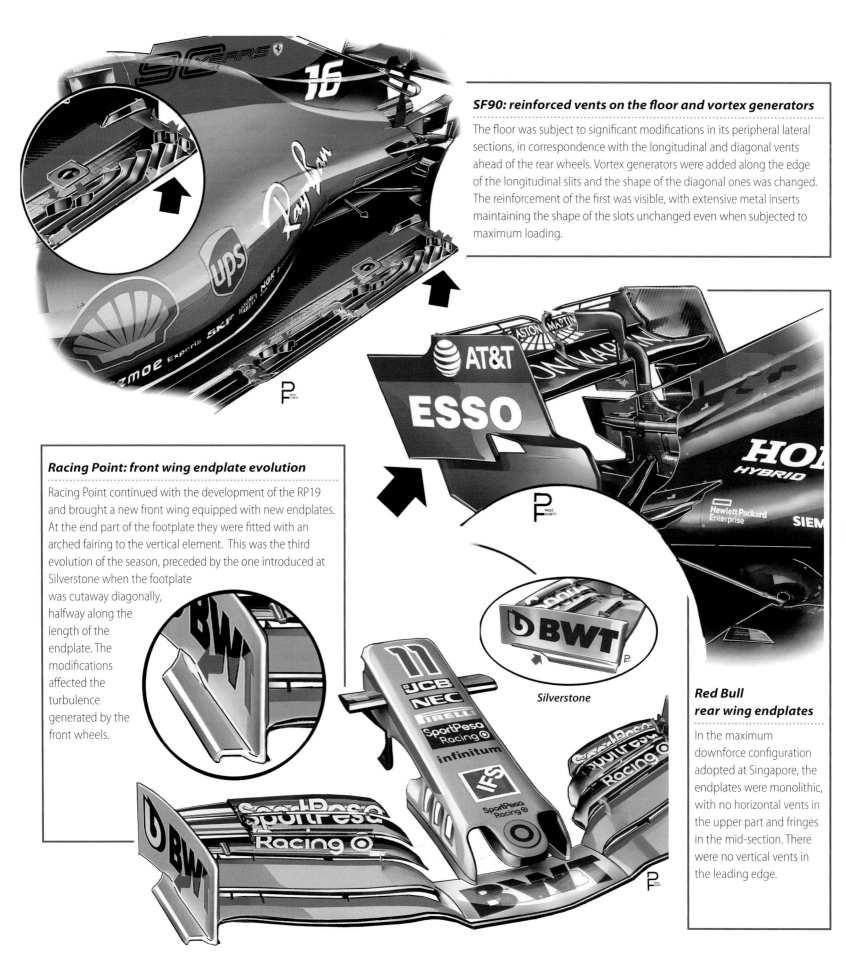

SF90: reinforced vents on the floor and vortex generators

The floor was subject to significant modifications in its peripheral lateral sections, in correspondence with the longitudinal and diagonal vents ahead of the rear wheels. Vortex generators were added along the edge of the longitudinal slits and the shape of the diagonal ones was changed. The reinforcement of the first was visible, with extensive metal inserts maintaining the shape of the slots unchanged even when subjected to maximum loading.

Racing Point: front wing endplate evolution

Racing Point continued with the development of the RP19 and brought a new front wing equipped with new endplates. At the end part of the footplate they were fitted with an arched fairing to the vertical element. This was the third evolution of the season, preceded by the one introduced at Silverstone when the footplate was cutaway diagonally, halfway along the length of the endplate. The modifications affected the turbulence generated by the front wheels.

Silverstone

Red Bull rear wing endplates

In the maximum downforce configuration adopted at Singapore, the endplates were monolithic, with no horizontal vents in the upper part and fringes in the mid-section. There were no vertical vents in the leading edge.

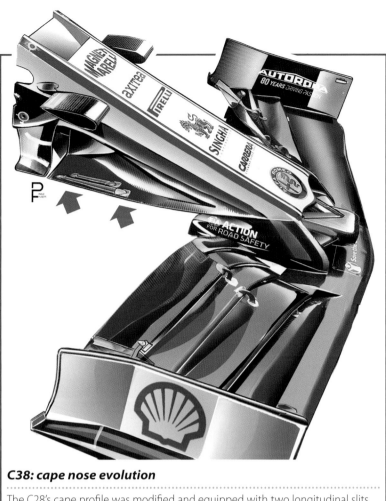

C38: cape nose evolution

The C28's cape profile was modified and equipped with two longitudinal slits in its rear section. They were designed to energize the lower flow and those on the floor, creating a kind of pneumatic seal.

Maximum downforce Renault T-wing

Like Alfa Romeo, Renault adopted a C-shaped triplane T-wing. Already seen at Monaco, it was characterised by sinuous elements; the lower one being more accentuated and traversed by a long longitudinal slit.

Alfa Romeo: triplane T-wing

The C38 was fitted with a C-shaped triplane T-wing. The lower element was traversed by a full-width vent that effectively split it into two profiles. A feature designed to increase the downforce generated on the rear axle.

DEVELOPMENTS OR TECHNOLOGICAL DÉJÀ VU?

RUSSIAN GRAND PRIX

SOCHI
SOCI AUTODROM
29 SEPTEMBER

Sochi is a circuit that despite demanding high downforce, similar to Singapore in fact, differed with respect to this last by the presence of long straights and a couple of fast corners. As the race was held just a week after that at Marina Bay, we could hardly expect many technical innovations with the exception of specific adaptations relating to the peculiarities of the two circuits. On the macro level the forecasts proved to be correct, with all the cars in their Singapore configurations, albeit with minor variations in terms of the incidence of the flaps and the front wing main plane. That said, in reality, the technical scene, at least at the start of the weekend, was characterised above all by a "novelty" concerning the front suspension of the Mercedes. In the first two free practice sessions, both W10s driven by Hamilton and Bottas adopted a mechanical heave damper in place of the hydraulic unit used from the start of the season. This third transverse damper, located between the suspension system's two rocker arms was responsible for controlling pitching and ride height variations. In effect, it tended to reduce oscillations along the longitudinal axis of the car caused by the transfer of loading from front to rear axle; the importance of this task and its response to the varying loads applied is clear. In practice, this element also controlled pitching rebound, that is to say the velocity with which the car returned to its ideal stance immediately after the braking or acceleration phase. The mechanical version had actually been tested in Singapore by Bottas alone in the first free practice session in order to evaluate its efficiency, in particular when turning in to and exiting corners. The feature was then shelved, without further testing on Hamilton's car, the balance and response obtained with the hydraulic version being considered adequate. However, qualifying and then the race had led to the emergence of an unexpected fact: in effect, one of the strengths of the W10 on high downforce tracks with corners with reduced radii such as Marina Bay – traction – had on that circuit become one of the most evident problems faced by the Mercedes.

At Sochi the team had planned on testing the mechanical system, this time on both cars, but not necessarily adopting it definitively for qualifying and the race. The fact that it was then adopted immediately with the intention of retaining it for the full weekend is a sign that the decision was taken as a consequence of the difficulties that had emerged a week earlier in Singapore. The adoption of the mechanical third damper equipped with Belleville cup springs made the W10's front suspension configuration very similar to that of the W08 from two years earlier. That car, it is only right to point out, was characterised by almost perfect balance, better than that of the W09 from 2018. Undoubtedly, this was a step backwards in terms of both time and technology and suggests that the three victories obtained by Ferrari prior to Sochi had effectively raised the performance bar and brought to light certain limitations in the Mercedes. It would appear to be correct to interpret this situation as a response to the performance the W10 displayed early in the season., revealing that of the SF90. With regard instead to the adaptation required for the characteristics of the Sochi Autodrom, it was interesting to note how Ferrari mutated the Sochi configuration with the only variation being the dished profile of the rear wing, combined with the high downforce endplates that had debuted at Marina Bay.

Red Bull instead brought a visible development of the "boomerangs" placed in the upper part of the bargeboards, characterised by a different sinuous leading edge profile. Naturally, this was a development designed to optimise the flows directed towards the sidepod mouths, to be considered as permanently operational even in races in which the thermal exchanged was significantly reduced, as in Mexico for example. There was an interesting adoption by McLaren of a front suspension pivot clearly inspired by the Mercedes design.

W10 third mechanical suspension element

Sochi saw a repetition of the functional testing of the mechanical heave damper on both cars, following the one conducted in Singapore where it was not adopted for either the race or qualifying. In Russia instead it was adopted from the outset and retained throughout

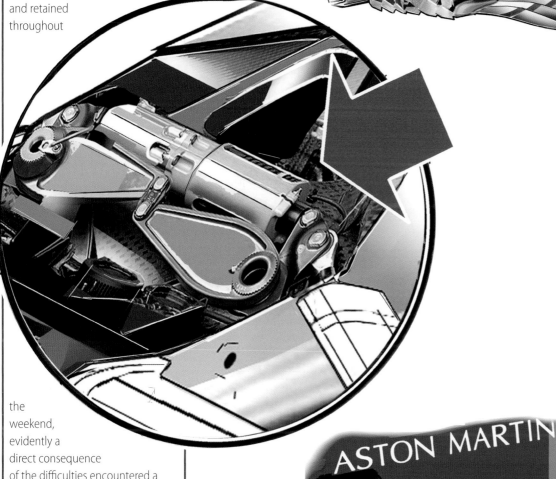

the weekend, evidently a direct consequence of the difficulties encountered a week earlier at Marina Bay. The adoption of the mechanical third damper equipped with Belleville cup springs made the W10's front suspension configuration very similar to that of the W08 from two years earlier.

Red Bull RB15: bargeboards development

At Sochi the bargeboards and the leading edge of the boomerang were modified. In detail, the profile of the bargeboard was no longer straight, but now had a sinuous cutaway that reduced the surface area in the lower part. Effectively, this modification increased the passage of air between the bargeboards and the diffuser while reducing the turbulence created by the flow exiting the lower part of the front wing. In the comparison we can see the difference with respect to the previous version used through to Singapore.

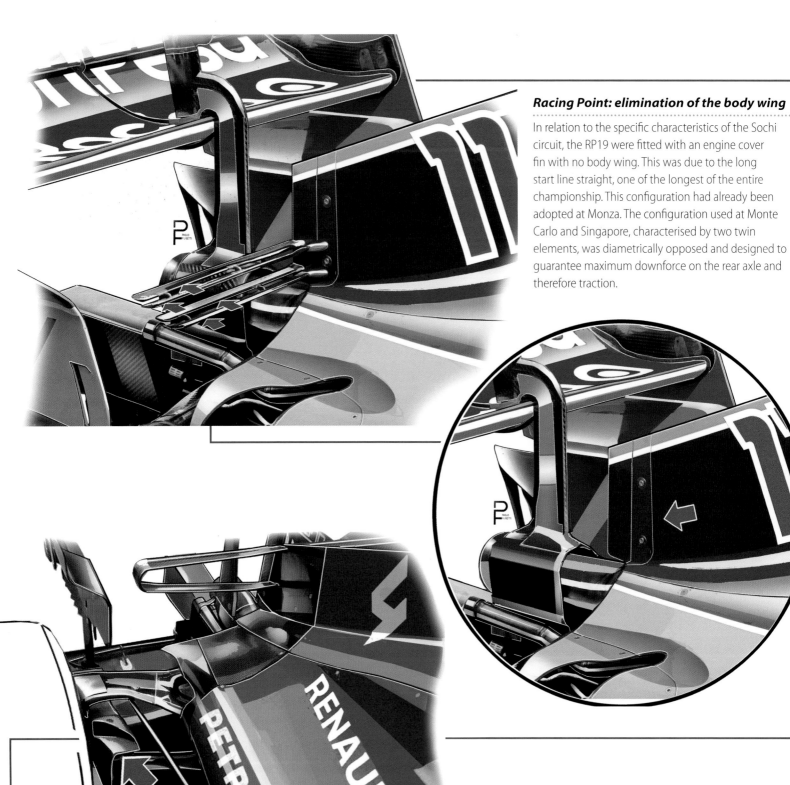

Racing Point: elimination of the body wing

In relation to the specific characteristics of the Sochi circuit, the RP19 were fitted with an engine cover fin with no body wing. This was due to the long start line straight, one of the longest of the entire championship. This configuration had already been adopted at Monza. The configuration used at Monte Carlo and Singapore, characterised by two twin elements, was diametrically opposed and designed to guarantee maximum downforce on the rear axle and therefore traction.

McLaren rear brake intakes

In reality, this was a modification introduced at Singapore and retained in Russia. Specifically, note the flared design of the intake mouth above the sinuous lower profile. This feature denoted great attention to detail and the subdivision of the flows, separated internally, for cooling the brakes and the uniform transmission of heat to the wheel rim via the drums.

McLaren MCL34: front suspension pivot

There was an interesting adoption of a larger pivot than previously used on the MCL34. In detail, there was a particularly conspicuous droplet fairing above the upper wishbone that concealed the extension of the double bracket to which the wishbone was connected.

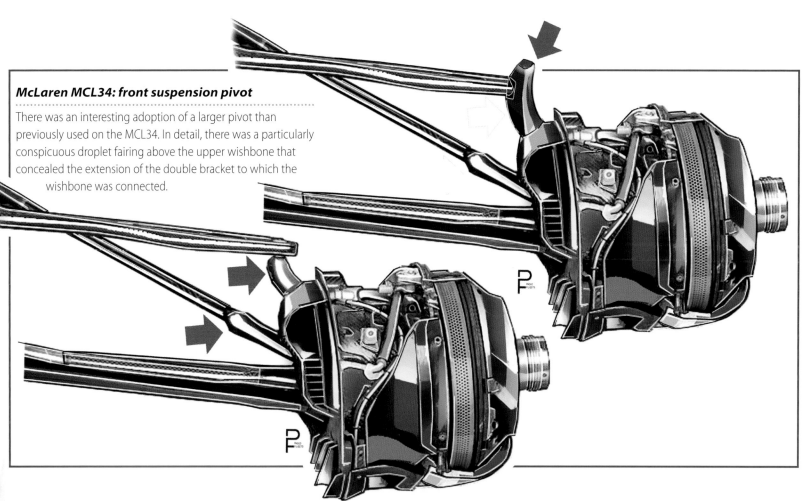

Ferrari SF90: rear wing endplates

At Sochi, Ferrari adopted its Singapore configuration in terms of the nose and floor, albeit with lower downforce wings. The rear wing was in fact a "hybrid", characterised by a dished main plane and the same high downforce endplates used at Marina Bay.

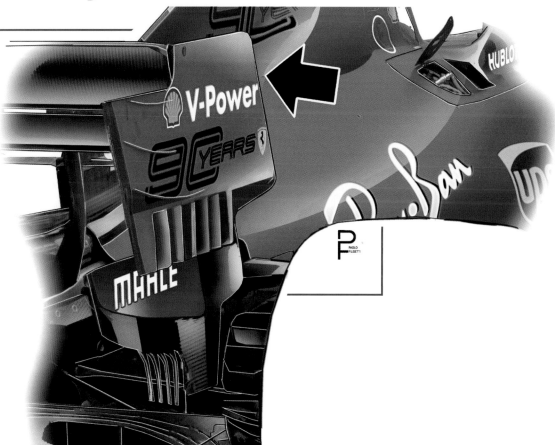

New deflectors for the W10 and a different S-duct for the RB15, but on track (in qualifying) it was the SF90

FINAL DEVELOPMENTS FOR MERCEDES AND RED BULL

JAPANESE GRAND PRIX

SUZUKA
SUZUKA CIRCUIT
13 OCTOBER

Suzuka, like Spa, represents one of the most complete and most technical circuits of the entire championship season. For this reason the characteristics of a car that is successful here effectively translate into aerodynamic efficiency and straight line speed, combined with traction in tight corners and balance in sweeping curves and rapid changes of direction (the esses).

The Japanese GP therefore represented the most severe proving ground and an excellent test of the performance of above all the Ferraris and the Mercedes. It would either provide a seal of approval attesting to the competitiveness of the SF90 displayed in the previous races, or confirm the superiority of the Mercedes on this specific circuit.

Ferrari arrived in Japan with a configuration identical to the one seen two weeks earlier at Sochi, characterised by variations to the flap incidence in a minor adaptation to the circuit. During the second of the only two free practice sessions held (due to the Hagibis typhoon that prevented any activity on the Saturday) it appeared that Leclerc had fitted a revised version of the front wing for the final 30 minutes. In reality, the wings used at Suzuka were exactly the same as those employed in Russia, the mistake being caused by the drastic increase in the incidence of the flaps which lent a different

appearance to the profile of the lower one, making it seem as if it had a different curvature. The modification tested on the Monaco-born driver's car represented the basis of the definitive configuration chosen for both qualifying and the race, which for the record was completed by a reduction in the incidence of the rear wing. This configuration, combined with a different front suspension setting in terms of the anti-roll bar and ride height, produced almost perfect balance on the SF90, which after having appeared to be around a second adrift of the W10 on the Friday, proved to be the fastest in qualifying by around three tenths. A remarkable performance boost that highlighted how balance and efficiency were two factors that with a set-up refined on the simulator at Maranello on the Saturday were perfectly integrated. With regards to the Mercedes instead, the results obtained over the weekend confirmed the downforce produced by the W10, but also highlighted its tendency to be "draggy", that is, to generate greater resistance than its rivals.

This characteristic had been clearly highlighted in qualifying, with the Brackley-based team introducing a final aero package as they tried to find a solution. Specifically, as well as adding an inclined, curving profile to the front wing endplates in order to increase out-wash, the novelties concerned the evolution of the bargeboards set outside the sides was shortened. In the previous version, the vertical profile was connected with a bridging vane running over the sidepod in correspondence with the intake mouths. In the new version, the two elements were instead separated rather than linked and the further intermediate profile connecting the bargeboard to the sidepod was shortened and curved upwards, connecting it to

the residual horizontal portion of the bridging profile. In this way the team tried to reduce the drag generated by the extreme complexity of the profiles present in this area of the car, opening a kind of channel that reduced the obstruction to the airflow in the peripheral section of the sidepod. The objective can be said to have been achieved only in part, with no magical solution being found to the excessive drag produced by the W10. While the comparison between the performance of the Ferrari and the Mercedes was the greatest issue of technical interest, it is nonetheless appropriate to mention the significance of that of the Red Bull on the circuit owned by its power unit partner, Honda. The RB15, equipped with the fourth example of the final version of the Japanese power unit, which had entailed a grid penalty for Verstappen at Sochi, presented interesting modifications to the S-duct vent. In effect, while up to the previous race it had been characterised by a full-width aperture in the transverse section of the vanity panel above the chassis, at Suzuka it featured a vent reduced to less than half the width. Consequentially, this led to a different management of the air flows running under the chassis and constituted a preview of the 2020 design. The rear wing was also revised, with modifications being made to the endplates. Two versions were taken to Japan and compared during free practice: one equipped with a vertical slot in correspondence with the leading edge and one without. The first, capable of enhancing the extraction and the grooming of the flow leaving the diffuser, was chosen for qualifying and the race. In any case, the modifications introduced to the RB15 did not appear to provide the cars from Milton Keynes with a performance boost sufficient to allow them to rival the Ferraris and Mercedes.

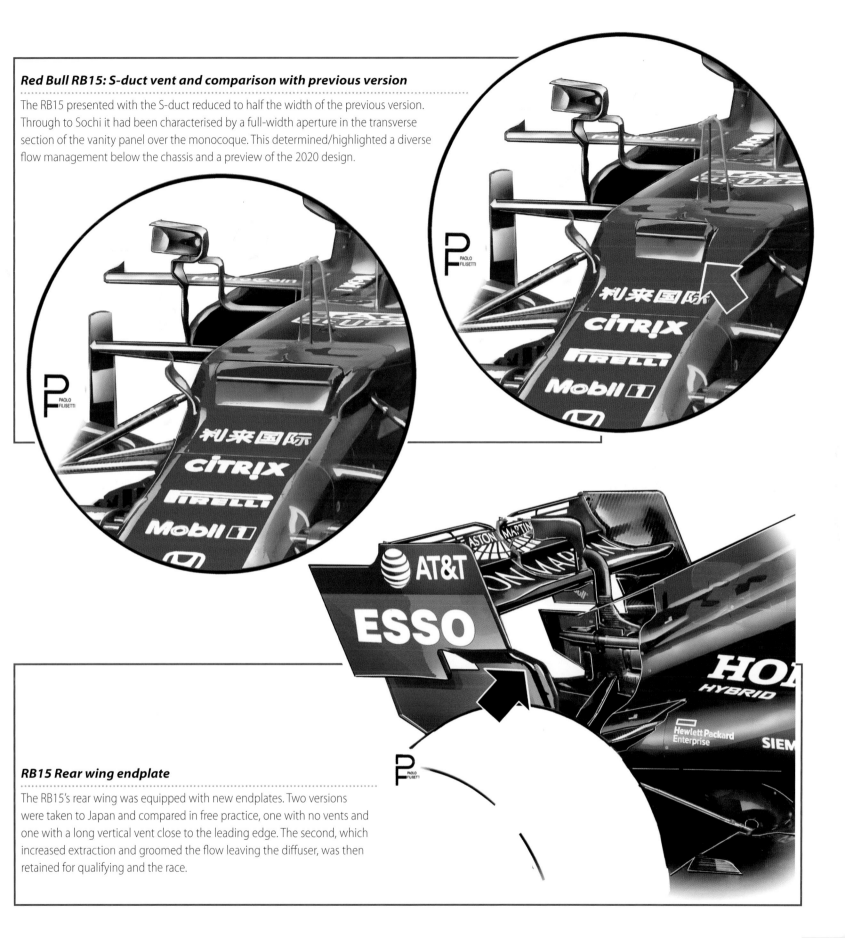

Red Bull RB15: S-duct vent and comparison with previous version

The RB15 presented with the S-duct reduced to half the width of the previous version. Through to Sochi it had been characterised by a full-width aperture in the transverse section of the vanity panel over the monocoque. This determined/highlighted a diverse flow management below the chassis and a preview of the 2020 design.

RB15 Rear wing endplate

The RB15's rear wing was equipped with new endplates. Two versions were taken to Japan and compared in free practice, one with no vents and one with a long vertical vent close to the leading edge. The second, which increased extraction and groomed the flow leaving the diffuser, was then retained for qualifying and the race.

RS19 front wing

At Suzuka, Renaul introduced an evolution of the front wing characterised by modifications that concerned the main plane and the flaps. The internal portion of the first presented a brief but deep rectangular vent that effectively split it into two elements. The first flap was characterised by a leading edge that mirrored the shape of the main plane trailing edge and was equipped with a small triangular cut-out in its lower internal extremity. Similarly, the chord of the two mobile flaps was also increased, more overtly on the last in the internal section with respect to the incidence adjustment mechanism. The comparison drawing illustrates the differences with respect to the version used in Russia.

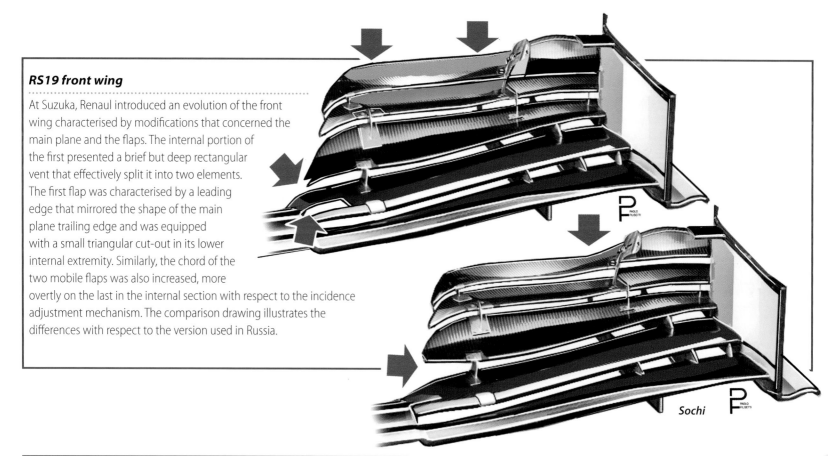

Sochi

W10 Rear wing endplate

A micro-aerodynamics modifications that concerned the front wing endplates: the addition of a small curved and inclined profile was designed to enhance the out-wash effect.

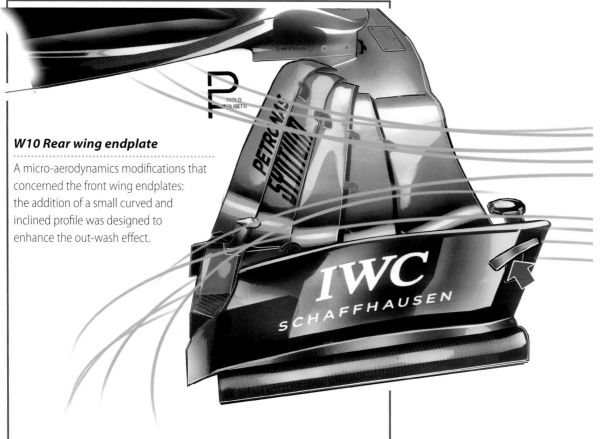

Mercedes W10: turning vane evolution

At Suzuka, Mercedes introduced the final evolution of its bargeboards. In the previous version, the turning vane had been connected to the bridging vane extending above the sidepods in correspondence with the intake mouths. In the new one, the two elements were separate rather than connected. In this way, the engineers attempted to reduce the drag generated by the complexity of the profiles in this area of the car. The previous evolution had been adopted at the German GP (see the drawing) when the five horizontal blades had been introduced in place of the vertical elements. Note the bridging profile, then still in place.

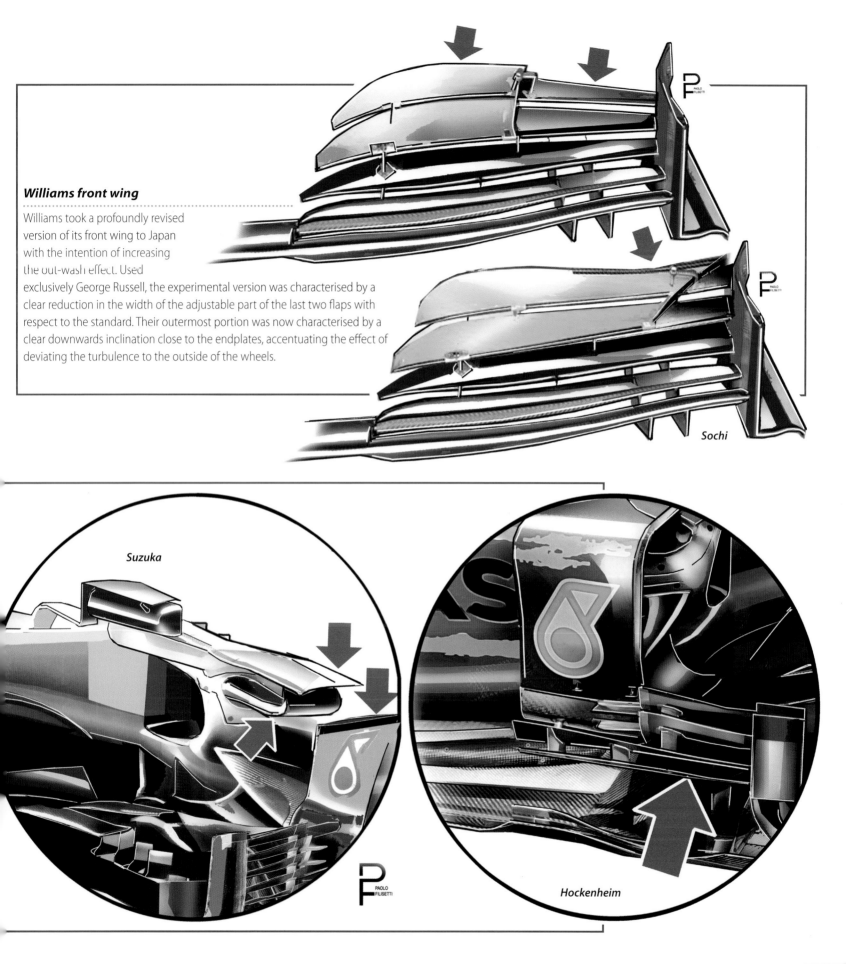

Williams front wing

Williams took a profoundly revised version of its front wing to Japan with the intention of increasing the out-wash effect. Used exclusively George Russell, the experimental version was characterised by a clear reduction in the width of the adjustable part of the last two flaps with respect to the standard. Their outermost portion was now characterised by a clear downwards inclination close to the endplates, accentuating the effect of deviating the turbulence to the outside of the wheels.

Sochi

Suzuka

Hockenheim

In search of lost downforce and effective thermal exchange at an altitude of 2250 metres

🇲🇽 HIGH ALTITUDE AERODYNAMICS AND TESTING FOR 2020

At this point in the season, the development of the cars was restricted to adaptations to the characteristics of the specific circuits as various design departments had for some time been devoting their time and resources to the definition of details on the 2020 car. In the case of this GP, in reality the specific demands of the Mexico City circuit forced all the teams to perform an overall "recalibration" of their cars. What does this mean? The rarefaction of the air at an altitude of 2250 metres is around 40% and entails the introduction of countermeasures designed to reduce its effect on aerodynamics, in terms of the low downforce produced, on the cooling of the power unit components and the brakes and lastly to compensate adequately for the loss of power. Mercedes was one of the most active teams, effectively preparing a configuration for the W10 that integrated a massive expansion of the intakes for cooling air with a tangible increase in the passage of air exiting from the radiators towards the rear of the car. It was no coincidence that the section of the aperture for the upper wishbone

was increased to ensure adequate heat exchange, above all in the area where the turbocharger is located. In parallel, grilles were adopted either side of the cockpit, as had already been done at the hotter Grands Prix such as Bahrain. In truth, the performance of the Brixworth Power Units was lacking in the final two versions (Phase2 and Phase 3), displaying a tangible gap with respect to the Ferrari 064 Evo 3. In order to attempt to bridge that gap, appropriately managing the environmental factors described above, the Mercedes engineers opted for a less conservative mode compared with those used in the preceding races. This was confirmed in the final part of this GP, when Hamilton was instructed from the pit wall that he could draw on the full power from his PU to keep the progressively more threatening Vettel at bay. The use of the most extreme turbo and rising internal temperatures were factors that the Mercedes engineers focussed on throughout the race. It is interesting to note the adoption of front brake drums characterised by the presence of a series of vortex generators along the front external edge. These were elements designed to facilitate management of the flows exiting laterally through the wheel rims. The optimization of cooling was also the leitmotif of the bodywork configuration adopted by Red Bull. The dimensions of the rear part of the RB15 had in fact been increased considerably and presented a kind of megaphone

section. In the upper part, in correspondence with the aperture in the upper wishbone, the bodywork featured a well-disguised "chimney" providing a tangible improvement in heat extraction. With regard to Ferrari, Vettel and Leclerc's SF90s presented an increase in intake area that was much less overt than that of their rivals. At the rear, the trailing edge of the bodywork presented a modified profile with a cutaway, thereby increasing the section of the air passage for the flow exiting the radiator packs. Rather more interesting was the adoption in FP3 of a strip of pressure sensors on the floor of the car ahead of the diffuser. This was a test in relation to the 2020 car, designed to measure the rate and pressure of the air flow in this area of the car, with the last version of the floor (introduced in Singapore). The data were to serve as a basis for comparison in the wind tunnel and CFD for the definition of this area of the following year's car. It should be pointed out that there was nothing new in this type of testing, this being a consolidated practice, adopted on multiple occasions over the past two seasons by Mercedes. Despite the development of simulator programmes, the precision of the data harvested on track remains a fundamental tool that integrates rather than being in conflict with the new technologies. Toro Rosso instead tested a new front wing characterised by a different main plane and a revision of the outwash configuration.

Red Bull: increased thermal exchange

Due to the rarefaction of the air, many teams tried to increase heat dispersal. The section of the rear end of the RB15 was increased, creating a kind of megaphone. In the upper part, in correspondence with the aperture for the upper wishbone, the bodywork featured a "chimney" providing a tangible improvement in heat extraction. At the base of the halo, as had been the case in Bahrain and also Hungary, a triangular vent was introduced on both sides of the cockpit.

Ferrari SF90: rear bodywork and sensors on the floor

On the SF90, the trailing edge of the rear bodywork presented a modified profile with a cutaway, thereby increasing the section of the vent for the air flow exiting the radiator packs. Moreover, during FP3, a strip of pressure sensors was fitted to the floor, ahead of the "elbow" created by the diffuser mount. This was a test in relation to the 2020 car, designed to measure the rate and pressure of the air flow in this area of the car, with the last version of the floor (introduced in Singapore).

Mercedes W10 brake drum evolution

There was an interesting micro-aerodynamic development in Mexico that concerned the front brake drums of the W10. In detail, in the upper part, at the centre of the ample cut-away profile, four pairs of micro vortex generators were introduced to energize the out flow. This was the fourth evolution of the drums, which as well as being designed to optimize the cooling of discs and callipers, through complex internal ducting, they also served to transmit heat to the wheel rims thereby maintaining correct tyre pressure, as well as having an

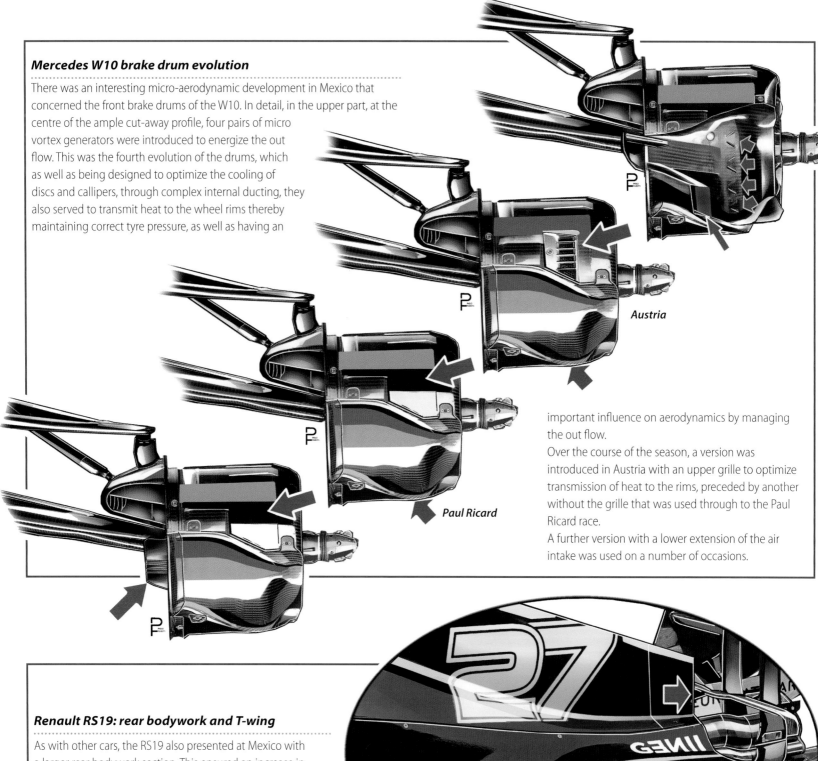

Austria

Paul Ricard

important influence on aerodynamics by managing the out flow.

Over the course of the season, a version was introduced in Austria with an upper grille to optimize transmission of heat to the rims, preceded by another without the grille that was used through to the Paul Ricard race.

A further version with a lower extension of the air intake was used on a number of occasions.

Renault RS19: rear bodywork and T-wing

As with other cars, the RS19 also presented at Mexico with a larger rear bodywork section. This ensured an increase in thermal exchange otherwise penalised by the rarefaction of the air. There was also an interesting adoption of a monoplane T-wing with the extremities curving downwards. This feature was used in order to avoid excessive increases in the drag generated on the long straights despite the lower density of the air.

Mercedes W10: increased thermal exchange

Mercedes also adapted the W10 to counterbalance the performance of the cooling system, penalised by the rarefied air at Mexico City's altitude of over 2000 metres. In reality, there was a combination of features, with a fairly closed rear end 2), in which the trailing edge of the bodywork was notably lower with respect to the upper wishbone. At the same time, however, supplementary grilles were adopted 1) either side of the cockpit in order to guarantee adequate thermal exchange.

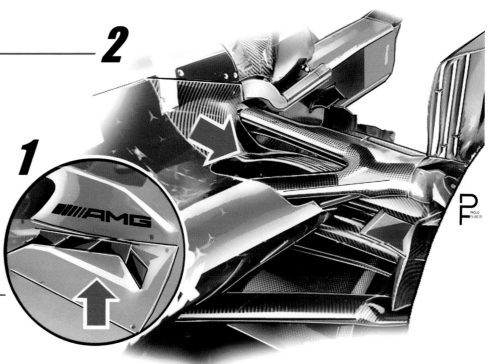

Toro Rosso STR14: rear bodywork

There was a very clear increase in the section of the STR14's rear bodywork. In detail, we can see how it was significantly higher than the upper wishbone, with the height of the rear vent considerably increased.

Toro Rosso front wing

A new front wing was tested, characterised by a different main plane without the flare between the neutral central section and the lateral portions and with a revision of the out-wash configuration of the air flows.

TEXAN ADAPTATIONS

USA GRAND PRIX
AUSTIN
CIRCUIT OF AMERICAS
3 NOVEMBER

As this was the second of two races in the space of a week, it was clear that there would be no particular developments introduced to the cars with the exception of the inevitable tweaks to adapt them to the Circuit of the Americas. This proved to be the case from the technical point of view with the weekend offering no elements of particular interest apart from a new front wing for Haas, which was profoundly inspired by that of the Ferrari SF90, (introduced in France). This apparently featureless scene in reality allowed attention to be focused on certain elements of the cars that could not really be defined as novelties but which were equally interesting as indicators of a design philosophy that evolved over the course of the season and, in some ways, anticipated concepts that would be applied to the 2020 designs. This was the case for example with the Red Bull RB15. From the introduction of a different vent at the exit of the S-duct a few races previously, it had also been fitted with a different configuration of the turning vanes under the nose and chassis. Specifically, it was interesting to look at how their lower horizontal profile, between the first vane connected to the

nose and the successive ones, formed a kind of full-length "rail". In effect, even though the feeding of the S-duct on the Milton Keynes car differed with respect to that of the Mercedes W10, a certain tangible convergence could be seen in the exploitation of the central channel via what has commonly been called a "cape". In substance, at Red Bull too the engineers positively evaluated the deviation outboard and the exploitation of the flows passing in the central section of the wing, better known as the Y250 vortex. This in fact represented the first clue to how in the design of the RB16 – the 2020 car – Red Bull has decided to follow the Mercedes path, with a nose with a reduced section with respect to 2019 and a lower cape.

From Singapore Ferrari had adopted a reduced cape and in this case too it was clear how important it was to be able to generate a low pressure zone downstream of the front wing, ahead of the T-tray, thereby increasing the downwards thrust of the flow heading towards the floor of the car. With regard to the most significant adaptations to this circuit, worthy of note was the adoption by Red Bull of the rear wing used at Suzuka, equipped with an ample vertical vent in correspondence with

the leading edge of the endplates. In practice, the Mexico version, characterised by endplates without vents, was specific to that circuit which demanded a configuration similar to Monaco and Singapore. The return to a lower altitude and therefore normal air density permitted the adoption of a configuration that guaranteed penetration on the return straights. In Texas, the car's braking systems are subjected to particular stress, hence the teams fitted drum configurations that guaranteed elevated thermal exchange values. In this case, it might be said, in contrast with what has been described in relation to the aerodynamics, the features associated with the cooling of discs and calipers were virtually unchanged with respect to the previous race given the greater demands on the systems. One emblematic example was that of the Mercedes drums, symmetrical in configuration, given the virtual equivalence between left-hand and right-hand corners, in the most complex version in terms of channels for the dispersal of heat. In reality, it is only right to underline how this configuration also guaranteed benefits in terms of management/control of tyre pressure thanks to the precise distribution of heat transmitted to the wheel rims.

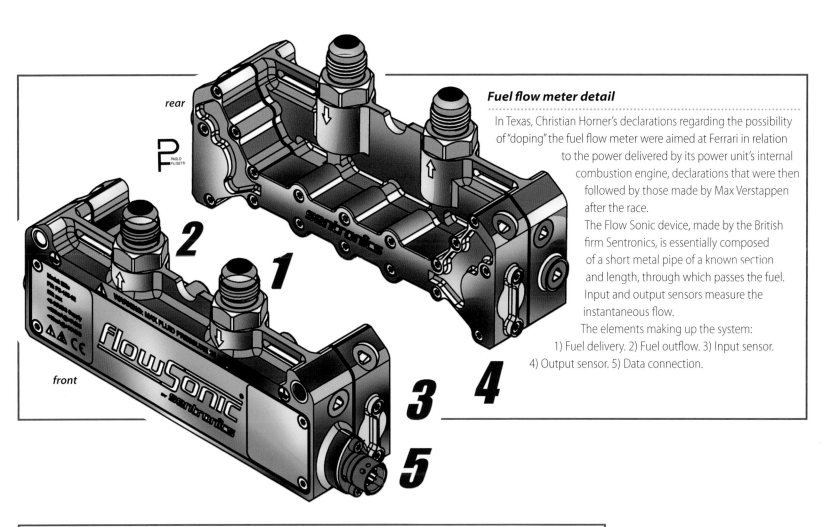

rear

front

Fuel flow meter detail

In Texas, Christian Horner's declarations regarding the possibility of "doping" the fuel flow meter were aimed at Ferrari in relation to the power delivered by its power unit's internal combustion engine, declarations that were then followed by those made by Max Verstappen after the race.

The Flow Sonic device, made by the British firm Sentronics, is essentially composed of a short metal pipe of a known section and length, through which passes the fuel. Input and output sensors measure the instantaneous flow.

The elements making up the system:
1) Fuel delivery. 2) Fuel outflow. 3) Input sensor.
4) Output sensor. 5) Data connection.

Mercedes W09 wheels with perforated spacers (2018)

The controversy over the fuel flow meter provides a cue for an examination of how in recent years the most bitter technical and regulatory disputes have always been triggered in the last part of the season. In 2018, the Mercedes wheels, which had debuted in Belgium with "rusticated" outer rims, were at the centre of attention in Mexico and then at Austin for the adopted of inner hubs with micro-perforations allowing the passage of heat towards the outside and towards the wheel through its hollow spokes. The feature was declared legal on several occasions by the scrutineers at each Grand Prix in which it was used. In Mexico, however, Mercedes had decided not to run it in order to remove any taint of illegality from its title conquest.

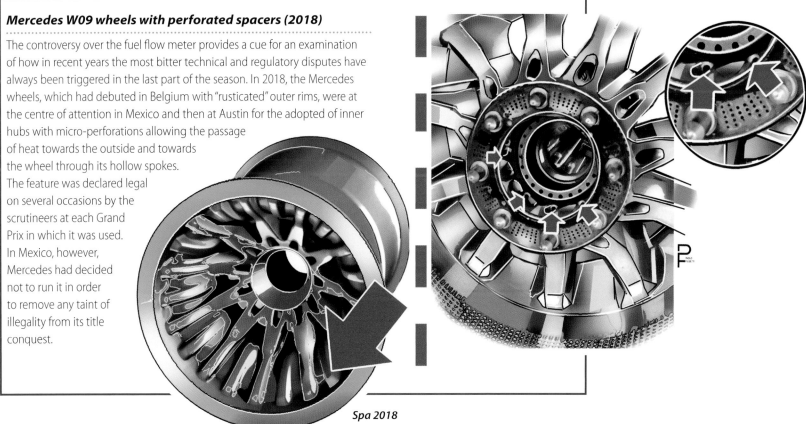

Spa 2018

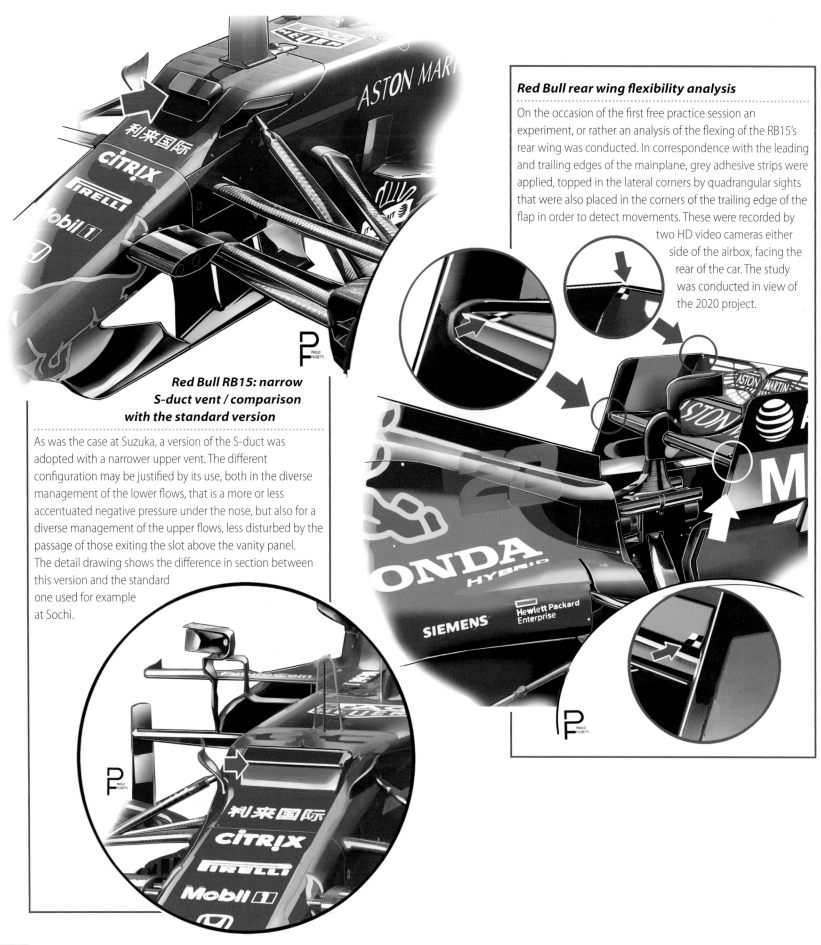

Red Bull rear wing flexibility analysis

On the occasion of the first free practice session an experiment, or rather an analysis of the flexing of the RB15's rear wing was conducted. In correspondence with the leading and trailing edges of the mainplane, grey adhesive strips were applied, topped in the lateral corners by quadrangular sights that were also placed in the corners of the trailing edge of the flap in order to detect movements. These were recorded by two HD video cameras either side of the airbox, facing the rear of the car. The study was conducted in view of the 2020 project.

Red Bull RB15: narrow S-duct vent / comparison with the standard version

As was the case at Suzuka, a version of the S-duct was adopted with a narrower upper vent. The different configuration may be justified by its use, both in the diverse management of the lower flows, that is a more or less accentuated negative pressure under the nose, but also for a diverse management of the upper flows, less disturbed by the passage of those exiting the slot above the vanity panel. The detail drawing shows the difference in section between this version and the standard one used for example at Sochi.

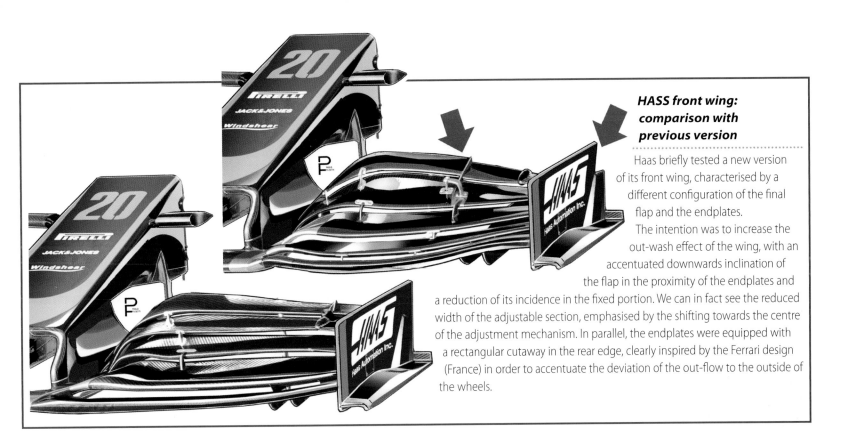

HASS front wing: comparison with previous version

Haas briefly tested a new version of its front wing, characterised by a different configuration of the final flap and the endplates.

The intention was to increase the out-wash effect of the wing, with an accentuated downwards inclination of the flap in the proximity of the endplates and a reduction of its incidence in the fixed portion. We can in fact see the reduced width of the adjustable section, emphasised by the shifting towards the centre of the adjustment mechanism. In parallel, the endplates were equipped with a rectangular cutaway in the rear edge, clearly inspired by the Ferrari design (France) in order to accentuate the deviation of the out-flow to the outside of the wheels.

Front wing out-wash accentuation

It is interesting to consider, starting with the final version of the front wing tested by Haas, how the progressive accentuation of the out-wash effect was imposed on various cars. In the case of Williams there was an emblematic comparison in Japan (subsequently seen in Mexico too) between the standard version used through to Sochi and the one with the accentuated deviation to the outside, characterised by the reduced width of the adjustable portion of the flaps and their minimal incidence with respect to the endplates. Another example is represented by the version introduced in Mexico by Toro Rosso, with modifications to the endplates, the main plane and, of course, the flaps which were strongly inclined downwards.

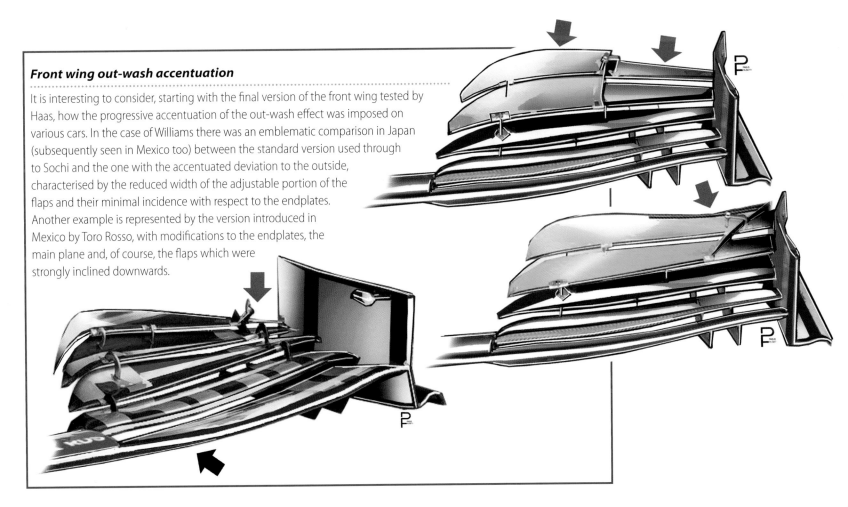

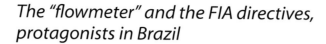

DISPUTES AND 2020 PREVIEWS

BRAZILIAN GRAND PRIX

INTERLAGOS
SAN PAOLO
17 NOVEMBER

The final races of the season are frequently lacking in technical interest or at best represent a kind of test bench for features destined for the following year's car. The Brazilian GP only partially respected this tradition. The Sao Paulo weekend was in fact characterised from the outset by a flurry of technical directives issued by the FIA which helped reinvigorate the climate of suspicion that had "poisoned" the race in Austin. For this reason, it is worth going back to the directive that the federation had issued in Texas that triggered the mother of all 2019 technical disputes. Ahead of the Austin race, Red Bull had asked the FIA for clarification regarding the adoption of a system that could vary the values read by the flow meter fuel consumption sensor, set to a maximum rate established by the regulations of 100 kg/hour. Christian Horner's claimed, in fact, that the signal generated by the two ultrasound sensors, which are an integral part of the device, could be "disturbed" by the interference of an electromagnetic field. In this way, according to the thesis developed by the Milton Keynes engineers, it would be possible to falsify the reading by default, providing a value that was lower than the true rate and thus permitting a flow of fuel greater than the permitted limit. Upstream of this theory was the declared suspicion that Ferrari's 064 power unit was exploiting a loophole in the

regulations to produce extra power. The below-par performances of the Rosse in the race at Austin were immediately seized upon by their detractors, including Max Verstappen, as evidence that after the FIA directive that had confirmed the illegality of this kind of system Ferrari had drastically reduced the output of its power unit and therefore that previously it had "cheated" (cit.). The fuel flow meter is produced by the British firm Sentronics and is installed within the fuel tank of each car. The device was subjected to extremely severe testing of both the reliability of reading and its sensitivity to the vibrations and electromagnetic fields present on an F1 car; in practice it had to resist extremely high stress in order to be homologated. In detail, it was composed of a metal tube with a capacity of around 15 ml, through which the fuel passes to the engine's injection system. Two ultrasound sensors for flow reading, one at the ingress and the second at the exit, with a frequency of 2.2 kHz, generate an impulse 2,200 times per second. The frequency of the sound wave varies as the velocity of the fluid in the tube varies, determining the volume of fuel running through it. The very high frequency produced effectively constitutes the clearest technical evidence of the difficulty in "tampering" with the system through the interference of a magnetic field. In fact, the frequency generated by the field should insert itself between the two impulses, with absolute precision, in order to have an effect on the flow, and the engine management software dealing with the injector openings would need to be equally precise. These and other technical motivations effectively ridiculed the suspicions and placated the dispute. However, a new directive emanated by the FIA on the 13th of November once again inflamed the paddock. In fact, FIA directive 38.19 ratified the illegality of emitting cooling liquid into the combustion chambers as a fuel

additive. To many, despite there clearly not being any direct reference, it appeared clear that this ban was a response to rumours once again concerning the Maranello power unit. In any case, the object of the dispute was the fluid used in the radiators and heat exchangers, generically identifiable with the well-known ethylene glycol. This colourless liquid (to which pigments are added for both industrial production and its use in competition) is produced on the basis of ethylene oxide. It is widely used in radiators and in competition permits the miniaturisation of the cooling circuit and the adoption of low internal pressure. Among its distinguishing features making it a valid fuel additive, is that it has a very high boiling point, over 170°, and self-ignition at over 410°C. In practice, it does not detonate, similar to the engine lubricant long at the centre of dispute and directives two years ago.

In terms of technology, there was more to the 2019 Brazilian GP however. In fact, a number of teams adopted features that prefigured concepts that would be integral parts of the 2020 cars. Haas, for example, adopted the final version of the front wing, which had appeared briefly at Austin, based on the evolution of the SF90 wing taken to France. In practice, not only was the outwash now accentuated through the inclination of the flaps which progressively sloped down towards the endplates but, additionally, these last were also characterised by a stepped cutaway in the upper corner facilitating the lateral exit of the peripheral flow. Red Bull also took this path, although only in free practice when the team tested a new front wing anticipating that of the RB16. As with Haas, in this case too, the sloping of the flaps towards the outside and the inclination of the endplates was clearly inspired by the Ferrari design. Additionally, the RB15 again adopted the nose characterised by the closed tip, as seen at Monaco and Montreal.

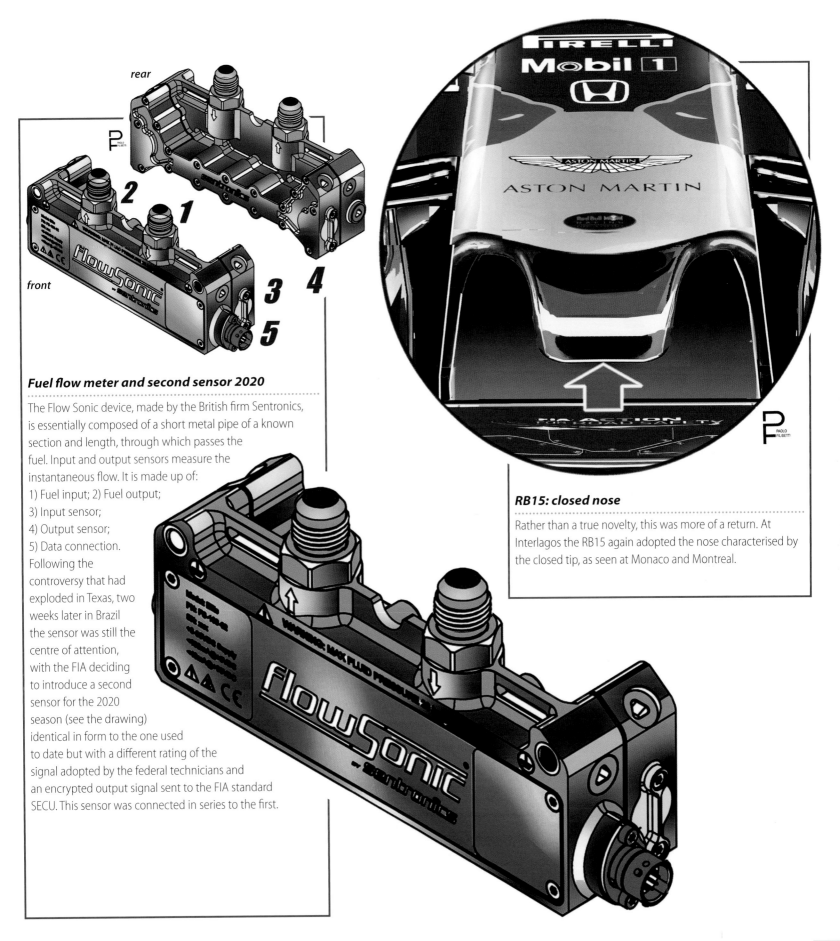

Fuel flow meter and second sensor 2020

The Flow Sonic device, made by the British firm Sentronics, is essentially composed of a short metal pipe of a known section and length, through which passes the fuel. Input and output sensors measure the instantaneous flow. It is made up of:
1) Fuel input; 2) Fuel output;
3) Input sensor;
4) Output sensor;
5) Data connection.
Following the controversy that had exploded in Texas, two weeks later in Brazil the sensor was still the centre of attention, with the FIA deciding to introduce a second sensor for the 2020 season (see the drawing) identical in form to the one used to date but with a different rating of the signal adopted by the federal technicians and an encrypted output signal sent to the FIA standard SECU. This sensor was connected in series to the first.

RB15: closed nose

Rather than a true novelty, this was more of a return. At Interlagos the RB15 again adopted the nose characterised by the closed tip, as seen at Monaco and Montreal.

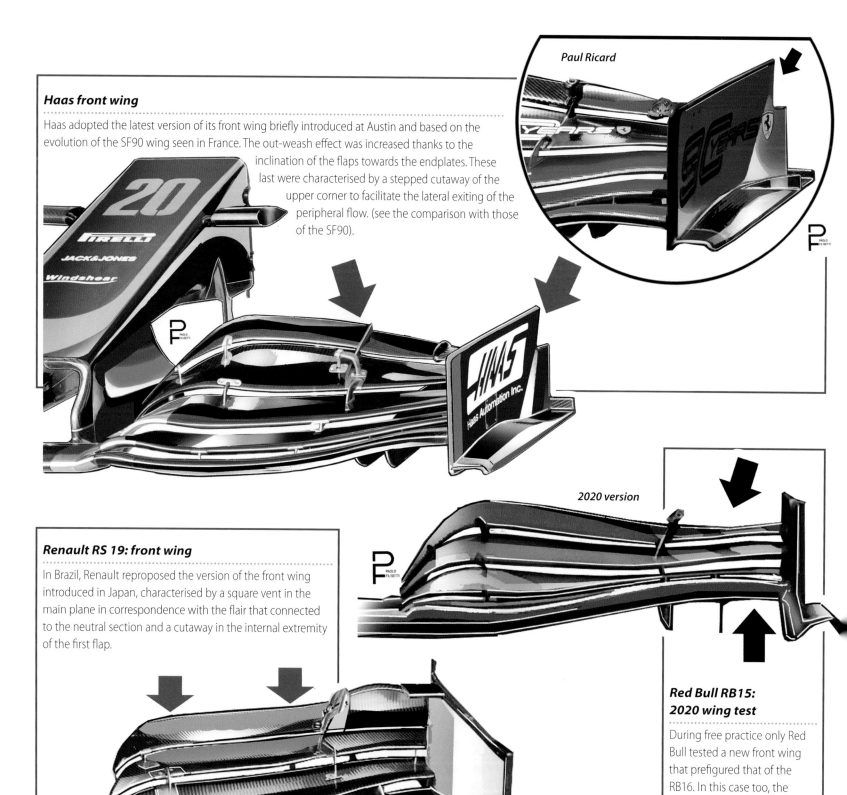

Haas front wing

Haas adopted the latest version of its front wing briefly introduced at Austin and based on the evolution of the SF90 wing seen in France. The out-weash effect was increased thanks to the inclination of the flaps towards the endplates. These last were characterised by a stepped cutaway of the upper corner to facilitate the lateral exiting of the peripheral flow. (see the comparison with those of the SF90).

Paul Ricard

2020 version

Renault RS 19: front wing

In Brazil, Renault reproposed the version of the front wing introduced in Japan, characterised by a square vent in the main plane in correspondence with the flair that connected to the neutral section and a cutaway in the internal extremity of the first flap.

Red Bull RB15: 2020 wing test

During free practice only Red Bull tested a new front wing that prefigured that of the RB16. In this case too, the configuration of the flaps sloping down towards the outside and the inclination of the endplates followed that adopted by Ferrari.

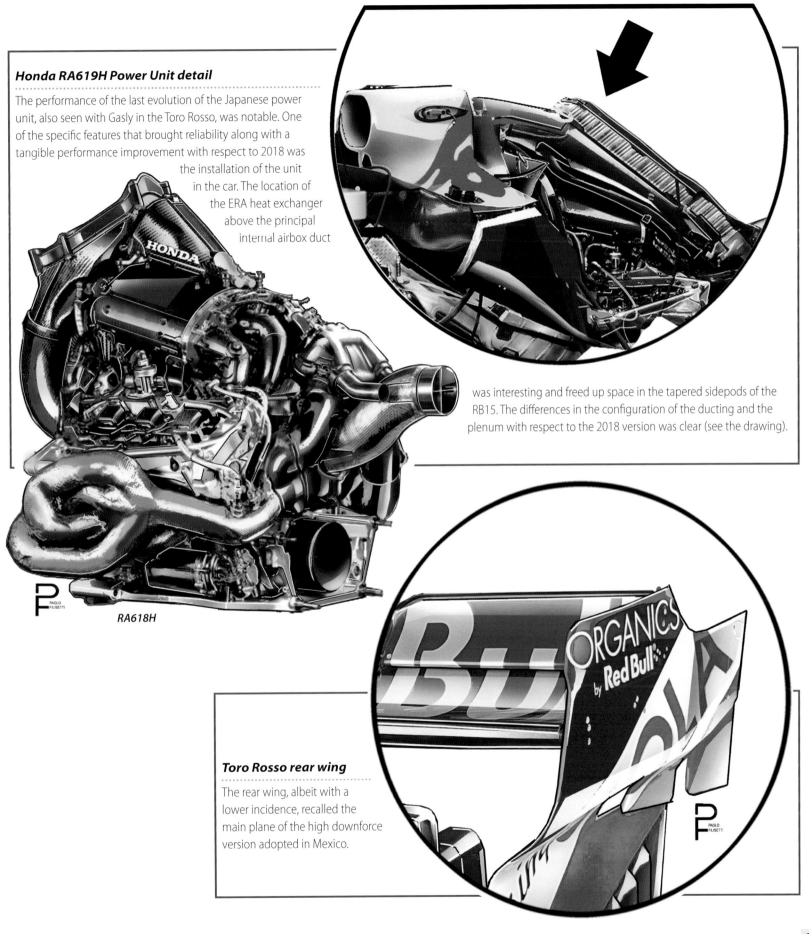

Honda RA619H Power Unit detail

The performance of the last evolution of the Japanese power unit, also seen with Gasly in the Toro Rosso, was notable. One of the specific features that brought reliability along with a tangible performance improvement with respect to 2018 was the installation of the unit in the car. The location of the ERA heat exchanger above the principal internal airbox duct was interesting and freed up space in the tapered sidepods of the RB15. The differences in the configuration of the ducting and the plenum with respect to the 2018 version was clear (see the drawing).

RA618H

Toro Rosso rear wing

The rear wing, albeit with a lower incidence, recalled the main plane of the high downforce version adopted in Mexico.

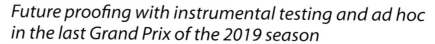
*Future proofing with instrumental testing and ad hoc
in the last Grand Prix of the 2019 season*

2020 AHEAD OF SCHEDULE AT YAS MARINA

GP ABU DHABI

ABU DHABI
YAS MARINA CIRCUIT
1 DICEMBER

The last GP of the season was of course a dead rubber in sporting terms, with both world titles having already been assigned and the top three positions in the Constructors' standings finalised. However, there was much of interest from a technical point of view, with the weekend effectively being a bridge to the forthcoming 2020 season. In practice, all the teams turned up with elements prefiguring features designed for their 2020 cars.

Ferrari was a protagonist in this sense, with both drivers running in free practice with components, aerodynamic and otherwise being tested in view of the definition of the new car. Mercedes, with Hamilton and Bottas, instead ran a front wing with a strong out-wash configuration, testing and comparing it with the standard version while collecting crucial data. Red Bull, the third force in this championship, had actually begun testing an out-wash aerodynamic configuration (with the airflows directed outside the front wheels) in Brazil, with a new Ferrari-influenced front wing. At Yas Marina, the same configuration seen in San Paolo was tested again, but above all the car was fitted with thermal imaging microcameras in the lower edge of the cooling air intakes in order to evaluate the behaviour of the tyres with diverse set-ups. Returning to the detail of the tests conducted by Ferrari, curiosity had been aroused by the adoption of a double wastegate valve exhaust above the principal exhaust exiting the turbocharger. In effect, the test aimed at harvesting data regarding an increase in the venting in the sections to the sides of the wing pylons, improving, at least on paper, the efficiency of the main plane, accelerating the lower flow and, at the same time, assisting the extraction of air via the diffuser. This modification was one of the aerodynamic corrections and an integral part of the 2020 car, generating greater vertical loading on the rear axle. As is well-known, in fact, one of the chronic problems with the SF90, only partially amended with the introduction of the "Singapore" package, was the lack of downforce generated by the body of the car, which was frequently an issue, especially on tracks where high downforce was required but penetration and correct tyre management also counted. In the race at Abu Dhabi, this factor was very clear, highlighting the rapidity with which the SF90's tyres decayed compared with those of Mercedes and Red Bull. In the first practice session, the SF90 had been fitted with an array of instruments on the floor, in the area ahead of the rear wheels, as had been the case in Mexico, in order to evaluate the pressure values in this area of the car. As previously mentioned, the W10s driven by Hamilton and Bottas were equipped with a front wing characterised by an upper flap inclined steeply downwards in the sections adjacent to the endplates, where its chord was also reduced with a curvature that brought the flap within the section of the endplate. Of technical importance was the sanction imposed by the race officials on Ferrari for a discrepancy regarding the team's pre-race declaration of the quantity of fuel loaded into Leclerc's SF90. In practice, the technical directive 14.19, published at the start of 2019, required each team to declare the amount of fuel carried by each car before the race. The weighing of the car and subtracted the dry weight revealed a significant discrepancy with regard to the figure declared by the team. Clearly, these checks were moving in the direction of increased attention to the maximum limit of fuel carried and useable, as the controversy provoked in Austin and the subsequently directives issued in Brazil highlighted.

SF90 dual wastegate exhaust test

There was an interesting test during free practice involving the adoption of dual wastegate exhausts above the principal exhaust exiting the turbocharger. The aim was to collect data regarding venting in the sections either side of the wing pylons, verifying whether this might enhance the efficiency of the main plane. In the comparison with the standard version note also the slight upwards inclination of the two exhausts at a maximum of 5° as per the regulations.

Mercedes front wing evolution

At Yas Marina the W10 presented a front wing equipped with a final flap strongly inclined downwards in the section adjacent to the endplates so as increase the out-wash effect. Its chord was reduced, with the curving trailing edge bringing the flap within the section of the endplate.

PETRONAS
SYNTIUM

P PAOLO FILISETTI

STR14 front wing

This feature was first introduced in Mexico and then again used briefly in Austin. For the last race of the season the STR14 was equipped with the final version of the front wing featuring endplates with the lower part of the leading edge inclined outwards and an accentuated inclination of the flaps that enhanced the out-wash effect adopted throughout the year.

Mexico City

RB15

2019

Comparison of tyre construction 2019-2020

In view of the tests to be held on the Tuesday following the race, Pirelli had taken to Abu Dhabi a version of its 2020 tyres which featured a different structure. The aim was to conduct a comparison with the 2019 version and collate the responses of the teams. The new carcass differed above all in the more rounded sidewalls and an increase in the depth of the shoulder of around 4 mm. The teams were unanimous in preferring the 2019 version on the basis that they had designed the 2020 cars around the data harvested during the course of the 2019 season.

RB15 front suspension

In its apparent simplicity, the installation of the front suspension elements within the chassis was very clean and skilfully integrated (see the detail in the oval) with the aerodynamic demands, as visible in the drawing with the vanity panel fitted, which highlights the two separate S-duct channels. The compactness, tidiness and attention to detail represent the ideal foundations for an even more extreme front end configuration in view of the 2020 season.

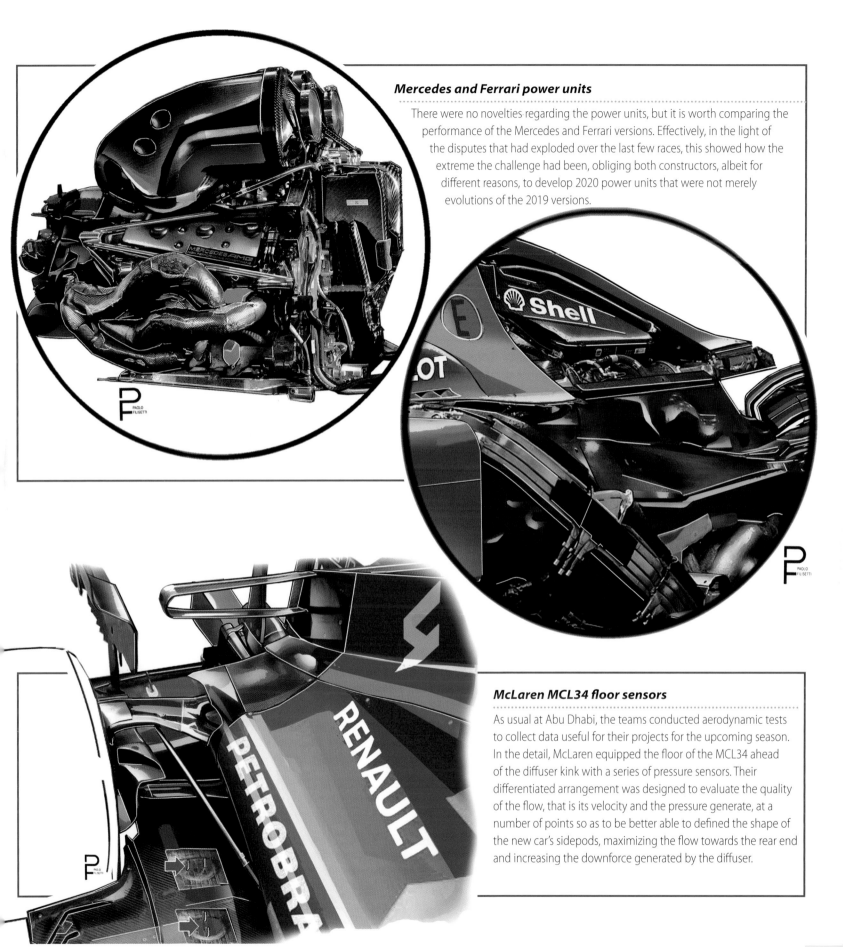

Mercedes and Ferrari power units

There were no novelties regarding the power units, but it is worth comparing the performance of the Mercedes and Ferrari versions. Effectively, in the light of the disputes that had exploded over the last few races, this showed how the extreme the challenge had been, obliging both constructors, albeit for different reasons, to develop 2020 power units that were not merely evolutions of the 2019 versions.

McLaren MCL34 floor sensors

As usual at Abu Dhabi, the teams conducted aerodynamic tests to collect data useful for their projects for the upcoming season. In the detail, McLaren equipped the floor of the MCL34 ahead of the diffuser kink with a series of pressure sensors. Their differentiated arrangement was designed to evaluate the quality of the flow, that is its velocity and the pressure generate, at a number of points so as to be better able to defined the shape of the new car's sidepods, maximizing the flow towards the rear end and increasing the downforce generated by the diffuser.

2020: YEAR OF TRANSITION IN EMERGENCY

E when the Pirelli tests at Abu Dhabi concluded a few days after the last GP of 2019 and the curtain dropped on the F1 season, the dominant impression was that 2020 would be a transitional year. The reasoning behind this belief was eminently technical. On the one hand, there was absolute stability of the regulations, the rules of the F1 game, and on the other the decision taken by the teams to adopt the 2019 carcasses for the 2020 Pirelli tyres. In effect, with a substantially unchanged scenario and in view of (at the time) a major technical revolution planned for 2021, it was clear that the teams would not have devoted significant resources to the 2020 projects given that any new technical features would have lasted only a year. It was inevitable that the changes that would be seen in F1 in 2021 would have been of such magnitude that everyone would immediately be obliged to devote resources to the preliminary study of the impact of the new regulations on their designs. As it worked out, this led to a need to establish from the outset an appropriate allocation of resources between the 2020 and 2021 projects. Naturally, despite the depth of their pockets, the budgets of even the top teams are finite, as are their workforces. In reality, this is only partially true in the sense that a team, especially one of the majors, conducts its strategic planning around a period of longer than a single year. That is to say, those who can afford it make staffing and infrastructure investments on a three/five year cycle. The top teams, in contrast with those in the midfield and especially those at the back of the grid, could up until a few months ago actuate business plans that spread the necessary resources over time without necessarily having to balance the books immediately. It was very different for those who have balance those books every year in order to be able to plan for the following season. These financial considerations precisely delineated the scenario for the 2020 season. Ferrari, Mercedes and Red Bull had the possibility of developing two programmes in parallel, reinforcing their operations in terms of infrastructure and staffing, as shown by the number of job adverts published towards the end of 2019. None of the three was holding anything back for 2020, with the objective of building a car capable of competing for the title while also planning an intensive development programme. So it was through to the eve of the first 2020 Grand Prix in Australia when Covid-19 struck like a tsunami. With the Melbourne race being cancelled at the very last moment and the same fate befalling the following races through to the French GP in late June, F1 has had to actuate a contingency plan that allows the 2020 World Championship to be disputed and creates the economic management conditions necessary for the survival of all the teams in the coming years.

The 2021 regulations were postponed for a year, a budget cap was introduced that will come into force in 2021 while the development of the power units was frozen (with the exception of reliability modifications) and that of the cars restricted, with the homologation of certain parts from the first race held (Austria) and others from 15 September 2020, with just two overall development tokens available.

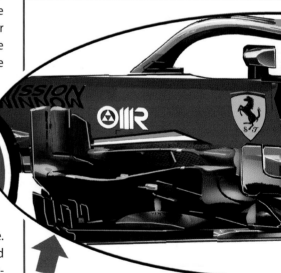

Ferrari SF1000 side view

Of particular note are the more complex bargeboards (detail) despite the car having clearly retained the front wing out-wash configuration. The rear part of the sidepods is sharply tapered with a profile similar to that of the Red Bull.

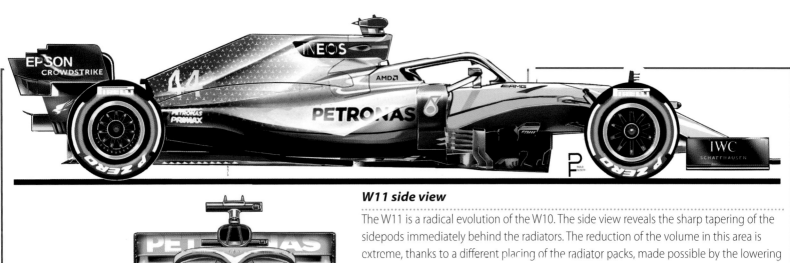

W11 side view

The W11 is a radical evolution of the W10. The side view reveals the sharp tapering of the sidepods immediately behind the radiators. The reduction of the volume in this area is extreme, thanks to a different placing of the radiator packs, made possible by the lowering of the side-impact cones.

W11: front view

Of note are the horizontal air intakes, set high up in accordance with the current fashion. The lower parts of the sidepods are preceded by bargeboards retaining an almost identical design to that of the W10. The rear wing reprises the final version from 2019.

Ferrari SF1000 front view

The nose equipped with the cape introduced in Singapore last year appears slightly narrower than on the SF90, but does not have a minimal section like those of Mercedes, Red Bull, McLaren and Renault. Note the vertical winglets either side of the triangular air intake designed to direct the flow towards the rear wing.

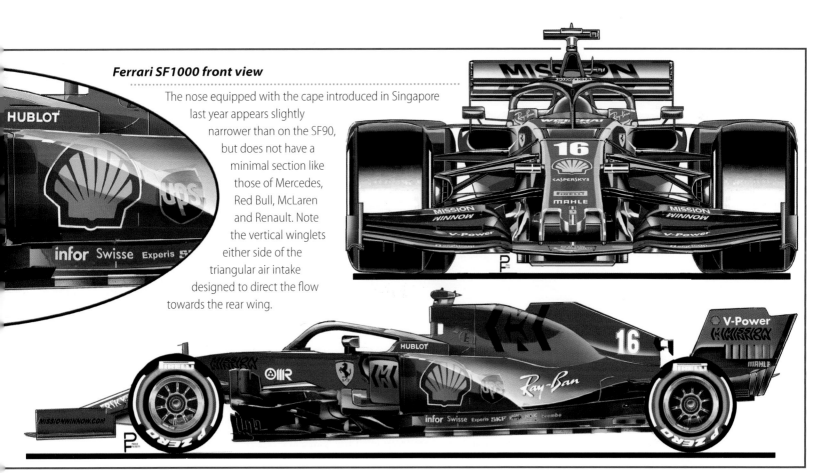

Red Bull RB16 front view (Barcelona test)

Note how the width of the nose has been reduced by around 40% with respect to the RB15. The cape directing the air downwards, increasing the flow under the car, is clearly visible and reflects the influence of the Mercedes philosophy. The front wing has greater out-wash with respect to last year and mirrors the version tested in Brazil.

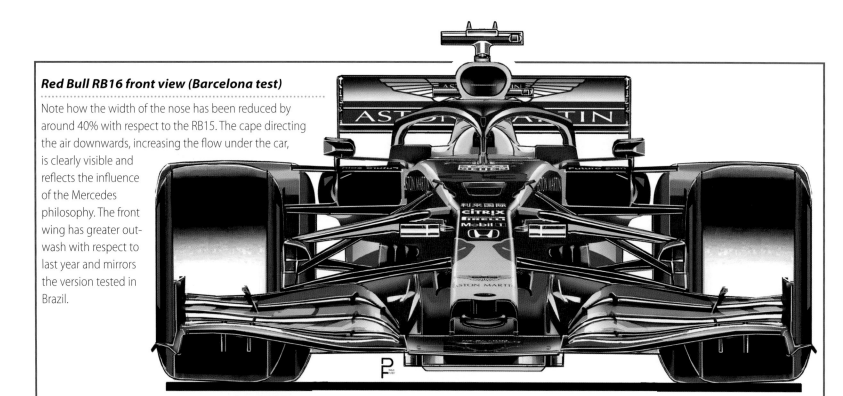

RB16 nose detail (Barcelona test)

Note the central air intake feeding the S-duct and the lateral channels feeding the cape, increasing the velocity of the flow downstream of the neutral section of the front wing. The two rectangular holes above the ovoid intake are interesting and destined to channel cooling air to the electronics and the cockpit.

Red Bull RB16: Austria, front view with nose detail

At the first race held at the Red Bull Ring, the nose cone of the Red Bull was characterised by a lower section with close-set front wing support pylons. In practice, they were no longer tangential to the maximum frontal section of the nose at that point but rather were overhung laterally, as in the case of the Mercedes and of course the Racing Point.

Austria

SF1000 Front Wing

A new version of the front wing made its debut at the Styrian GP. In visual terms it differed with respect to the earlier model only slightly, but in reality the modifications were quite significant. (1) The main plane was more extensive than before and inclined downwards close to the endplates. (2) The profile of the final flap no longer had a twist close

to the endplate to reduce its incidence: its chord was shorter and it was rounded in the innermost section where previously it was straight. (3) The leading edge of the footplate was arched rather than angular. (4) The vortex generator on the footplate was now larger and no longer triangular.

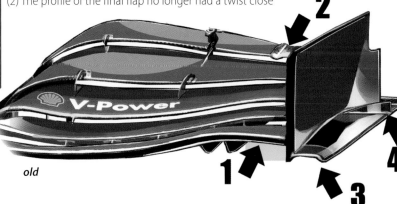

old

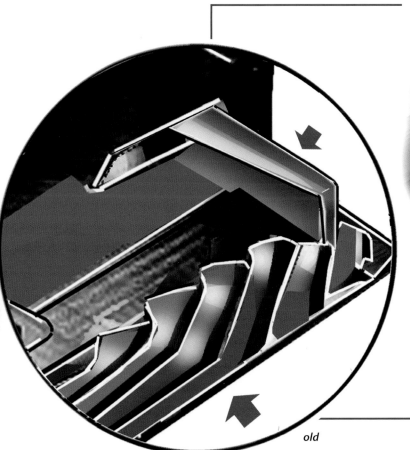

old

SF1000 new floor: comparison with old version

The floor is characterised by the presence of nine vents inclined at 45° ahead of the rear wheels, which effectively replace the series of rails that had been a feature of the previous version (see detail). Note also the different bridge profile in the rear section, characterised by a vaguely triangular section, with the larger area in the centre anchored to the vertical mini-deflector.

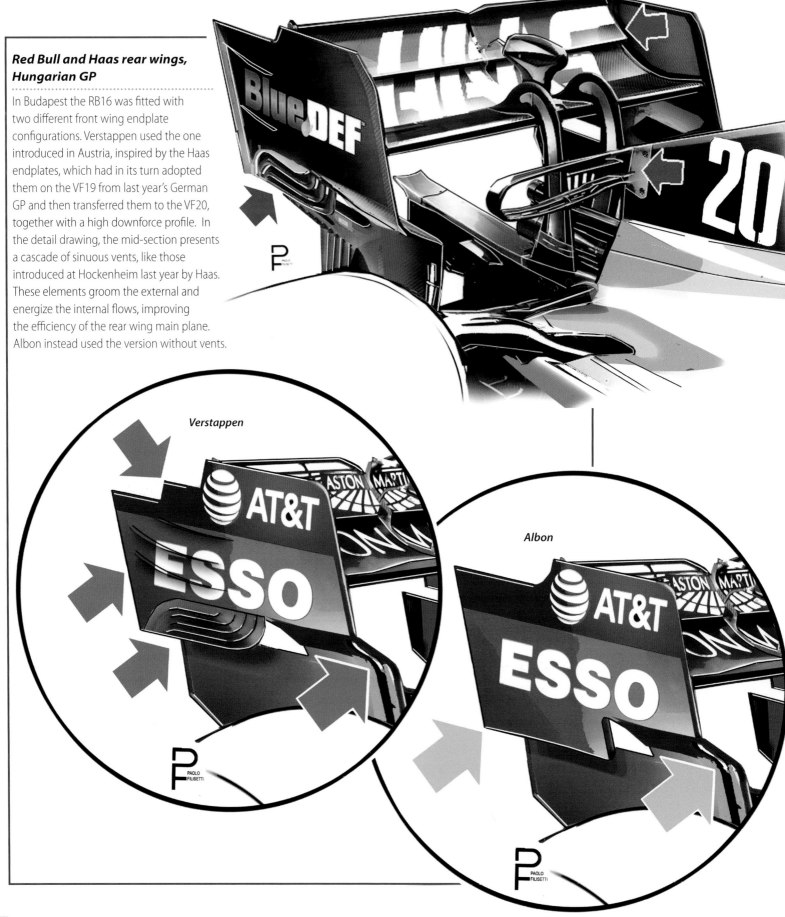

Red Bull and Haas rear wings, Hungarian GP

In Budapest the RB16 was fitted with two different front wing endplate configurations. Verstappen used the one introduced in Austria, inspired by the Haas endplates, which had in its turn adopted them on the VF19 from last year's German GP and then transferred them to the VF20, together with a high downforce profile. In the detail drawing, the mid-section presents a cascade of sinuous vents, like those introduced at Hockenheim last year by Haas. These elements groom the external and energize the internal flows, improving the efficiency of the rear wing main plane. Albon instead used the version without vents.

Verstappen

Albon

W11: front suspension with third mechanical damper

The front suspension equipped with a third mechanical damper tested last year in Russia, efficiently manages ride height variations. It is interesting to note how the passage from the hydraulic to the mechanical version came about not solely in terms of the type of dynamic response desired, but also because its lower weight compensated for the increase generated by the DAS.

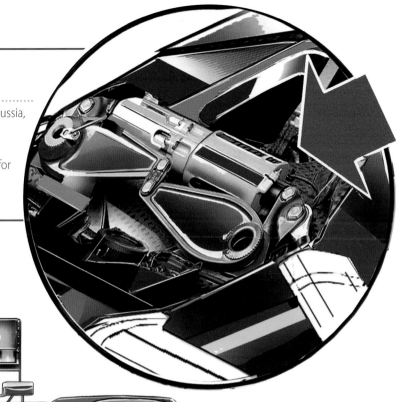

W11 front view, DAS location

Highlighted in the circle, concealed behind a fairing, the steering box integrated with the DAS (Dual Axis Steering) system. The red arrows indicated the hydraulic actuators that permit the opening of the convergence and the realignment of the wheels via the axial movement of the steering wheel.

DAS: W11 steering box detail

In the detail drawing of the Mercedes W11 steering box note, indicated by the red arrow, the housing for the "single" rack and pinion coupling. The yellow arrows instead indicated the two lateral "lobes" on the hydraulic power steering system that contain the hydraulic actuators that open or close the convergence, realigning the wheels.

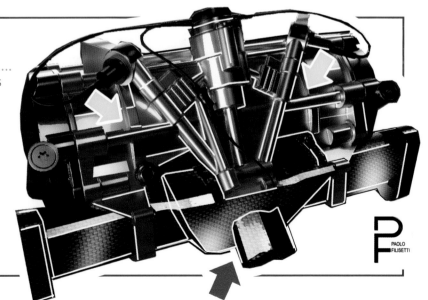

PAOLO FILISETTI

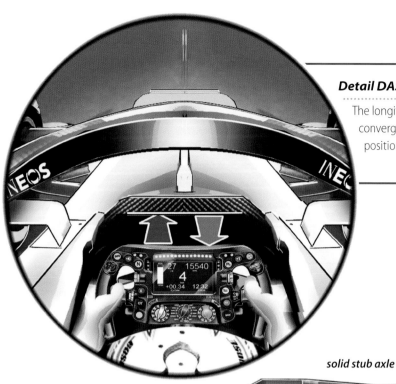

Detail DAS action

The longitudinal movement of the steering wheel along the steering column opens the convergence (steering wheel forwards) and realigns the wheel (steering back to normal position).

solid stub axle

The Mercedes W11's second secret: the front stub axles

We were all struck and even dazzled by the DAS, Dual Axis Steering, system that from the Barcelona tests was considered to be Mercedes' secret weapon, but Montmelò also revealed how Mercedes had tried two different versions of the brake disc bell and stub axle assembly. Specifically, one characterised by an abnormal number of holes of various diameters, carefully arranged on the stub axle. The impression is that the number of holes is not justified by a lightening of the component in order to reduce unsprung weight, but that it is instead a painstaking creation of ventilation channels in order to create, through the rotation of the wheels, efficient extraction of the air towards the outside of the wheels. This effectively appears to be an attempt to exploit a loophole regarding the regulation banning the blown hubs widely up to a couple of years ago by firstly Red Bull and then Ferrari. The precise directing of the flows, drawn towards the outside through the complex brake ducts characterising the Mercedes W11, produces aerodynamic benefits towards the rear end, with a tangible increase in diffuser efficiency.

Perforated and solid stub axles

In the drawing note the perforated stub axle characterised by a radial pattern in the holes which the Brackley engineers define as a simple lightening of the flange. Their function in extracting the air in the area adjacent to the hub is clear. There is a clear difference with respect to the solid version which has no holes at all, as can be seen in the two drawings. In this case, in fact, the component is extremely conventional, as on the rival cars.

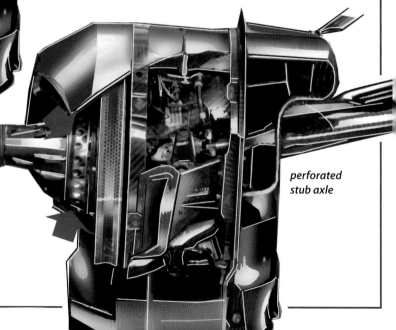

perforated stub axle

Racing Point RP20: side view and comparison with the Mercedes W10

Note how, concealed by the BWT livery, the shape of the car corresponds exactly with that of the Mercedes W10, in every detail. The exact correspondence of the endplates, bargeboards and turning vanes flanking the sidepods is evident. The differences are minimal: in the rear view mirror supports and in the absence of grilles either side of the cockpit.

RP20 front view and comparison with the Mercedes W10

In this view, note the precise correspondence between the various profiles making up the front wings of the RP20 and W10: the identical shape of the nose, the cape and the vanity panel area. The sidepod mouths correspond to the millimetre to those of the Brackley team's car. The air scoop is also identical.

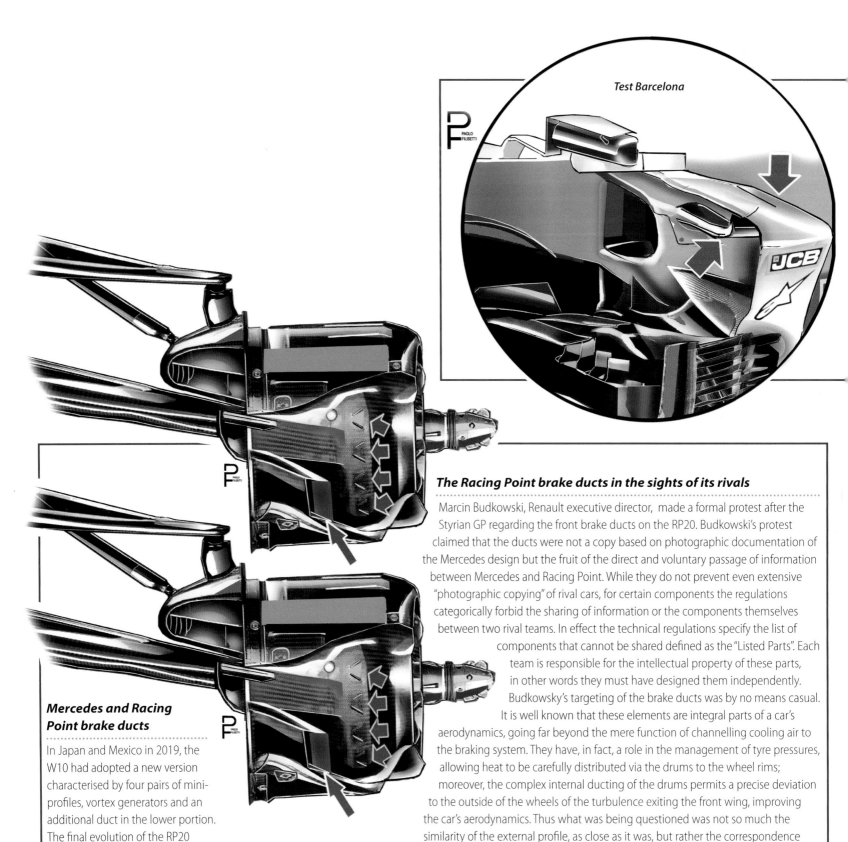

Test Barcelona

The Racing Point brake ducts in the sights of its rivals

Marcin Budkowski, Renault executive director, made a formal protest after the Styrian GP regarding the front brake ducts on the RP20. Budkowski's protest claimed that the ducts were not a copy based on photographic documentation of the Mercedes design but the fruit of the direct and voluntary passage of information between Mercedes and Racing Point. While they do not prevent even extensive "photographic copying" of rival cars, for certain components the regulations categorically forbid the sharing of information or the components themselves between two rival teams. In effect the technical regulations specify the list of components that cannot be shared defined as the "Listed Parts". Each team is responsible for the intellectual property of these parts, in other words they must have designed them independently. Budkowsky's targeting of the brake ducts was by no means casual. It is well known that these elements are integral parts of a car's aerodynamics, going far beyond the mere function of channelling cooling air to the braking system. They have, in fact, a role in the management of tyre pressures, allowing heat to be carefully distributed via the drums to the wheel rims; moreover, the complex internal ducting of the drums permits a precise deviation to the outside of the wheels of the turbulence exiting the front wing, improving the car's aerodynamics. Thus what was being questioned was not so much the similarity of the external profile, as close as it was, but rather the correspondence of their internal parts (which cannot be photographed). While it is plausible that a visible element may be copied photographically, this is not the case with its internal configuration which requires information not provided by spy cam shots.

Mercedes and Racing Point brake ducts

In Japan and Mexico in 2019, the W10 had adopted a new version characterised by four pairs of mini-profiles, vortex generators and an additional duct in the lower portion. The final evolution of the RP20 brake drums reprised the Japanese-Mexican version of the W10 drums.

Racing Point RP20: turning vanes evolution

In the comparison between the two details note the differences between the version adopted in the Barcelona test and the one introduced in Melbourne. Specifically, there is a visible separation between the upper horizontal and the vertical portions; the reduction of the blockage of the flows directed towards the outside of the sidepods is clear.

Melbourne

Red Bull RB 16: turning vanes development

In the direct comparison between the RB16 turning vanes seen in the first session at Barcelona and the version introduced on the last day of the second session – subsequently adopted in Australia – the differences are evident. The central vane, in fact, was replaced by the series of Venetian blind-like elements that, as is well-known, permit more precise management of the flows as well as reduced drag.

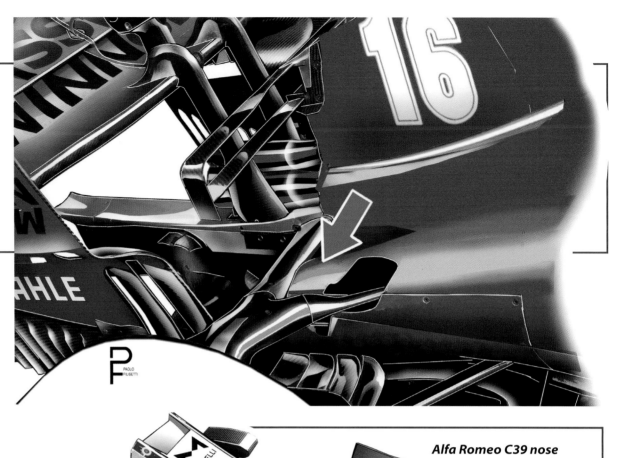

Ferrari SF1000 rear end

At the Hungarian GP Ferrari tested a different third suspension element at the rear in order to improve the traction that had proved to be wanting in the two Red Bull Ring races.

Haas VF20: sidepod detail

Note how the car is a development of the VF19 and drew heavily on the aerodynamic concepts seen on the Ferrari SF90, modifying them with original details.

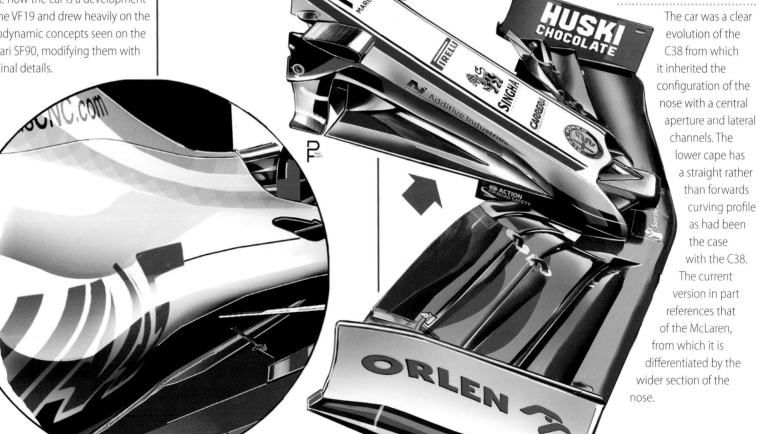

Alfa Romeo C39 nose

The car was a clear evolution of the C38 from which it inherited the configuration of the nose with a central aperture and lateral channels. The lower cape has a straight rather than forwards curving profile as had been the case with the C38. The current version in part references that of the McLaren, from which it is differentiated by the wider section of the nose.

Renault RS20: nose (test livery)

With the RS20, Renault joined the ranks of cars with narrow noses. The cape, already introduced in France on the RS19, extends backwards almost as far as the splitter. It is fed by the tusk-like lateral channels that project forwards like those of the Mercedes and the Racing Point.

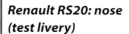

Alpha Tauri AT01: rear suspension detail

Note the closely form-fitting rear bodywork which reprises that seen on last year's Red Bull RB15. Painstaking attention has been paid to detail on a car that appears very well constructed around the Honda power unit.

3D VIRTUAL TECH TO ANALYSE AND EXPLAIN REALITY

Alongside the two-dimensional illustrations that are traditionally found in a printed technical analysis, digital 3D graphic tools today allow us to create virtual models of the cars and their components with the highest level of detail and to animate them, thereby increasing the interaction with the public.
This represents an expansion of the means of technical divulgation which the author embraced in 2018, introducing it to television and the social media.
Rather than competing with one another, the two worlds of illustration and virtual reality co-exist perfectly, allowing a multiple and diversified fruition of Formula 1 technology.

Mercedes W11, 3D model, presentation version

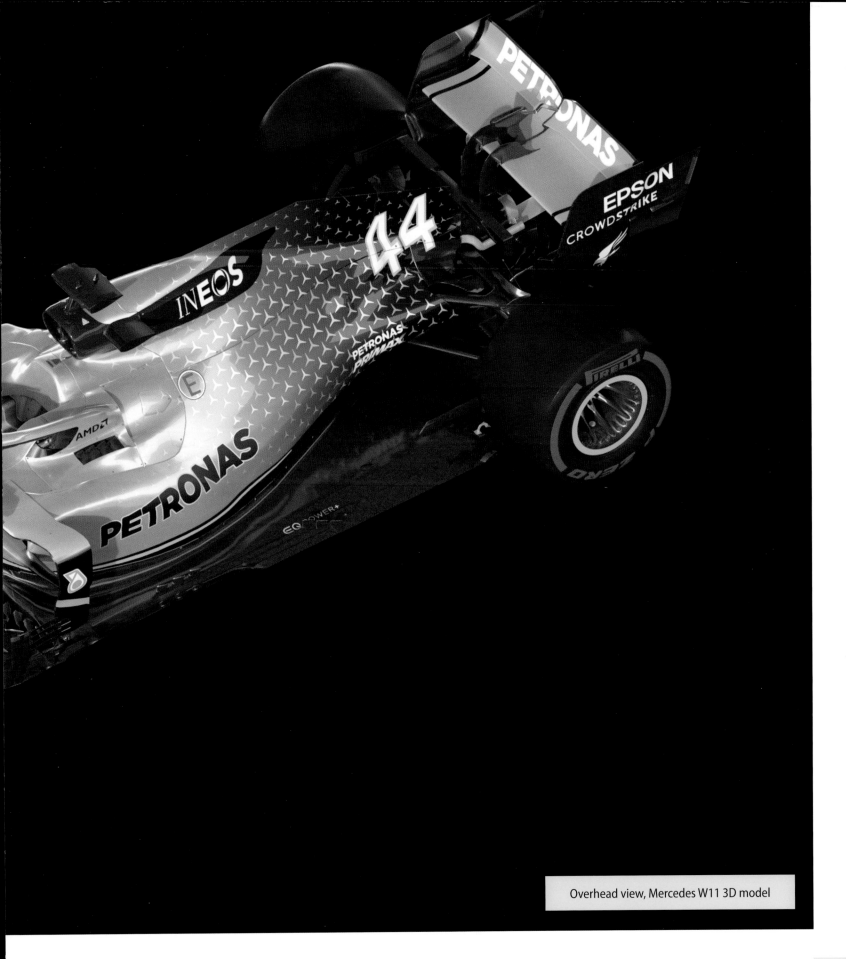

Overhead view, Mercedes W11 3D model

General three-quarters view, Ferrari SF1000
(Charles Leclerc) 3D model

Rear view, Ferrari SF1000
with LED rear lights illuminated

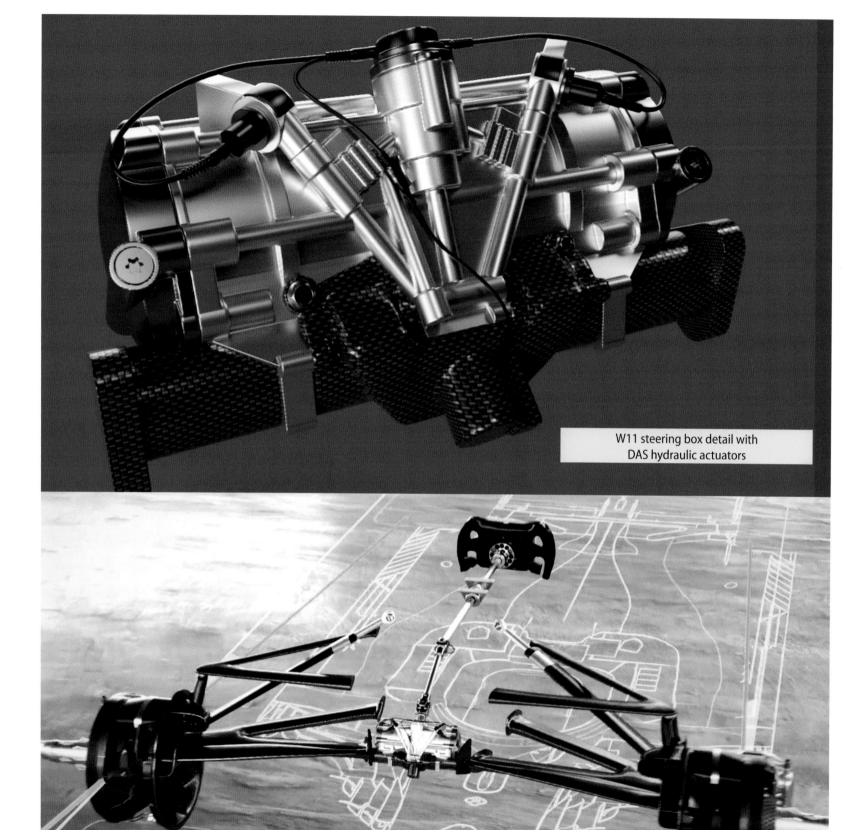

W11 steering box detail with
DAS hydraulic actuators

Convergence angle variation

DAS, steering column and wishbones

DAS, visualization of aerodynamic and thermal effects on tyres

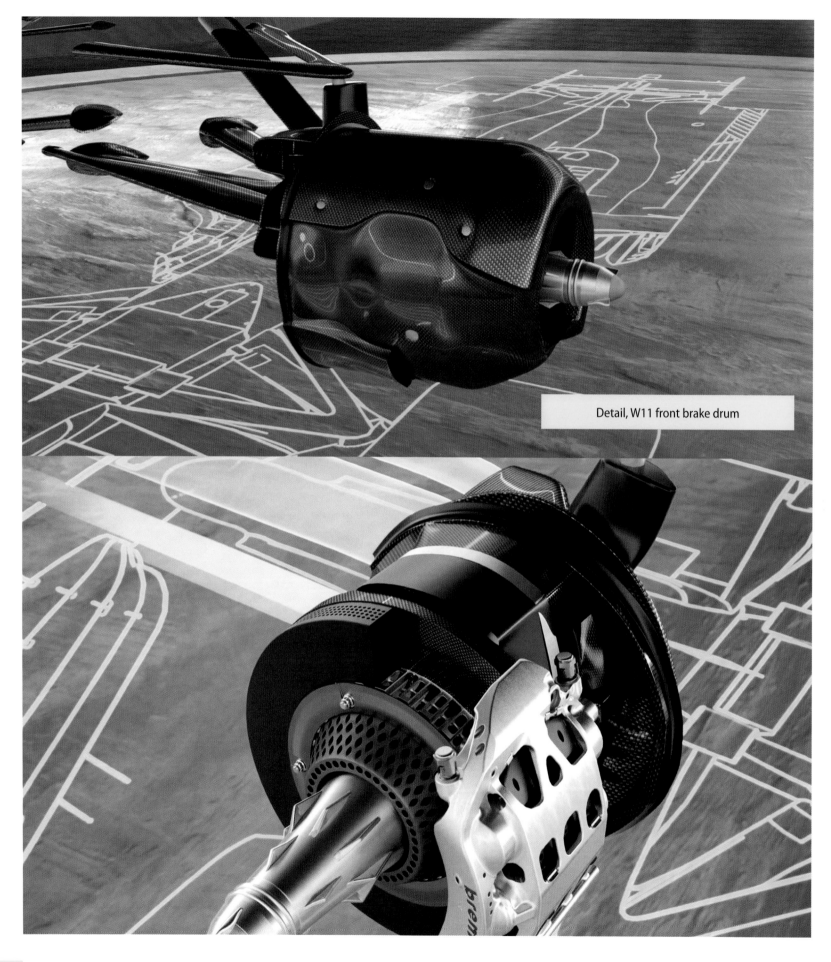

Detail, W11 front brake drum

If you would like regular updates on the latest news regarding publications and the events and meetings Giorgio Nada Editore organizes

Please visit our websites to find out how to register:

www.giorgionadaeditore.it
www.libreriadellautomobile.it

Don't forget to follow us on social media too

Printed by D'Auria Printing - Ascoli Piceno (Italy) - September 2020